T0319728

# Social Capital, Networks and Economic Development

De Pedro, para Pedro

# Social Capital, Networks and Economic Development

## An Analysis of Regional Productive Systems

María Semitiel García

*Reader in Economics at the University of Murcia, Spain*

**Edward Elgar**

Cheltenham, UK • Northampton, MA, USA

Published by
Edward Elgar Publishing Limited
Glensanda House
Montpellier Parade
Cheltenham
Glos GL50 1UA
UK

Edward Elgar Publishing, Inc.
136 West Street
Suite 202
Northampton
Massachusetts 01060
USA


A catalogue record for this book
is available from the British Library


**Library of Congress Cataloguing in Publication Data**
Semitiel García, María, 1970-
    Social capital, networks, and economic development : an analysis of regional
    productive systems / María Semitiel García.
       p. cm.
    Includes bibliographical references and index.
    Contents: The network perspective and the concept of productive system –
    Data characteristics and methods explanation – Regional productive
    structures and production systems – Regional productive systems and
    development processes.
       1. Industrial productivity–Social aspects. 2. Economic development–Social
    aspects. 3. Social capital (Sociology)–Economic aspects. 4. Social networks–
    Economic aspects. 5. Regional economic disparities–Spain–Case studies. I. Title

HC79.I52S46 2006
338.9–dc22                                                        2005052820

ISBN-13: 978 1 84542 596 8
ISBN-10: 1 84542 596 0

Printed and bound in Great Britain by MPG Books Ltd, Bodmin, Cornwall

# Contents

# Acknowledgments

I am grateful to the Department of Economics at the University of Sheffield, for the financial support that I obtained from them, and also to the Department of Applied Economics at the University of Murcia, for allowing my visits to the United Kingdom, which enabled my work on my PhD thesis that resulted in the present book. My thesis benefited greatly from the supervision of Professor Andrew Tylecote and Dr. Pedro Noguera Méndez, as they provided a great deal of guidance and direction throughout the work, whilst allowing and encouraging freedom of thought in its development. For this I am truly grateful to them.

# 1 Introduction

The objective of this research is to study productive systems and their relation to development from a structural, interdisciplinary and holistic view. In order to do so an appropriate epistemological perspective should be adopted to consider the social nature of economic actors, the importance of historical and geographical aspects and the relational character of socio-economic institutions. Moreover, an appropriate set of methods should also be selected in accordance with the adopted epistemological perspective. The selected methodology should consider the relational character of economic actors. Once the epistemological perspective of the research has been decided, it will be applied to study regional economic structures and their relationship with regional development.

The main aspects of the methodological view assumed in this research are: the consideration of the territory as a crucial economic factor; the concern that economic research should be holistic, including diverse actors, aspects and relations; and the focus on the relational and structural character of socio-economic systems.

The consideration of territory as a crucial economic factor leads to the selection of regions, instead of nations, as the units of analysis. Cultural and institutional conditions underlying the regional economies are some of the main causal factors that contribute to their development, having a localized character and constituting the relational specificities and abilities of economic actors. Those factors are difficult to reproduce in other regions, and therefore they constitute regional qualities that explain the economic success of some regions and thereby contribute to particular national development processes. However, economic research has traditionally focused on nations. Particularly, economic development and growth studies concentrate on national attributes and policies, emphasizing macroeconomic considerations and forgetting the substantial differences existing in economic performances across regions belonging to the same country.

To approach economic systems localized in regions, considering the area's cultural and institutional conditions makes it necessary to accept a holistic perspective. Diverse actors and factors have to be taken into account. In that sense, formal and informal interdependencies are taking place in economic systems, among firms and other institutions. Moreover, these are purposive interdependent actors and not independent agents looking for maximum benefit, as is the case in mainstream economics. The social and relational character of economic actors should be considered according to the links both maintained among them, in a formal or informal sense, and being affected by the economic history and the location factor of their area.

Traditional economic research generally considers nations instead of regions, average agents instead of differentiated actors, and their attributes instead of their relationships. Moreover, usually only economic aspects are taken into account while the social, geographical and historical character of economic systems and processes are ignored.

From this research perspective, the whole set of related actors constituting diverse economic systems at regional level make particular structures. These relational structures can be compared among regions and over time to consider their evolution. In order to do so a relational structural analysis should be followed. In line with a structural view, the elements of a set cannot be defined according to their intrinsic value but by their relationships with the other elements in the same system. Therefore, the scientific analysis should concentrate on clarifying and explaining the composition and relations maintained in the structures.

In the particular case of economics, the main characteristics of a structural analysis should be the consideration of a global perspective, the interdependence of the analysed components, the consideration of historical and social factors and a dynamic view of the economic situation. Then the objective of an economic structural analysis should be the study of interdependence relationships, having some permanent character, linking the main components of a comprehensive economy.

Following these ideas, this research offers two different and related contributions, one on the methodological and theoretical side, in the first part, and the other, empirical, in the second part. The research is structured as follows.

Chapter 2 focuses on the methodological approach adopted in this research: the network perspective. It offers the necessary foundations to study economic systems from a relational and structural view. Although it allows for the consideration of the social character of economic structures, it has rarely been adopted in economic research, as economic agents are generally assumed to be independent and therefore researchers focus on their attributes, forgetting relations and structures. The objective of Chapter 2 is to show the benefits of applying the network perspective to the economic research. Social capital and embeddedness are among the main concepts favouring the use of network methodology in economics, and allowing for the consideration of the social character of economic actors and relationships. Territory and history are also fundamental factors when studying economic relations, because economic actions and relations take place in, and are affected by, a particular geographic and historical context. The network perspective has the necessary interdisciplinary character to study economic structures.

When studying economic systems, the sets of their related interdependent complex components constitute structures inside structures, considering different micro and macro levels, therefore the research can be focused on different stages. In Chapter 2, different concepts, which aim to consider the whole set of economic agents and links acting in a particular geographic context, are also discussed. The 'regional productive system' term is considered the most appropriate for studying economic structures from a network interdisciplinary perspective. Productive systems, comprising firms, formal and informal institutions and their relationships, are embedded in the regional net made by the whole complex of social relationships, constituting a basic part of the regional structure.

The structural analysis is then approached in this research by studying the structure and evolution of regional productive systems. In the economic literature, the terms 'structure' and 'structural analysis' have been widely applied, but usually to mean the separate study of the main factors of economic systems. One of the aspects that has been more generally studied as structural is the characterization and evolution of the main economic sectors, according to their weight in GDP and employment. Moreover, structural studies generally use econometrics and descriptive statistics without using a specific method for their analyses. The use of relational analysis to study the main structural factors and the dynamics of those relationships has not received enough attention when referring to the meaning of the economic structure concept.

One of the most important structural analyses in the economic literature is the input–output study, which considers that the economic structure is represented in an input–output table through the exchange relations maintained among economic sectors. These data have been widely used in empirical national studies. Usually, they have been applied: to the calculation of several coefficients to classify productive branches; to descriptive analyses of final demand, consumption, imports and employment; and through models to measure separate effects (volume of final demand, composition of final demand, technical coefficients) of changes in production. But they have not been studied from a network perspective, focused on relations, and matching perfectly the structural character of the input–output information, and offering very enriching economic interpretations. It is remarkable that, even at international level, a proper structural input–output analysis has not been developed; only some studies applying graph theory and minimal flow analysis to study the trade relations in national input–output tables can be found.

The methods selected in this research, to study the productive systems from a relational view, are explained in Chapter 3. The main method corresponds to social network analysis, offering a whole set of specific measures to value relationships taking place in a particular network or system. Input–output indices are also used and therefore they are explained, together with the main characteristic of the selected data, in Chapter 3.

Input–output data are analysed in Chapter 4 to identify regional production systems, as sets of productive branches related by their intermediate transactions and therefore by their productive processes. This will be the first step for the empirical study of regional productive systems as they constitute their technical side. In Chapter 4, the main production systems in Andalusia and the Basque Country are identified and characterized using several network measures, input–output indices, a particular algorithm and regional historical information. Once they have been studied and compared, institutional information is added in Chapter 5 to transform them into regional productive systems.

Regional production systems and regional productive systems are identified in the two selected Spanish regions for time and spatial comparisons. These regions have been chosen because they are representative of the lowest and highest level of regional development in the country. Andalusia, located in the south of Spain, is considered an 'objective 1' region in the European Union, with a relatively large territory, low development level and high specialization in agriculture and in the agro-food industry. The Basque Country is an industrialized region in the north of Spain, with high development, a relatively small territory and socio-political problems. The geographical level of this study is regional, and its economic level is situated in the productive system, instead of considering the whole country and the complete set of economic relations. Regional, instead of national, data and productive systems, as opposed to the whole exchange net, have been chosen in the analysis to avoid excessive generalization in the study and in the conclusions, to provide a more realistic research and to retrieve more credible findings. There are particularities at regional level, showing the country's heterogeneity, that have great importance when trying to understand their productive structures and their differences in development and growth. The two selected regions are compared in two different years, 1980 and 1995, looking for conclusions related to the existence and persistence of development interregional differences.

Productive systems have a fundamental role in the explanation of interregional development differences – therefore regional systems are compared in order to test, in Chapter 5, a set of hypotheses establishing relationships between productive systems structures and differences in regional development. The research intends to clarify the importance of structural factors in regional development paths.

The proposed hypotheses are tested by applying mechanism causality. The basis is that through the application of social network analysis the explanations of phenomena occurring at a macro level are found in their underlying structure. That is, explanations are in the process occurring at an inferior level, which in this analysis is the level of the firms that form productive branches making the production and productive systems.

Finally, the main conclusions that can be drawn from this work have been summarized in Chapter 6.

# 2   The Network Perspective and the Concept of Productive System

## 2.1   INTRODUCTION

The aim of this chapter is to show the main aspects of the methodological perspective adopted in this research. The main methodology applied is the network perspective, and therefore it seems necessary to expound first of all the basic ideas of this perspective, its foundations and its main concepts. Complementary to this, input–output analysis is applied as well, but this is already a well known perspective in economics and does not constitute the main methodological approach.[1] Its main characteristics are explained in Chapter 3, which examines the method and the data.

As one main objective of this research is the identification of linked groups of productive sub-sectors, the explanations presented in this chapter will show the suitability of the selected network methodology to cover this.

The network perspective is considered a research methodology that offers a particular view for the study of agents of any type as related social actors. The distinctive character of this methodology is its structuralist nature, as the focus for analysis is the relationships maintained among the agents under study.[2] There are basic concepts brought to or accepted in this perspective, contributing to the development of a proper method of analysis, and therefore contributing to the acknowledgement of the perspective as a methodology, or even a paradigm. These concepts include network, embeddedness, weak and strong ties, bridges, structural holes and social capital; all of these focus on the understanding of diverse types of groups of related social actors.

The network methodology can be applied to the analysis of groups of actors of any kind, and therefore it is applicable to the study of economic organizations acting in a social structure as related agents. When this methodology is used for economic studies there are contributions of both economics and sociology in the analyses, and the concept of embeddedness allows for coordination between both disciplines. Therefore, the approach and the concepts offered by network analysis are available for the study of economic organizations, allowing for the proposal of theories, depending on the kind of research to be done, such as exchange theories. There are several empirical studies explaining the behaviour and performance of economic organizations as exchanging economic actors, each of them focused on concrete agents such as firms, groups of firms, other economic institutions, or productive sectors, and in particular relationships such as organization charts, input–output relationships, trust or friendship (Scott, 1987; Krackhardt, 1992; Perrow, 1992; Uzzi, 1996, among others).

More specifically, when the units of analysis are groups of exchanging firms or productive sectors, there appear in the literature a set of concepts proposed to study the behaviour of such groups, such as those of productive systems, production systems or industrial districts, among others. These can all be considered as networks of economic organizations and therefore can be analysed from the network perspective. Of all these the productive system is the most general concept, considering the possibility of a broad set of relations and economic agents in addition to the exchanging firms. For this reason this is the chosen concept in the present research, for the identification of groups of related productive sub-sectors and institutions in selected geographical areas inside Spain, through the application of the network perspective. In addition to the identification and analysis of regional productive systems, the input–output analysis is applied through several indices, for a better explanation and characterization of the selected systems.[3]

The next section of this chapter is dedicated to the explanation of the main characteristics of the network perspective, as a methodology for analysis in several disciplines. Section 2.3 adapts the methodological foundations of the perspective to the case of economic organizations, presenting a literature review in that area. The last section is even more concrete, adapting the network perspective for economic organizations to several concepts appearing in the economic literature to name and identify groups of firms or of productive sectors. With reference to those concepts, the regional productive system appears as the most relevant, and therefore it is selected for its identification and characterization in the next chapters.

## 2.2   THE NETWORK PERSPECTIVE

This section shows the basic aspects of the network perspective as a research methodology, considered by several authors as a paradigm,[4] according to which the analysed agents, as any group of social actors, are embedded in networks of social relations. The structure of social nets is crucial to understanding the opportunities and restrictions of actors, in accordance with their positions in them. The networks and their structures are studied by analysing the relations maintained among agents, in contrast to traditional analyses focused on the attributes of the actors.

As any network is embedded in a more complex one, the establishment of limits is necessary, and therefore the researcher chooses the kind of agents and relations under analysis. Depending on this choice, and on the planned objective, several theories have been proposed following the present perspective,[5] all of them applying certain concepts that are essential for the approach, such as those of embeddednes and social capital. All these terms are necessary for the explanation of the structure and evolution of the network and for the identification of actors in special positions.

In an attempt to offer a clearer exposition, this section is divided into two parts: the first refers to the presentation of the perspective as a methodology that focuses on the relationships maintained among any kind of actor; the second part is dedicated to the definition and explanation of the main theoretical concepts applied by the network perspective.

### 2.2.1   The Network Perspective as a Relational Methodology

Social network analysis, generally known as the network perspective, is considered a methodology, even a paradigm, applicable to several disciplines, offering a set of methods for the systematic study of social structures.

As we will be able to see throughout this chapter, the network perspective has its own concepts, methods and, what is more important, a methodological view, according to which the main aspect for analysis is the existing set of relations among the agents under study. It is, therefore, also considered a structuralist perspective, given that the structural position of individuals, or groups, in the set of relations they maintain explains the regularities in their behaviour and the opportunities for and restrictions on actions of the actors involved.

Any kind of agent can be analysed: individuals, organizations, institutions, countries or regions. In general terms the unit of analysis is not the individual, but an entity that consists of a collection of individuals, and the linkages among them. The agents are studied from the point of view that the main explanation for their behaviour, and the results of such behaviours, are the relationships maintained among them. The ties or linkages among the members of the network analytic framework may be any relationship existing between units. The perspective is therefore focused on the relational structure of a group of entities and the properties of that relational system.

According to Degenne and Forsé (1999, p. 2): 'Network analysis analyses *overall relations* in an inductive attempt to identify behaviour patterns and the groups or social strata that correlate with those patterns. Then, it sorts out the pertinent groups *a posteriori* and *identifies the concrete constraints of structure on behaviour at the same time as it uncovers constraints on structure from group interactions (their emphasis).'*

From a methodological point of view the network perspective is not reductionist but holistic, as opposed to individualistic, and interdisciplinary. Actors are purposeful, intentional agents, with social and economic motivations, and their actions are influenced by the net of relations in which they are embedded. The homo economicus, studied by economic theory, is compatible with the network perspective and the inclusion of social relations, as actors are considered rational and acting to achieve goals according to their personal preferences.[6] Nevertheless, there are constraints in the structure of the network interfering with individual actions and influencing the probability of achieving some goals.[7]

By giving precise formal definitions to aspects of the political, economic or social structural environment, the network perspective makes it possible to answer social and behavioural research questions. In general, the environment in which agents act is characterized by a particular structure in which they behave according to their preferences and, therefore, with the capacity to modify the original structure through the effect of interactions among them. In this manner, the network in which agents are embedded is evolving and changing.[8]

The agents and the relationships maintained among them form a social network, where the position of every agent is a key element shaping its general structure, implying opportunities as well as restrictions for the actors involved. The structure of the network explains the results of actions; moreover, the form of the network has a major impact on the process of exchange of any kind, in the way in which the structure affects the exchanges. At the same time, it is the product of elementary interactions.

According to Wasserman and Faust (1994), the central principles underlying the network perspective, in addition to the use of relational concepts, are as follows:

- Actors and their actions are viewed as interdependent rather than independent, autonomous units.
- Relational ties, or linkages, between actors are channels to transfer or for the flow of resources, either material or non-material.
- Network models focusing on individuals view the network structural environment as providing opportunities for or constraints on individual actions.
- Network models conceptualize structure (mainly social, economic and political) as lasting patterns of relations among actors.

In Emirbayer and Goodwin (1994), the underlying theoretical presuppositions and conceptual strategies of network analysis are the priority of relations over categories, and that relational and positional analyses are ways of representing social structure. In accordance with the first presupposition, the authors focus on what they call the 'anticategorical imperative', according to which network theories build their explanations from relations instead of attributes, from patterns of relations. Regarding the second aspect, referring to the relational analysis, it is noted that both direct and indirect connections among actors explain social networks. With respect to positional analysis the importance of the ties' nature is emphasized, not from one actor to another, but to third parties.

For the application of the network perspective there is not only one particular theory or model recommended, as this will depend on the kind of actors and relations under study and on the necessity to focus on some aspects to develop the research. When choosing a theory it is important to bear in mind that any structure is always embedded in a larger one, which consists of all the influences that remain outside the defined model. Therefore, it is one of the researchers' tasks to decide on the limits of the network, the level of network or sub-network, the kind of relations and the unit or entity to be studied, everything according to theoretical and practical considerations and to the subject proposed in the analysis.

As has been pointed out, structural and relational information is used to study or test theories; nevertheless, information about attributes of actors can be very useful to complement the analysis.[9] Monge and Contractor (2004) present the following theories as explaining the emergence of networks, considering that the theoretical basis for any study can be diverse, and therefore it could be useful to use aspects from more than one theory in a particular study.

- Theories of self-interest: theory of social capital and transaction cost economic theories.
- Theories of mutual self-interest (jointly rather than individually self-interested) and collective action: collective action and mobilization and collective action and adoption of innovations.
- Exchange and dependence theories: power, leadership, trust and ethical behaviour, resource dependency theory and power in interorganizational networks, corporate elites and interlocking groups of directors, creation, maintenance, dissolution and reconstitution of inter-firm links and network organizations.

- Contagion theories: general workplace attitudes, attitudes towards technologies, behaviour through contagion and interorganizational contagion.
- Cognitive theories: semantic networks, network organizations as knowledge structures, cognitive social structures and cognitive consistency.
- Theories of homophily: general demographic homophily and gender homophily. [10]
- Theories of physical and electronic proximity.
- Uncertainty reduction and contingency theories.
- Social support theories.
- Theories of network evolution.

Therefore, there is a wide set of proposed theories to apply the network perspective to different objectives, actors and relations. All the theories follow the principles of the network approach presented before, and all of them use the main concepts explained next.

### 2.2.2    Main Theoretical Concepts in the Network Perspective

There are some network concepts that are essential in this perspective, from a theoretical and from a practical point of view. They are interrelated, as each one refers to the characteristics of the agents, the relationships or the network as a whole.

The notion of a network has already been mentioned in the previous section, as a concrete set of actors and the defined relation or relations connecting them. Actors can be individuals or groups, and ties can be formal or informal. Therefore, a group of related organizations is considered a network but, at the same time, the organization itself is considered a network. Moreover, as networks are made of agents and relationships, they change according to both of them: 'Networks are constantly being socially constructed, reproduced, and altered as the result of actions of actors ... Therefore networks are as much process as they are structure, being continually shaped and reshaped by the actions of actors who are in turn constrained by the structural positions in which they find themselves' (Nohria, 1992, p. 7).

As every network of agents and relations is embedded in a more complex one, social networks have no natural frontiers and, therefore, it is a methodological problem, faced by the researcher, to decide the boundaries and the relations to be studied. For Tichy *et al.* (1979) and Brass and Burkhardt (1992), the basic network types are defined by the following relations: exchange of goods and services, exchange of information and ideas and affective relationships or liking.

The relationships maintained among actors, the ties, have different intensity depending on which actors they are linking. According to Granovetter (1973) it is possible, and useful, to distinguish between strong and weak ties. For Granovetter, there are four factors defining the strength of a tie: amount of time, emotional intensity, intimacy and reciprocal services.[11] But the notions of strong and weak ties have been applied to any kind of network, even to organizations and institutions. The important thing is that strong ties are linking actors belonging to the same group, actors interacting with high frequency. But a weak tie will be one between the member of a group and the member of a different group, that is, the agents linked by a weak tie do not belong to the same group and, therefore, that link constitutes a bridge. Weak ties, acting as bridges, provide agents with access to information and resources beyond those available in their own social groups.

When there is more than one path to connect, or link, two agents belonging to different groups, but one of them is particularly short in relation to the others, such a weak tie constitutes a local bridge. As every group, or net, is embedded in a more complex one, bridges imply cohesion and accessibility to resources and information. Weak ties are especially useful in the diffusion of innovation among agents; in this case, individuals with many weak ties are often called 'liaison persons'. This person, or actor, connects two network sectors, and all his ties, into one or both sectors, are weak. For Granovetter (1973, p. 1368) this situation is particularly important when talking about the diffusion of risky innovations.

When analysing the structure of a network it could be feasible to find groups, or small networks, which are weakly connected. Then, between every two weakly tied networks, there is a hole, or what Burt (1992, 2001) calls a structural hole, showing the opportunities for some strategic agents to allow for the flow of any exchange among groups or networks. The existence of structural holes, and therefore bridges and weak ties, implies a potential for some agents as a characteristic of the structure of the network. At the same time, a high cohesion of the net with many strong ties, and therefore high density, implies feasible cooperation and coordination among the agents building the network. This is, again, a characteristic of the network structure with positive implications.

Consequently, the relational structure of the network is a resource emerging from it, available for its exploitation to the benefit of the group. This structural resource is the social capital, which is present in every network, regardless of its size and scope, as all social relations and social structures facilitate some forms of social capital. However, it acts with different intensity according to the structure, because it emerges from the relations or links maintained among the actors constituting the network. Therefore, the social structure is a kind of capital, social capital, that can create for certain individuals or groups, occupying a certain position in the structure, advantages in pursuing their ends; and therefore better connected actors enjoy higher returns: 'By analogy with notions of physical capital and human capital – tools and training that enhance individual productivity – "social capital" refers to features of social organization, such as networks, norms, and trust, which facilitate coordination and cooperation for mutual benefit. Social capital enhances the benefits of investment in physical and human capital' (Putnam, 1993, p. 2). According to the same author, and others such as Coleman (1988), the productivity of social capital makes possible the achievement of certain ends that would not be attainable in its absence.

Social capital is seen, at present, as a vital factor for economic development at any level, which helps to formulate new strategies for development:[12] relationships are a strategy for development and growth. For Coleman (1988), the notion of social capital is a way of introducing social structure into the rational action paradigm and, therefore, connecting sociology and economics. With rational action, and through social capital, each actor has control over certain resources and interests in certain resources and events.

The relationship between structural holes and social capital is not clear at all, although it seems generally accepted that social capital is bigger in the case of networks with strong links inside them, with high closure, and many weak ties acting as bridges through structural holes linking them with other networks (Burt, 2000). For Burt (2001), the network mechanisms that theoretically define social capital are network contagion and prominence, network closure and structural holes. The first mechanism refers to the case in which the social structure facilitates the transmission of beliefs and practices among actors (people or organizations). The network closure mechanism explains that, in dense networks, the risk of cooperation is lower and the facilities for retrieving information are greater. For the last (structural holes) mechanism, there is connection with other groups and, therefore, access to a higher volume of information that is, in turn, less redundant and attainable in less time.

According to all the above, and continuing with the main ideas presented in the previous section, the structure of a network, and the position of actors in the net, offer essential information. The position of agents makes it possible to obtain inferences about which agents are strategic in the network, by checking whether they occupy a central position or a bridge position. This can also be linked with the existence of power, prestige, dependency relationships or even vulnerability. In the case of actors in vulnerable positions, that is, positions in which they depend on one or very few other agents to maintain their relationships in the network, the existence of social capital through structural holes gives them some possibilities to reduce their vulnerability. A possible strategy is the extension of their network relations, by establishing links with other actors, and another way to act is to consolidate their networks by linking the weaker vulnerable actors among them (Monge and Contractor, 2004).

One type of agent for which the situations described in this section are clearly applicable is economic organizations and, from this point, the analysis will be focused on them.

## 2.3   NETWORK THEORIES FOR ECONOMIC ORGANIZATIONS

This section shows the adaptation of the network methodology and concepts to the particular case in which actors are economic organizations. A literature review is offered, together with the exposition of the link between economics and sociology through the concept of embeddedness proposed by Granovetter in 1985. After that, the application of the perspective as a structural analysis, with its complete set of terms and concepts for economic organizations as related actors, will be explained. Finally, a specific set of theories belonging to the network methodology, which are named 'exchange theories' and which are clearly applicable to economic analysis, and some empirical studies that have already applied them, will be described.

### 2.3.1   Economics and Sociology: the Concept of Embeddedness

The embeddedness argument, which constitutes one of the main bases of the network perspective, proposed by Granovetter (1985), offers a potential link between sociology and economics to explain business behaviour. For Granovetter, economic interactions are embedded in a net of social and personal relationships, and explaining them by abstracting them from such a net will lead to a misunderstanding of the phenomenon analysed. A similar idea is that of Wilkinson (1983) offering an alternative methodology for the study of economics, by necessarily including the economic, social and political perspectives in all research.

What Wilkinson proposes as an alternative methodology has been present from the time of the classics. In the texts of Adam Smith, David Ricardo,

John Stuart Mill and Karl Marx it is not possible to understand the economy without considering at the same time the ongoing political, institutional and philosophical aspects. Nevertheless, at the time that Wilkinson defended such an alternative methodology, the leading economic paradigm was and is the neoclassical, in which positivism is the prevailing theoretical perspective, and it seems necessary to propose that kind of interdisciplinary methodology again.[13]

In the application of network analysis to economic studies, according to Uzzi (1996, p. 674): 'Embeddedness refers to the process by which social relations shape economic action in ways that some mainstream economic schemes overlook or misspecify when they assume that social ties affect economic behaviour only minimally or, in some stringent accounts, reduce the efficiency of the price system'; while the definition offered by Granovetter (2005, p. 35) is 'the extent to which economic action is linked to or depends on action or institutions that are non-economic in content, goals or processes'.

The coordination of both perspectives, sociological and economic, embraces the concept of rational action, superimposing on it – endogenously or exogenously – social and institutional organizations. Following Granovetter, the concept of man applied in economic analysis is under-socialized and, therefore, economic researchers forget the importance of personal relations and of networks of relations, in generating trust, in establishing expectations and in creating and enforcing norms. For Coleman (1988, p. S97), the embeddedness is an 'attempt to introduce into the analysis of economic systems, social organizations and social relations not merely as a structure that springs into place to fulfil an economic function but as a structure with history and continuity that give it an independent effect on the functioning of economic systems'. Agreeing with the notion of embedded economic networks, pre-existing social relations lead to trust and, in turn, to embedded ties trust generates subsequent commitments, which leads to reciprocated exchanges, to concrete trust, and concrete trust again to embedded ties.

### 2.3.2    Structural Analysis for Economic Organizations

A set of the network theories is focused on the analysis of organizations, considered networks and at the same time actors in bigger networks. In Nohria (1992), the basic premises underlining a network perspective of organizations are as follows:

• All organizations are, in important respects, social networks and need to be addressed and analysed as such. The relationships in the whole network would comprise the formal or prescribed, such as organizational charts and input–output tables, as well as informal or emergent relations.

• An organization's environment is properly seen as a network of other organizations. The most significant elements in an organization's environment are the other organizations and the pattern of relations among them – the 'interorganizational field'.[14] Organizations in this field would be suppliers, resources and product consumers, regulatory agencies, other organizations producing similar products or services, and so on.

• Actions, attitudes and behaviour of actors in organizations can be best explained in terms of their position in networks of relationships.

• Networks-constrained actions are, in turn, shaped by them.

• The comparative analysis of organizations must take into account their network characteristics.

Nohria (1992) describes the importance of applying the network perspective, which has been maturing as an academic discipline, to economic analysis, especially to study the emergence of new entrepreneurial firms, the formation of regional districts, the expansion of new industries, the dynamics of Asian economies and the evolution of technological developments such as new information technologies.[15] In the case of economic organizations, as for any actor in general, the structure of the network and the position of each organization in it define the opportunities and constraints of actors forming the group: 'The type of network in which an organisation is embedded defines the opportunities potentially available; its position in that structure and the types of inter-firm ties it maintains define its access to those opportunities' (Uzzi, 1996, p. 675).

According to the network perspective, and its application to economic organizations, a market is considered a network, constituting a group of agents and the relationships among them. In that case, the effects of maintaining concrete relations in the net can be evaluated with data on economic transactions. For market relationships, a better performance is predicted for groups with strong relations among their agents and spanning structural holes allowing access to diverse perspectives, skills, resources and technologies. Creativity and learning would be stimulated by structural holes, increasing in turn the competitive advantages of actors in the group. The organization's ability to learn and, consequently, the capacity of the firm to manage technical change, would be greater: 'Organizations with management and collaboration networks that more often bridge structural holes in their surrounding market of technology and practice will learn faster and be more productively creative' (Burt, 2000, p. 24).

The analysis of structural holes for the study of economic organizations is particularly interesting. For Burt, holes imply entrepreneurial opportunities, with organizations in bridge positions having access to information, resources and innovations. This situation would increase the social capital of actors in these positions.[16] Although cohesion or network closure would also increase it, a network rich in entrepreneurial opportunities is considered by Burt (2000) an entrepreneurial network, with actors building bridges and spanning structural holes.

Firms, or organizations in general, in strategic exchange positions with other firms and institutions are key diffusers of innovation, knowledge and behaviour strategies. Such organizations are potential participants in common projects and investments, among other sharing opportunities. In this way, the profits obtained owing to their position are reinforced, allowing them to achieve even better results. As a consequence, even inside their own networks, made of groups of firms exchanging goods and services, these organizations are considered very attractive firms.

In market studies the social capital of network closure and that of structural holes are considered complementary. There is high performance when spanning structural holes beyond the group and showing strong relations within the group, mainly through communication and coordination. In market relations, an economic organization acts as a rational agent according to its preferences and, at the same time, establishes relations of coordination and trust with other organizations, working in embedded networks instead of in an atomistic mass of discrete firms. Nevertheless, firms can decide to maintain strictly competitive or commercial relations with some firms, and to develop informal relations with another group of firms. In the first case, there are firms needed for the productive process, without or with a minimum of embeddedness; in the second case, there are multiple, formal and informal, and therefore embedded, relations.

At the same time, routine trade relations and embedded ties are maintained. The embedded ties exist among firms maintaining a continued and high level of transactions, while competitive relations are those that are specifically necessary for developing the business. These necessary relationships, maintained with a specific group of firms, would be dependency relations that, according to the dependency theory, would imply power relations, as dependency is considered the basis of power.[17] This would be the case where a firm decided to trade with a particular firm for economic reasons, cost decisions, scarceness of resources or distance problems, among others.

In the case of economic sectors as the unit of analysis the main dependency reason is a technological one, owing to the productive process. In most cases the economic sector, acting as an actor in the network, cannot choose alternative sectors. Although it is convenient to consider (probably over a longer period and under less flexible conditions depending on each productive process ) the possibility of certain intermediate inputs that can be replaced by others, focusing on economic reasons as in the case of firms. One of the decision factors considered by a productive sector or branch, when selecting another branch for exchanges, would be that of location. Proximity determines, to an important degree, the exchanging partners for cost reduction, the search of reputation and trust, information and innovation exchange, and other important aspects.

### 2.3.3    Exchange Theories and Empirical Studies

As has been explained and underlined before, the network perspective is applied as a methodology to several areas of research, with different objectives, focuses, actors and relations. It is the researchers' task to decide, according to their particular study, the theory to be applied in each particular case. Some researchers, especially those interested in the study of economic relations, apply exchange theories following the network perspective, deciding the actors, relations and limits of the network to be analysed:

> We also need a distinction between the competitive market situations dear to economists, and networks of local elites or organizational actors. In an ideal free market environment, any two actors can theoretically exchange resources. In a network, more parameters are involved. In particular, actors must share mutual trust and links may be direct or indirect. In addition, each position has a specific 'value', e.g. cutpoints have options of control and exchange not available to other nodes. All these factors must be taken into account to determine the power, prestige and influence of each actor. (Degenne and Forsé, 1999, p. 146)[18]

According to Markovsky *et al.* (1988), following Cook *et al.* (1983), an exchange network can be defined with the following characteristics:

- A set of actors, either people or corporate groups.
- A distribution of valued resources among those actors.
- For each actor a set of exchange opportunities with other actors in the network.
- A set of historically developed and utilized exchange opportunities, called exchange relations.

• A set of network connections linking exchange relations into a single network structure.

Jones *et al.* (1997) provide a theory of exchange, to explain under what conditions network governance has comparative advantages. Following that theory, economic organizations use social mechanisms to coordinate, adapt and safeguard exchanges. By doing this, the network governance form shows advantages over both hierarchy and market solutions: 'The theory says that the network form of governance is a response to exchange conditions of asset specificity, demand uncertainty, task complexity and frequency. These exchange conditions drive firms toward structurally embedding their transactions' (Jones *et al.*, 1997).

Network governance is understood by the authors as inter-firm coordination, characterized by organic or informal social systems, in contrast to bureaucratic structures within firms and formal relationships among them. The theory is proposed for the case of sets of autonomous firms and non-profit agencies, engaged in creating products or services based on implicit and open-ended contracts. The set of organizations taking part in those exchanges are persistent, working repeatedly with each other over time, and structured according to exchanges that are patterned to reflect a division of labour.

For organizations working according to the above conditions, the frequency of exchanges is fundamental, as it facilitates transferring tacit knowledge in customized exchanges, mainly for specialized processes. According to Jones *et al.* (1997), frequent interactions are what establish the conditions for relational and structural embeddedness, which in turn provide the foundations for social mechanisms to adapt, coordinate and safeguard exchanges effectively. The necessary conditions for network governance to emerge are: demand uncertainty with stable supply; customized exchanges high in human asset specificity; complex tasks integrating diverse specialists; and frequent exchanges among parties comprising the network.

In the condition of demand uncertainty with stable supply, it is considered that unknown and rapid shifts in consumer preferences, rapid changes in knowledge or technology and seasonal variations lead to demand uncertainty and outsourcing or subcontracting. When the second condition, of customized exchanges high in human asset specificity, is included, then participant knowledge and skills, and therefore human asset specificity, are considered in the exchanges through customization. Moreover, this participation increases the dependency among the exchanging parties, and thus the necessity for coordination among them. In that sense, cooperation, proximity and repeated exchanges are required to transfer tacit knowledge effectively among parties. Coordination is not enhanced by market mechanisms, but there is a tendency to disaggregation and therefore the necessity for coordination and integration. In such circumstances, network governance enhances the rapid dissemination of tacit knowledge across firm boundaries.

According to the third condition, of complex tasks integrating diverse specialists, the fact that task complexity requires different specialized inputs to complete a product or service is taken into account. Therefore, there should be behavioural interdependence and a need for coordinating activities. Simultaneously, time pressure makes it necessary to reduce lead-time in rapidly changing markets or to reduce costs in highly competitive markets. Therefore, team coordination means that diversely skilled members are working simultaneously to produce a product or service in more efficient conditions. Following the last condition (frequent exchanges among parties comprising the network), frequent exchanges and human asset specificity help the transfer of tacit knowledge among parties. Moreover, with reciprocity in frequent exchanges, embeddedness is being developed. The combination of all four conditions promotes structural embeddedness among exchange parties through the following social mechanisms: restricted access to exchanges in the network, macroculture, collective sanctions and reputation.

When there is restricted access to exchanges in the network, continued interaction may 'substitute for internal socialisation process, and permit exchange partners to learn each other's systems, develop communication protocols, and establish routines for working together, all of which enhance coordination' (Jones *et al.*, 1997). Restricted access generates more interactions, more knowledge about each other, fewer incentives for opportunism, fewer costs of monitoring and higher coordination. Macroculture refers to shared assumptions and values, leading to specific actions and therefore to behaviour patterns. Macroculture is enhanced by close geographic proximity, increasing the likelihood and ease of interaction. Network governance is expected to be found in geographically concentrated areas. Collective sanctions involve group members punishing other members who violate group norms, values or goals, reducing behavioural uncertainty. Reputation increases and improves information about the reliability and goodwill of others, reducing behavioural uncertainty.

The interaction of the above social mechanisms decreases coordination costs, enhances the safeguarding of customized exchanges and increases the likelihood of emergence of network governance: 'Since network governance is a select, persistent and structured set of autonomous firms, it is not enough to call an industry or region a network without examining relations among firms and how these relations complete a product or service' (Jones *et al.*, 1997).

Another exchange theory is proposed by Degenne and Forsé (1999), which talks about a global dynamic theory of exchange, for which there could be positively and negatively connected networks. The connectivity in exchange networks would cause an exchange occurring through a link to be affected by other exchanges through other links. In the case of positive connectivity, coordinated action and group integration depend on cooperation among network members. With negative connectivity, coordinated action and group interaction depend on competition. Moreover, when there is positive connectivity an exchange increases the probability of other exchanges; in the case of negative connectivity that probability declines.

According to Degenne and Forsé (1999), in most real life situations there is a mix of positive and negative exchanges. Moreover, following Coleman (1973), rational behaviour of actors generates an interactive mix of self-interest and control. Usually there is collective action in those networks, and there is uncertainty affecting the links: 'If no single actor can achieve the goal alone or award herself the total payoff, the system of actor is defined as a network of mutual dependencies. Each actor and her special interests are dependent on the other actors for achievement' (Degenne and Forsé, 1999, p. 143).

In the research conducted by Perrow (1992) the network perspective is applied to the study of small firm networks. Firms in the network compete and interact by sharing information, equipment and personnel, among other things, with one another. In the group there are firms supplying raw materials, other groups supplying equipment, energy, and so on; there are business and financial service firms.[19] The number of producers is high and there are distributors and customers together with an infrastructure surrounding them, consisting mainly of local and regional government, trade associations and unions. Applying these characteristics, the author asserts that 'industrial districts' is another term for small firm networks. In the defined situation firms can react more quickly and fruitfully to changes in technology and markets. Firms act by maximizing their individual self-interest, but trust and cooperation coexist with competition, there are external economies of scale derived from networks, and this environment has positive effects for the efficiency of the region and of the industry.

One of the main conclusions obtained from the application of the network perspective to exchanging organizations is the importance of trust relations. As we are showing at this point, according to the results obtained through several studies, trust and embedded relations emerge in situations of continuous exchanges. In the case study developed by Krackhardt (1992), the relationships of a selected firm are analysed, concluding that informal relations implying trust are the prevailing ones in situations of crisis or radical change. But, under normal conditions, it is possible to know the structural positions of such an organization by attending to formal network relationships. Moreover, when there are informal relationships among economic organizations based on trust, there is a continuity of their relationships, and the organizations concentrate on the exchange and reduce their search for alternative information sources. For those reasons, a relation of trust is behind an exchange relationship maintained continuously among organizations, even if the value of trust cannot be seen or checked. In consequence, the existence of trust increases the embeddedness of the firms in such groups.

According to Gulati (1995), through ongoing interaction, firms learn about each other and develop trust, and inter-firm trust is increasingly built as firms repeatedly interact. Therefore, the author proposes prior alliances between firms as a proxy to measure trust. Moreover, trust is more likely to be built in reduced geographic areas, as it is expected that firms will trust domestic partners more than others. When distance among organizations is short, there is more and better information available about firms and the consequences for reputation of opportunistic behaviour are greater in a domestic context. For the author, and following Bradach and Eccles (1989), the primary control mechanisms governing economic transactions among firms are price, authority and trust.[20]

The research done by Uzzi (1996), through the analysis of questionnaires sent to a group of firms, shows that there are embedded ties among the firms maintaining a stronger trade relationship. Following this idea, the author measures embeddedness by applying indices built with data on intermediate goods exchanges. The main result is that there is high embeddedness when firm exchanges are concentrated in trade relations maintained with a few other firms; in the opposite case, with low or non-existent embeddedness, there is a large number of contracted firms.[21] Uzzi's conclusion is that a firm sending more than 20 to 25 per cent of its business to an exchange partner maintains an embedded tie, otherwise it represents a competitive tie. According to the answers in the questionnaires received, it was unlikely for a firm to have concentrated exchanges with another firm unless an embedded tie existed. There are other studies focused on relations among economic organizations applied to particular sets of actors and relations, for example Levine (1972, 1985, 1987), Mintz and Schwartz (1981a, 1981b), Stokman and Wasseur (1985), Palmer *et al.* (1986), Scott (1987) and Berkowitz (1988).

## 2.4   RELATIONSHIPS AMONG FIRMS AND PRODUCTIVE BRANCHES: THE CONCEPT OF REGIONAL PRODUCTIVE SYSTEM

Firms and productive branches are two types of actors complying with the conditions expressed in the previous sections.[22] For them, all the analysed aspects of methodology and concepts, as actors in general and as economic organizations in particular, are applicable. Nevertheless, when these groups have been studied in the literature, the network perspective has rarely been considered, especially in the case of productive sectors and branches. Some references are Leoncini and Montresor (2000) and articles included in Lahr and Dietzenbacher (2001).

There are several concepts appearing in the literature for the identification of groups of related firms or of productive branches, all of which can be identified and analysed by applying the network perspective. Some of these concepts have already appeared in the previous sections, as is the case of small firms networks and industrial districts, but there are some more, depending on the actors that are considered to be the unit of analysis, but mainly depending on the selected relations for the research.

More specifically, the literature focused on the identification of linked productive branches or firms, and uses one term or another, depending mainly on the emphasis on social relations, if any, as well as on the geographical factors affecting them. In that respect, we can find research studies trying to identify productive systems (Wilkinson, 1983; Lawson, 1999), production systems (Storper and Harrison, 1991), regional business clustering (Lawson, 1999), industrial districts (Harrison, 1992; Feser and Bergman, 2000), industrial complexes (Streit, 1969; Roepke, Adams and Wiseman, 1974), technological regimes (Breschi, 2000), Industrial Clusters (Feser and Bergman, 2000) or regional productive systems (Asheim and Dunford, 1997).

The wider concept, considering a broad range of relations, and therefore concerned with social relations and informal linkages together with market formal relations, is that of productive systems. A productive system is understood as being created by complex interactions of technical, economic, social and political nature taking place in historical time. For Wilkinson (1983) the concept of productive system is so general that it provides the basis for analysis at any level: firms, industrial districts, regions or even nations. The understanding of the productive system in an identified social context differentiates it from the more common concepts of industrial complexes and production systems.

The two concepts mentioned, industrial complexes and production systems, relate only to formal market relationships, without explicitly considering any kind of informal, social or interpersonal linkage. In Roepke *et al.* (1974) an industrial complex is a group of industries having similar patterns of transactions and including other industries, which are major suppliers or markets for those within the group. The industrial complex can be understood in a spatial (Campbell, 1970; Czamanski, 1971) or aspatial context (Israd and Smolensky, 1963; Streit, 1969). A production system refers to a set of production units linked by their input–output structure and, as Storper and Harrison (1991) assert, it can be identified by considering factors territorially.

Economic transaction is the characteristic linking firms and groups of firms in the two concepts above. Therefore, interrelated groups are identified by applying the trade criterion. But, when other kinds of factors are specifically taken into account, different concepts appear. This is the case of regional business clustering, industrial district, industrial cluster, regional cluster and socio-economic regions. All of these are sub-sets of the wider productive system, as they include some of the following factors: untraded interdependencies, industrial atmosphere, local institutions, informal and formal cooperation, learning and knowledge, collective technical culture, personal interactions, trust and experience or collaboration. That is, some kind of non-economic or non-formal relation is added to the trade one, but without considering the whole social net in which such relations are embedded, as would be the case for productive systems.

For all the above terms the location fact is determinant for the linkages among productive units, reinforcing and facilitating them. Location is shown as an important determinant of relations, as it comprises distinctive institutional, cultural and historical characteristics. Considering the importance of location factors, the concept of productive system would be that of regional productive system.

We should be aware that, for the terms listed above and considered sub-sets of the productive system concept, there is not only one accepted definition, as different authors add more or fewer social factors to their particular analysis in the necessary establishment of boundaries. In the case of industrial clusters the focus is input–output relationships, but, sometimes, with consideration of linked institutions influencing the competitiveness of the group (Redman, 1994), the synergies achieved with geographical concentration (Rosenfeld, 1995) or the effects of a specific spatial context in the more particular case of regional clusters.

Having in mind that regional productive systems (Asheim and Dunford, 1997) are viewed as productive systems for which location and non-economic factors are of great importance, a characteristic form of regional productive system is industrial districts (Harrison, 1992; Feser and Bergman, 2000). In industrial districts local intra-firm linkages are substantial and occur at local level. Firm boundaries are flexible and there is cooperative competition among firms. Therefore, trust is very important as there is continuous collaboration in the district. Firms belonging to the district are small and medium ones, and the relationship among them does not have to be an input–output one necessarily. They can be related through the sharing of tools, information or skilled personnel. According to Becattini (1989) firms in a district are held together by a complex of external economies and diseconomies of joint and associated costs and historical and cultural vestiges, enveloping both inter-firm and interpersonal relationships. For some authors, such as Granovetter (1985), trust, which comes from experience, is a key to the emergence of informal ties that are deeper than mere contracts, with trust requiring personal contacts and, therefore, geographical proximity. Firms inside an industrial district experience a combination of cooperation and competition among themselves.

When talking, in most general terms, about this kind of associational structure considered in location terms, the proper term including the whole set of relevant factors is that of 'regional productive systems'. According to this, the consideration of institutions, social structures and even cultures and traditions is necessary to understand the most important links among firms. Those links are based on knowledge, learning, know-how, disembodied technology and positive externalities coming from innovation processes. Agglomeration is of great concern for the better understanding of knowledge, learning and innovation flows. For this reason, and because of the existence of a collective technical culture and institutional framework, the geographical question is fundamental to the study of such regional productive systems (Storper and Scott, 1995; Desrochers, 2001; Porter, 1996). Other very important factors are untraded interdependencies, and tacit and codified knowledge generating learning by doing, learning by using and learning by interacting and, moreover, interactive learning by cooperation among firms and also with local authorities.

For Wilkinson (1983) the parts constituting a productive system are labour power, means of production, methods by which production is organized, structure of ownership and control of productive activity, and the social and political framework within which the production process operates. Therefore, the success of a productive system will depend on its comparative advantages in terms of its economic, technical, political and social organization. In such a way it would acquire a strong competitive position.

The existence of this kind of net, or regional productive system, can be fully understood when the importance of trust and cooperation are considered. These two factors, in the context of a particular institutional framework, create a structure of social relations in such a way that, in the explanation of a production process, it is not possible to talk only about physical and human capital and production process, since social capital appears as another production factor, which is becoming essential for firms.

Recognizing the role of social capital in modern capitalism, understood as a learning economy (Morgan, 1997), know-how and tacit knowledge are the intangible and invisible key factors for the production processes of any firm. Therefore, knowledge, competence, skill and organizational culture become very important for groups of interrelated firms located in a particular area and working as a social net. In Morgan (1997), and following Storper (1995), to study productive systems inside their regional location is so important because there are two main roots of learning playing a key role. These roots are localized input–output relations and untraded interdependencies leading to coordination. The latter includes, mainly, labour markets, regional conventions, norms and values, and public or semi-public institutions, all of which should be explained in a localized or regional context. For the case of localized input–output relations, they form a net of firms related by trade flows and, at the same time, these flows include information and innovation flows. Therefore, assuming the importance of a learning process in production, it is important to realize that firms are most likely to learn from other firms, especially those which are customers, suppliers and competitors, which are related by input–output flows.

Three definitions and a theoretical claim have been discussed in this chapter in relation to the concept of social capital. Morgan's definition of social capital constitutes a particular application of the concept given by Putnam, which in turn can be placed within the most general definition referring to it as social structure, used by Burt (both concepts are discussed in Section 2.2).

Burt's use of the term is the most general one, as it refers to the relational structure of every network. Moreover, according to this, all social structures facilitate some form of social capital. Nevertheless, as explained in Section 2.2, Burt argues that, depending on the structure of the network, the social capital factor will be more or less intense. In this sense, networks with high closure, and therefore strong links inside them and many weak ties linking them with other networks, will show the highest level of social capital. The social structure definition includes Putnam's concept. His definition also refers to the relational structure of the networks, but it specifies the particular features that create and define this structure. Those features are mainly networks and norms. The existence of a net of interrelations (network) and of norms acting on the network structure makes coordination and cooperation easier for the mutual benefit of actors in the social organization. The concept of networks in Putnam corresponds to the relational structure in Burt's definition. Moreover, network closure and weak ties in the social structure explanation correspond, in a more abstract form, to the facilitation of coordination and cooperation involved in Putnam's definition. From both perspectives, social capital reduces the risk of cooperation and facilitates access to information.

The way in which Morgan makes use of the social capital concept fits perfectly with the two definitions discussed above. In Morgan's application of the concept, the emphasis is on the identification of the current capitalist system as a learning economy. From this viewpoint, tacit knowledge, competence, skills and organizational culture are the key flows in the networks of interrelated firms working in a social network. Therefore, the concept of networks given by Putnam and the social structure in Burt's definition correspond to the concept of social networks used by Morgan for the particular case of networks of interrelated firms. Depending on the structure of the network – as a function of its closure and weak ties – coordination and cooperation will be easier, and therefore tacit knowledge will flow in a more efficient form. In fact, Morgan explicitly points out that untraded interdependencies leading to coordination constitute a main root of learning in firms' networks. Among the untraded interdependencies, Morgan includes norms and values, and these are also major factors in the social capital concept given by Putnam, which emerge in the relational structures of networks in the social structure definition.

Finally, it should be emphasized that the role of social capital as a means of linking the functioning of networks, when there are actors with a different and vulnerable position, does not constitute a definition of social capital *per se*. It is instead a theoretical claim aimed at accounting for the empirical relevance of social capital in particular situations, where the process of integration is characterized by complexity, uncertainty and tacit knowledge. Traditionally, markets and hierarchies have been put forward in the literature as the two basic devices for integrating networks. All this will be discussed in Chapter 5, where the relevance of social capital, in the particular case of markets and economic structures, is discussed in relation to the efficiency of the socio-economic system and to development, and where markets, hierarchies and networks, as analysed by Williamson (1983) and Ouchi (1980), are discussed and compared.

The wider regional productive system concept is the one to be studied in the present research, as it is the concept that considers the broadest set of relations, by applying mainly the network perspective and additionally input–output analysis. Clearly, it will not be possible to identify complete systems according to the stricter theoretic sense of the concept; rather it will be necessary to identify limited systems. Following the network methodology, some actors and specific relations will be selected from the broad net, depending on the quantity and quality of the available information and on the research objectives.

More specifically, the data offered by regional input–output tables for a time period of 15 years (1980–95) are applied, and therefore formal trade relations are considered. Complementing that information, specific data about regional firms working in the branches classified by input–output tables are also used, in order to search for frequent trade interactions generating trust and embeddedness. Data about relevant institutions, such as technology and research institutes, are also included. Historical references considering the productive situation of every place under analysis, as well as other studies available for the same or comparable locations, are of great help in the identification of the systems. This set of information is used to consider dynamic and historical factors and to provide a context for the systems' identification and characterization. The characteristics of the data and the explanation of the specific methods applied in the research are the focus of the next chapter, before the applied study is presented.

## NOTES

1. The economic literature focused on input–output analysis is very vast; some of the basic references are Leontief (1951, 1967, 1977, 1985), Rasmussen (1956), Dorfman, Samuelson and Solow (1958) and Schultz (1977).
2. Although information about attributes is considered in some studies applying network analysis, this is done only in a complementary form to enrich the research. The main characteristic of this approach is its relational character.
3. The input–output indices are explained, together with a brief exposition of the input–output theory, in Chapter 3, which is focused on description of the methods and data used.
4. Some authors who refer to it as a paradigm are Nohria (1992), Emirbayer and Goodwin (1994), Degenne and Forsé (1999) and Wasserman and Faust (1994).
5. See Monge and Contractor (2004) for an overview of theories applying network analysis.
6. This is based on Granovetter (1985) and will be discussed in Section 2.3.
7. 'The structural perspective is deductively superior to normative action since its use of network models provides a rigorous algebraic representation of system stratification from which hypotheses can be derived. It is descriptively superior to atomistic action since it explicitly takes into account the social context within which actors make evaluations' (Burt, 1982, in Degenne and Forsé, 1999, p. 11).
8. Deeper-reaching arguments in this respect can be found in Burt (1982), Leydesdorff (1991) and Degenne and Forsé (1999).
9. For some authors, such as DiMaggio (1992), it is not possible to disregard the actors' attributes when studying social networks.

10. Homophily, understood as the extent to which members of the group have their closest ties to members who are similar to themselves, requires attribute data on all nodes in addition to relational data.
11. 'The strength of a tie is a (probably linear) combination of the amount of time, the emotional intensity, the intimacy (mutual confiding), and the reciprocal services which characterise the ties' (Granovetter, 1973, p. 1310).
12. 'Where you live and whom you know – the social capital you can draw on – helps to define who you are and thus to determine your fate' (Putnam, 1993, p. 6).
13. Friedman (1953) and Scott (1984) are among the most influential references discussing the concept of positivism in economics.
14. DiMaggio and Powell (1983) explain that, when an organizational field is consolidated, the organizations in it start to become more similar to one another, a phenomenon called isomorphism, as a process of homogeneity. Isomorphic change can happen through coerciveness, imitation (mimetic processes) or normative pressures. According to the authors, diversity is more convenient than isomorphism, and for this reason it is necessary to know its causes for political purposes. In knowing the causes, a theory of institutional isomorphism is necessary because the theories of natural selection (the invisible hand of Adam Smith) and elite control (represented by Marx) are not satisfactory to explain the shifts towards homogeneity.
15. This leads to new production arrangements, new means of internal organization and new ways to organize ties to firms with which they transact and, therefore, creates manufacturing and telecommunication networks.
16. Social capital is, in essence, social structure, as will be seen in Section 2.4.
17. For Benson (1975) organizations are dependent upon their positions in the network, because networks are mechanisms by which organizations acquire and dispense scarce resources and, therefore, create and perpetuate a system of power relations. Following this idea, Pfeffer and Salancik (1978) formulate a resource dependency theory.
18. 'Node' is the technical name for an actor in the network. A cutpoint is a node in a network whose removal would increase the number of connected components in the net. A component is a group of nodes which are all interconnected among themselves and without connection with any node outside the group. The removal of a cutpoint divides the network into more sub-sets without connection.
19. Supplying, basically, business surveys, technical training, personnel administration, transport, research and development, and so on.
20. The author mentions Arrow (1974) asserting that trust is perhaps the most efficient mechanism for governing economic transactions, as it reduces costs.
21. The author uses two different complementary indices, a first-order network coupling (1) and a second-order network coupling (2), with values between 0 (no embeddedness) and 1 (embedded relations):

(1) $\sum_{j=1}^{n_m} p_{ij}^2$ where $p_{ij} = \dfrac{x_{ij}}{x_i}$, and $x$ are outputs; (2) $\dfrac{\sum_{j=1}^{n_m} Q_j}{n_m}$, where $Q_j = \sum_{i=1}^{n_s} D_{ji}^2$, $D_{ji} = \dfrac{x_{ji}}{x_j}$, and $x$ are inputs.

22. 'Branch' is the name for groups of firms, or groups of parts of firms, dedicated to related productive activities and, therefore, leading to a more disaggregated classification than that of the productive sectors.

# 3 Data Characteristics and Methods Explanation

## 3.1 INTRODUCTION

According to the previous chapter, the focus of this research is the study of regional productive systems as networks of productive branches and other institutions, following a network perspective. The systems will be identified and characterized at regional level. They will then be compared in time and space to explain, from a relational structural perspective, different regional development processes. The adopted perspective implies an alternative epistemological view according to its basis, presented in the previous chapter, and its methods, explained in this chapter. For this purpose, a specific set of data has been collected, and the available methods have been studied.

Input–output analysis has been widely used in empirical studies looking for groups of interrelated sectors or branches, mainly through the application of indices to measure and classify every relation appearing in an input–output table. These indices are explained in this chapter as they are used to complement the main method of analysis, network analysis, for a better understanding of the identified regional productive systems.

The characteristics of input–output analysis generated the need to look for another method for the groups' identification process. Such a method should be more in accordance with the adopted methodological perspective, explained in Chapter 2; should allow for the presentation of data and results in a more simplistic form than input–output indices do; and should also allow for a structural analysis of the systems. The needed method, focused on the structure of a relational system, is network analysis, which can be interestingly complemented by input–output indices. Network analysis offers a wide set of measures for the identification of productive systems and for the analysis of their structures. The most important measures are explained in this chapter, simplified as much as possible. The main concepts and indicators are presented in such an elementary way to allow, in the next chapter when those measures are applied, for a fuller explanation when necessary.

Once the regional productive systems have been identified and characterized, their structures and evolution will be related to differentiated development patterns. This will be done through the proposal of a set of hypotheses that will be tested with mechanism causality. Therefore, this type of hypotheses testing method will also be expounded in this chapter.

In summary, this chapter seeks to explain the main characteristics of the data under analysis and the methods mentioned. For quantitative data, regional input–output tables will be used and therefore there is a section focused on the explanation of their characteristics. Other sources of information are also used, at firm level and for other institutions taking part in the productive systems, and therefore they are also briefly explained. These data will be analysed in the next chapter applying the two selected methods, social network and input–output analyses. Then the regional systems structure and evolution will offer some explanations for diverse regional development paths through mechanism causality testing.

## 3.2 RELEVANT CHARACTERISTICS OF THE DATA USED

The principal quantitative data source for this research is regional input–output flows, originally elaborated by Leontief in 1951 at national level for the US economy, together with the Leontief model, which allows for the study of intersectoral relationships. Input–output data can be used in different ways and, therefore, the researcher should choose, according to the investigation, some data aspects. In this study, input–output flows are considered in value terms, all their circularity direct and indirect connections are taken into account, focused on intersectoral relationships eluding intrasectoral links, regional data are used and therefore extrapolations from national flows are avoided, and domestic instead of total values are considered.[1]

Complementary data sources are also used: information at firm unit level for different regions and productive branches; data on regional technological centres, parks and other institutions; comparative studies for the same regions and others with similar characteristics; and historical bibliography to provide a context for the productive systems embedded in every region.

### 3.2.1 Sectoral Relationships in Input–Output Flows

Leontief offered his model in an attempt to combine an economic theory with empirical research. He explains the necessity to establish that kind of combination in the economic investigation, even if abstraction has to be done:

> This chapter is concerned with a new effort to combine economic facts and theory, known as *interindustry* or *input–output* analysis ... It is true, of course, that the individual transactions, like individual atoms and molecules, are far too numerous for observation and description in detail. But it is possible, as with physical particles, to reduce them to some kind of order by classifying and aggregating them into groups. This is the procedure employed in input–output analysis in improving the grasp of economic theory upon the facts with which it is concerned in every real situation. (Leontief, 1951, p. 3)[2]

When Leontief proposed the elaboration of a table made of input–output flows and developed an analysis according to that information, he named it 'Input–Output or Interindustry Analysis' (Leontief, 1951). 'Input–Output Analysis is a method of systematically quantifying the mutual interrelationships among the various sectors of a complex economic system' (Leontief, 1986, p. 19). The information offered by these tables is a quantification of all the trading flows taking place among the productive branches of an economy. The model built by Leontief allows for the design of measurements to obtain specific information about inter- and intra-industry relationships. Consequently, input–output tables and analysis, together with network analysis, explained as a method in this chapter, are used further on in this research to identify and characterize regional productive systems. Briefly, the well-known Leontief model can be expressed as follows.[3]

For each productive branch, production goes partially to intermediate sales and partially to final demand; therefore, in the case of the output of branch $i$, $x_i$, in a system of $n$ branches, the following equation is obtained, where $FD$ is final demand and $x_{ij}$ indicates the amount of $i$ production sold to branch $j$:

$$x_i = \sum_{j=1}^{n} x_{ij} + \mathbf{FD}_i \, . \tag{3.1}$$

Once technical coefficients are defined as in (3.2), equation (3.1) can be transformed into (3.3):

$$a_{ij} = \frac{x_{ij}}{x_j} \, , \tag{3.2}$$

$$x_i = \sum_{j=1}^{n} a_{ij} x_j + \mathbf{FD}_i .$$  (3.3)

As this last equation holds for all $n$ branches, it can be presented in matrix terms, where $\mathbf{A}$ is the matrix of technical coefficients and $\mathbf{B}$ is the Leontief inverse matrix:

$$X = \mathbf{A}X + \mathbf{FD} \Rightarrow X = (I - \mathbf{A})^{-1} \cdot \mathbf{FD} \Rightarrow X = \mathbf{B} \cdot \mathbf{FD} .$$  (3.4)

The values of the input–output matrix, made of $x_{ij}$ elements, are used as measurements of trade flows among sectors. Matrix $\mathbf{A}$ of technical coefficients will be used as a picture of the internal structure of the system. Matrix $\mathbf{B}$, or inverse Leontief matrix, comprising $b_{ij}$ elements, considers all direct and indirect dependence relationships among productive branches. Two other matrices can be built, one of them made up of (3.5) coefficients, and therefore considering the weight of a trade relation on the intermediate sales of the selling branch, $\mathbf{IS}$. The other, made up of (3.6) coefficients, considers the importance of a relation on the intermediate purchases for the purchasing branch, $\mathbf{IP}$.

$$\frac{x_{ij}}{\sum_{j=1}^{n} x_{ij}} = \frac{x_{ij}}{\mathbf{IS}_i} ,$$  (3.5)

$$\frac{x_{ij}}{\sum_{i=1}^{n} x_{ij}} = \frac{x_{ij}}{\mathbf{IP}_j} .$$  (3.6)

The five matrices offer enough information to identify the kind and magnitude of intersectoral and intrasectoral trade relationships and, therefore, to apply network analysis and to build input–output indices, helping such identification and better characterization.[4]

Once the general model has been presented, the following sub-sections are dedicated to go deeply into some aspects of the Leontief model and data.

### 3.2.1.1    Value or physical terms

Input–output tables usually show trade flows in value terms. Therefore, when comparing two different tables or the coefficients obtained from them, changes in prices are included. There are arguments for and against the use of values or quantities. Nevertheless, it is evident that prices themselves constitute a relevant variable offering important information. Bharadwaj (1966, p. 317) establishes that 'if the value coefficients are to be the basis of an incentive mechanism working via the market, price changes, in themselves, play an important role'.

For Chenery and Watanabe (1958), value terms are preferred to physical terms. Their main argument refers to practical reasons, owing to the availability of data but also because, at the same time, the comparison in value terms is more meaningful when the interest is in the overall pattern of interdependence rather than in its details.

The Leontief model (1951, 1985) allows obtaining the prices of all the branches in the system in the following way:

$$P = \mathbf{B}'VA_u .$$                              (3.7)

Where matrix **B** is transposed and $VA_u$ is the value added in terms of one unit of production. Both **B** matrix and $VA_u$ vector are needed in physical terms to achieve this vector of prices, which is quite unusual information from a practical point of view.[5]

For the identification of productive systems through input–output flows the value of the transaction is of great importance, when looking for the most important linkages. Value terms could be more helpful, even in the comparison among regions.[6] This is because the relations maintained among sectors are tradable ones and therefore they are done in value terms and their changes are due to variations in quantities bought and also in price terms. Consequently, to identify a productive system in a place and at a particular moment, current values are preferred, although, to compare years, values in constant and current prices could be used for comparison and to identify the characteristics of the changes.

### 3.2.1.2    Direct and indirect effects

In the literature using input–output tables and model, the terms 'direct' and 'indirect effects' and 'linkages' are widely used, but the meaning of these terms is not clear as there are two different interpretations, depending on the author doing the investigation. It is necessary to clarify both perspectives to determine which will be used in this research.

For some authors the distinction between both terms refers to the last step in the relation between two branches, without intermediary branches.[7] That is, one term refers to the straight flow between two sectors, without going through intermediary branches (direct), and the other considers all the flows in which a sector has participated to build a particular product through its sales to other intermediate sales (indirect).[8] Therefore, direct linkages can be measured with the input–output matrix of flows and with the technical coefficients of matrix **A**, while total (direct and indirect) linkages will be measured with the inverse matrix **B**.

There is an alternative use of both terms, direct and indirect. According to Rasmussen (1956), Dorfman *et al.* (1958) and Hewings (1982), a direct effect is identified with the amount of product *i* going directly to final demand and not with the amount of *j* sold to *i* as the final step in the elaboration of product *i*. In that case, **B** can be used to identify total (direct and indirect) linkages, while to measure only indirect effects (total intersectoral relationships without considering the last flows going to final demand) the calculation should be done with the coefficients of $(\mathbf{B} - I)$.[9] Coefficients in matrix **A** and in the input–output matrix of intersectoral relations measure the last indirect relation in the production process according to that terminology.

We shall call 'intersectoral linkages' the ones using the coefficients of **A** and the flows of the input–output matrix, and 'total linkages' the ones using the coefficients of **B**.

### 3.2.1.3 Intersectoral and intrasectoral relationships

Another discussion in the use of the input–output information is whether intrasectoral flows and linkages should be considered. Rasmussen (1956) suggested the use of $(\mathbf{B} - \hat{b})$ to identify key sectors, where $\hat{b}$ is a diagonal matrix representing intrasectoral links. The remaining coefficients will consider only intersectoral relationships.[10] For Rasmussen, the inclusion of the diagonal in **B** would tend to equalize the indices, because of the dominating effects of intrasectoral relationships. Therefore, the highest values of indices would be obtained when applying $(\mathbf{B} - \hat{b})$ instead of $(\mathbf{B} - I)$, and this in turn would show higher coefficients than when applying **B**.

It seems quite reasonable to operate only with intersectoral relations for the identification of productive systems. However, the level of sectoral disaggregation should be taken into account in the following way. If the sector classification is detailed enough (high disaggregation and therefore high number of branches), eliminating the relations that branches have between themselves will allow for a better picture of the productive system, following the idea of Rasmussen. But if the level of aggregation is too great (low number of branches representing the whole productive system), the inclusion of intrasectoral relations should be taken into account to include the characteristics of the region under analysis. In the latter situation it could be the case of a particular sector being too aggregated, with high participation in the economy under study, including within itself a productive system identifiable at a lower level of aggregation. For this reason it is of great importance to characterize productive systems according to the particular context of the region in which it is identified, and therefore to include other sources of information. A key sector could be acting in a region inside a system in a hardly perceivable way if the level of aggregation does not allow distinguishing particular branches that are relevant for the region.[11]

### 3.2.1.4    Extrapolation of national data to other countries and to regions

It is a common practice, when using input–output information, to adapt in some way the national trade flows to the country's regions or even to other nations.[12] Sometimes there is no adaptation at all, but it is assumed that technical coefficients are the same across regions or countries.[13]

To carry out that kind of extrapolation, it is necessary to assume that there are no differences in the productive processes of goods and services among countries or regions. This is considered mainly true for the case of developing countries among themselves, underdeveloped countries among them, or regions belonging to the same country.[14]

When that homogeneity is assumed, the effect of a different location, and the characteristics of different regions for transportation, available technology, productive specialization, culture, institutions, history or tastes, are not considered significant factors. However, these are key elements to be included for the productive systems under identification, not only when comparing countries but even when comparing regions inside the same country. For such reasons it is extremely important to find input–output tables at regional level to identify, not national, but regional productive systems. Once such identification is done, development strategies could be designed according to the specific characteristics of the area.

Moreover, it should be remembered that, when geographical differences affecting sectoral relationships in different places are ignored, each productive branch comprises, not a unique product, but products from many other sub-branches, depending on the aggregation level. And some sub-branches have a higher weight in some regions, or nations, than in others, therefore technical relations should be different and extrapolation has no sense. Even if extrapolation is done, being aware of this fact, it is not possible to establish straight conclusions and affirmations when comparing two different places, at national or at regional level.

Some examples that discuss the opportunity of extrapolations are Hirschman (1959), Bharadwaj (1966) and McGilvray (1977). A more specific reference is Harrigan *et al.* (1980), which tries to establish whether it is possible to use UK national data to study the region of Scotland, but obtains a negative conclusion.

### 3.2.1.5   The meaning of backward and forward effects

Looking, in general, at the information offered by an input–output matrix, we could see that most inter-branch relationships are circular. Therefore, most branches are buyers and sellers for other branches at the same time. When considering the effect of a branch as an intermediate buyer for other branches to obtain its product, we are looking at the backward effects. Looking at the other side, that is, the effect of a branch as an intermediate seller for other branches to obtain their products, forward effects are considered.

According to the Leontief model, backward effects are defined as the effects of the final demand of one sector on the production of several sectors, as intermediate sellers. In the same way, forward effects are defined as the effect of several final demands on the production of a sector, as an intermediate seller. Both effects are calculated using the inverse Leontief matrix.

Several authors have asserted that the significant effects in selecting key sectors, or key relations, are the backward and not the forward effects.[15] A key sector, identified as one with high backward effects and then stimulated to generate growth, will encourage and drag the production of the sectors that sell it intermediate goods. However, a key sector identified as one with high forward effects has the uncertain effect of its perturbation on growth. In that case, once the branch has been invigorated, its production is affected by the final demands of the branches that are buyers for it. With the stimulation, its production is increased but there is not a clear effect on the other branches. Its impulse can promote investment in other sectors buying its intermediate goods, but this cannot be taken for granted. Backward effects are more powerful in that sense and therefore they can be used as a basis for investment decisions. The same situation applies when linkage effects are understood in the sense of agglomeration industries, as in Hirschman (1959).[16] In that case, the forward effect is not an independent inducement mechanism, but a powerful reinforcement to backward effects.

The discussion about the importance of backward and forward effects, when identifying key sectors or key intersectoral relationships, can go further. Following Jones (1976), when both effects are calculated applying the Leontief model, the backward effect will measure the effect of final demand of branch *i* on the production of all the branches selling to it. The forward effect will be measuring the effect of all final demands on the production of branch *i*. Therefore, in both cases the effects are measured from increases in final demands and looking at the effect, backward, on the production needed to allow for such final demands. For Jones both of them are backward relations. The author suggests calculating forward effects in a different way, explained further on.

Nevertheless, when calculating forward effects with **B** coefficients, through the sum of the rows in that matrix, the value obtained is the amount of *i* needed in the elaboration of one unit of all the goods being produced in the system, and this is generally understood as a forward effect of branch *i*. To obtain backward effects the sum of the columns of the **B** matrix is calculated and the amount obtained means the quantity of every product needed to get one unit of good *i*, and this is generally understood as a backward effect.

### 3.2.1.6    Total or inside values

Usually, input–output tables offer information about trade flows between branches for inside and total values and, therefore, also consider imports. In the case of regional tables, we find three values measuring the same flow between two branches: the inside, corresponding to the trade happening inside the region; the national, which corresponds to the inside plus the imports from the rest of the country; and the total, that is, the national plus the imports from the rest of the world. Therefore, a prior question to solve, before using input–output data, is which of them is the most relevant for the analysis. In the case of this research, data are applied to identify regional productive systems and therefore inside values should be the ones under consideration. Nevertheless, the other two values offer useful complementary information for the characterization of the identified productive systems.

In the search for regional productive systems the target is to identify groups of related sectors and firms, to explain the kind of relation they maintain and to understand their characteristics and evolution. Thus, national or total values do not allow the acquisition of that necessary information, as other firms, not working inside the region, will be included. Considering national, or more clearly total, values, regional productive systems cannot be found and even less explained. With total values the agro-food, steel or automobile productive system would be basically the same in every region, and in every country, because the required inputs for the whole process are similar in every place. In that sense, it is worthwhile to remember the distinction (offered in Chapter 2) between production systems, considering only trade relations, and productive systems, taking into account other economic, social and historical factors.

### 3.2.1.7    Data classification and homogeneity

The input–output data used consist of two tables for each analysed region (Andalusia and the Basque Country), one for the year 1980 and another for 1995. According to these tables' methodology, either CNAE-74 or CNAE-93 (*Clasificación Nacional de Actividades Económicas*, National Classification of Economic Activities) has been the classification used. However, every table shows a different number of productive branches and therefore they have a dissimilar aggregation level. This situation is justified in the methodological notes as an attempt to adapt each classification to the productive characteristics of the region.

The unification of all these tables involves great difficulty and the appearance of unavoidable incongruities; therefore the decision regarding this research has been to homogenize branches in time inside each region but not in space. That is, the research is done with the same number of branches for 1980 and 1995 inside each region, but with every region having a somehow different classification. This decision does not impede the comparison of results among regions but avoids incurring too many biases that necessarily appear when data homogenization is carried out.

### 3.2.2    Regional Qualitative and Quantitative Information

The application of network and input–output analyses to the productive branches of the selected input–output tables will allow for the identification of regional production systems. Thereafter, other information is used to go from production to productive systems. Each type of system will be explained and characterized.

### 3.2.2.1    Directorate of firms and technology institutions

Since each branch is made up of firms, regional firms belonging to the branches constituting the selected production networks or systems have been selected and interviewed. Also, structured questionnaires were sent to a group of firms.[17] Other complementary sources refer to regional institutions such as technology parks, innovation and training centres and associations. The structure of the productive networks will be explained, including these data, checking whether firms are related to the regional institutions and studying what type of relation they maintain. Through those relations there are diverse flows, such as for information, technology or workers, and it is necessary to be aware of this to study regional productive systems. Substantial conclusions can be obtained as the existence of these links allows for a better performance of regional firms and for regional development processes. All these data will be better understood when complemented by the information obtained from comparative references for locations with similar characteristics.

### 3.2.2.2    Regional economic history

Regional historical information is highly important for the identification of the productive systems and for their selection and characterization. Several authors, such as García Delgado and Carrera Troyano (2001), Bernal and Parejo (2001) and Fernández de Pinedo and Fernández (2001), emphasize the importance of history in understanding regional economic behaviour in Spain, and in particular in Andalusia and the Basque Country.

The historical specialization of every region allows for deductions referred to as regional productive systems, because the past productive structure determines the present one, and this is obvious for the selected regions in this analysis. According to its economic history, for the Basque Country a system integrating the iron, steel and machinery industries should be studied. In Andalusia the agro-food industry and mining sectors should be analysed.

The historical specialization of every region, their comparative advantages, their workers' skills, and their trade and traditions offer strong arguments in support of the necessity of considering the systems mentioned in the selected cases. Therefore this type of information is included in the processes of selection and characterization of regional productive systems.

## 3.3 MAIN METHODS APPLIED IN THIS RESEARCH

The two main methods applied to the data described above to study regional productive systems are social network analysis and measures obtained from input–output analysis. This section explains the main concepts belonging to both techniques and the measures applied in the next chapter to the kind of data discussed in the previous section. In order to identify and characterize regional production systems in the next chapter, the main measures used to value input–output relations are explained first, following the input–output model appearing in section 3.2. After that, there is a section focused on the concepts and measures proposed by network analysis, some of which will be explained more deeply when applied in the next chapter. The last section is dedicated to mechanism causality, because this is the hypotheses-testing method selected to analyse the relationship between regional productive systems and regional development processes.

### 3.3.1 Measures to Value Input–Output Relations

Input–output analysis has been widely used to develop measures to value relationships among productive branches. These measures are very useful for a general understanding of the production systems working in a region, for the characterization of such systems once they have been selected using social network analysis and for the identification of key sectors.

In that sense, two of the most important applications of input–output analysis were made by Rasmussen in 1956 and by Chenery and Watanabe in 1958. These authors showed ways to quantify and classify the relationships maintained among productive sectors. Their proposals have been widely used in economic analysis to identify key economic sectors, to plan development strategies and to identify clusters of interrelated firms, among other things. In Hirschman (1959) the use of both proposals is suggested to measure linkage effects (backward and forward), understood as the effects exerted by one or more firms to attract other firms to the same location, since they have some kind of supply or demand relationship.

The measures proposed by both authors, as well as the one of Streit (1969), not so generally used, are explained below. Moreover, some comments will be made that refer to several studies applying these techniques, with some suggestions on their use.

### 3.3.1.1    Rasmussen indices

The measurements proposed by Rasmussen (1956) are the following indices of power of dispersion, for $j$ (3.8), and of sensitivity of dispersion, for $i$ (3.9), in a system of $n$ productive branches:

$$U_{.j} = \frac{\frac{1}{n} b_{.j}}{\frac{1}{n^2} \sum_{j=1}^{n} b_{.j}}, \text{ where } b_{.j} = \sum_{i=1}^{n} b_{ij}, \qquad (3.8)$$

$$U_{i.} = \frac{\frac{1}{n} b_{i.}}{\frac{1}{n^2} \sum_{i=1}^{n} b_{i.}}, \text{ where } b_{i.} = \sum_{j=1}^{n} b_{ij}. \qquad (3.9)$$

The above indices are averages of the backward and forward total linkages of a productive branch, normalized by the overall average to allow for inter-industry comparisons.[18]

There are several versions of these indices, as they have been quite often used in applied research works. The most general form is the named absorption and diffusion effects, calculated as the sum by rows and by columns of $b$ coefficients.[19] Moreover, Jones (1976) proposes to calculate forward effects using a different **A** matrix to obtain a new **B**; the new **A***, made of $a_{ij}^{\bullet}$, is named in de Mesnard (2001) and in Lantner (2001) as the 'matrix of allocation coefficients':

$$a_{ij}^{\bullet} = \frac{x_{ij}}{x_i}. \qquad (3.10)$$

With the sum, by rows, of the new inverse, according to Jones (1976), the starting point is at the beginning of the production process, with an increase in primary inputs and tracing the effect forward through the system. The argument of de Mesnard (2001) and Lantner (2001) is that technical coefficients, $a$, measure the absolute direct influence of a sector over other sectors, while allocation coefficients, $a^*$, measure the relative direct influence of a sector over other sectors, and therefore there is elasticity.[20]

Both Rasmussen indices can be modified, by including a system of weights, to consider the importance of the measured branch in the whole economic system. Rasmussen proposed final demand for the weights, to obtain weighted indices of power and sensitivity of dispersion ($U_j^w$ and $U_{i.}^w$).

Rasmussen indices of power and sensitivity of dispersion are known in a sector of the literature as absorption and diffusion effects, or even as Hirschman indices.[21]

Rasmussen was aware that the above indices might not tell the whole story about branches' interrelations, as they are average measures. For this reason, he proposed to calculate, at the same time, measures of variability using the coefficients of variation of power and sensitivity of dispersion ($V_{.j}$ and $V_{i.}$).

Both variability measures can also be recalculated with weights, as for the indices of power and sensitivity of dispersion. Rasmussen established that a branch could be distinguished as a key industry when it has high $U_{.j}$ and small $V_{.j}$. This would mean that such a branch has high backward linkages, and those linkages are maintained with a relatively high number of other branches.

### 3.3.1.2 Chenery and Watanabe measures

Another important proposal was made in Chenery and Watanabe (1958), presenting two measures of interdependence as expressed in (3.11), indirect use of factor, for *j*, and (3.12), indirect demand, for *i*; where *IP* is intermediate purchases, *IS* means intermediate sales and *TD*, total demand. The indices consider the importance of every branch's intermediate purchases and sales for its production and demand, and both can be calculated in relative terms, with respect to the value of the index for the whole system.

$$u_j = \frac{IP_j}{x_j} \text{ with } IP_j = \sum_{i=1}^{n} x_{ij} , \tag{3.11}$$

$$w_i = \frac{IS_i}{TD_i} \text{ with } IS_i = \sum_{j=1}^{n} x_{ij} . \tag{3.12}$$

Chenery and Watanabe established a two-way classification, based on whether each sector's values are above or below the mean values. In that form, interdependence among sectors is understood as their relation on both sides, demand and supply. According to that classification there are four kinds of productive branches:

- Intermediate primary production: branches with low $u$ and high $w$.
- Intermediate manufacture: branches with high $u$ and $w$. This group is made up of very dependent sectors.
- Final manufacture: branches with high $u$ and low $w$.
- Final primary production: branches with low $u$ and $w$. This group is made up of relatively independent sectors.

According to the indirect use of factors, $u$, branches can be classified as primary or manufacture. When the value of $u$ is relatively low the branch is called 'primary', as most of its purchases are coming from primary factors (labour and capital) instead of from intermediate commodities. For values of $u$ that are relatively high the branch is classified as manufacture, because most of its purchases are coming from intermediate goods instead of from primary factors. For the indirect demand, $w$, sectors are classified as intermediate or final. When that value is relatively low, most of the branch sales are going to final demand (final). For a high $w$ instead, most of the branch sales go to intermediate trade for other branches (intermediate).

These indices are generally known in the literature as backward and forward linkages, and most of the time both of them are calculated in terms of production, and not of total demand as Chenery and Watanabe did for the indirect demand index.

The main difference between the Rasmussen and the Chenery and Watanabe proposals is that the first defines the indices with the elements of the **B** matrix, and therefore considers direct and indirect effects of the production of one branch on the final demand of another. However, in the Chenery and Watanabe indices the elements of the input–output matrix are used and therefore only intersectoral relations are considered. Consequently, both techniques should be considered complementary.

### 3.3.1.3    Streit coefficients

Streit coefficients are measurements of the economic linkages taking place between two branches, proposed in 1969 in the following way:

$$ST_{ij} = ST_{ji} = \frac{1}{4}\left( \frac{x_{ij}}{\sum\limits_{j=1}^{n} x_{ij}} + \frac{x_{ij}}{\sum\limits_{i=1}^{n} x_{ij}} + \frac{x_{ji}}{\sum\limits_{i=1}^{n} x_{ji}} + \frac{x_{ji}}{\sum\limits_{j=1}^{n} x_{ji}} \right) = \frac{1}{4}\left( \frac{x_{ij}}{IS_{i}} + \frac{x_{ij}}{IP_{j}} + \frac{x_{ji}}{IS_{j}} + \frac{x_{ji}}{IP_{i}} \right)$$

(3.13)

Once the coefficients have been obtained for every couple of branches, a unique index for each branch can be calculated:

$$ST_{j} = \sum_{i=1}^{n} ST_{ij} .$$ 

(3.14)

The $ST_{ij}$ coefficient shows all intersectoral relations maintained for every couple of branches, as sellers and buyers, on average. In the case of $ST_{j}$ coefficients, that information is summarized, showing all kinds of intersectoral relations taking place for each branch with all the others linked to it. In this last case it is not possible to know with which branches the relations are established, as it is a condensed index; such information is obtained from the first of the two indices (3.13).

### 3.3.1.4    Calculation and comparison of coefficients of variation

As has already been mentioned, the coefficient of variation is considered by several authors to be another important measure to be included in the analysis of input–output relations. According to most of the researchers, key sectors would show low coefficients of variation for their relations with all the productive branches. The variation coefficients can be applied to **B** and **A** coefficients. A high coefficient of variation will show that the analysed branch relates with a small number of other branches, even just with one. A low coefficient of variation will indicate that the studied branch relates with most of the branches in the system, even with all of them. Key branches, with low coefficients of variation, are disseminating in the system. In that sense those coefficients can be calculated as complementary measures to backward and forward indices.

Variation coefficients can also be applied for a better understanding of productive systems. The development trajectory of productive systems can be observed by checking their evolution, complementarily to backward and forward indices. It could be the case that the coefficients of variation have decreased in general terms, a situation that could be identified with diversified economies. But there could be observed the case of a change, where some sectors show an increase in the coefficients while others have a decrease. In such a case the first group of sectors could be identified as less integrated, and the second as more dynamic.

### 3.3.1.5    Application of the input–output measurements

All the above mentioned indices, mainly the Rasmussen ones, have been widely used, sometimes in the terms proposed by their authors and sometimes with variations. In some cases, the indices are even used without giving recognition to their authors, which has happened especially in the case of Rasmussen.

Publications using the mentioned indices to identify economic key sectors include Bharadwaj (1966), Hazari (1970), Yotopoulos and Nugent (1973), McGilvray (1977) and Schultz (1977). Some of these works are discussed below, because they apply the proposed measurements for specific purposes after including some variation. Therefore, this short bibliographical discussion can serve to identify the type of context where the measures have been applied and in which terms.

In most cases, authors look for key sectors applying Rasmussen – and in some case Chenery and Watanabe – measures. More concretely, Schultz (1977) calculates the two Chenery and Watanabe indices with respect to production. Moreover, he modifies them by considering imports, including weights, and eliminating intrasectoral relations. The power of dispersion of Rasmussen is also applied to check its effect on some economic aggregates. For Bharadwaj (1966) key sectors have high power of dispersion and low coefficient of variation. Therefore he applies Rasmussen together with Chenery and Watanabe indices, naming them backward and forward linkages.[22] In the case of McGilvray (1977), key sectors are identified to propose an industrial development programme. He calculates Rasmussen indices but names them backward and forward linkages.[23] Hazari (1970) applies Rasmussen indices and coefficients of variation, and key sectors are identified with power and sensitivity of dispersion higher than one and with relatively low coefficients of variation. He names the Rasmussen weighted indices using relative final-demand backward and forward effects.

A different perspective is offered in Yotopoulos and Nugent (1973) when trying to check the relationship between linkages and growth in developing and under-developing countries.[24] In order to do this, they define total linkage as the Rasmussen power of dispersion index without the averages.

Other research studies applying the measurements from a theoretical perspective are Jones (1976), calculating the Chenery and Watanabe indices in relation to production and, Cuello and Mansouri (1992), applying Rasmussen indices and coefficients of variation modified with a likelihood function and considering elasticities.

Finally, there are some studies for Spain such as the following: in Dominguez Hidalgo (1999) and Prado Valle (1999), Chenery and Watanabe, Rasmussen and Streit coefficients are applied to identify productive systems inside the Basque Country;[25] in Santamaría Martínez *et al.* (1999), Chenery and Watanabe indices are used to characterize the agro-food productive system in the Basque Country; in Prado Valle and González Gómez (2001), Chenery and Watanabe and Streit indices are calculated to analyse strategic economic sectors.

### 3.3.2 Social Network Analysis

Social network analysis uses graph theory and matrix analysis for its empirical application. Proceeding with these two techniques, mathematical calculations should be done to obtain particular measures, such as size, density and centrality, to identify social networks and to study their structure. In the application of the measures, the first step is to know the kind of group to be identified, as there are several possibilities from a conceptual and practical point of view.

Depending on the characteristics of the available data, and on the restrictions imposed on them according to the current research, there are several kinds of groups that network analysis can study. Once data have been collected, and relationships identified, there could be a group made by the collection of all actors on which ties are to be measured and of all kinds of relations linking them. A set of these actors can be selected, identifying sub-groups.[26]

A less restrictive definition than group is social network, defined in Iacobucci (1994) and in Wasserman and Faust (1994) as a finite set of actors and the relations or relation linking them. It is less restrictive because only a selected set of relations is considered, not all of them.[27] A particular kind of social network is the component, understood in Borgatti (1994) and Iacobucci (1994) as a social network with ties between all pairs of actors or nodes, and there is no link with actors outside the network. This is a very strict term, considered a strong alliance, which has been relaxed by some authors in their application. A strongly connected component is known as a 'cluster', as in Degenne and Forsé (1999) and Aroche-Reyes (2001), where the term is applied to the case of Mexican input–output tables for the year

1980 after applying several thresholds or filters.[28] The type of group in which each actor is directly and strongly linked to most but not necessarily all others[29] is the social circle. It is also labelled 'social cluster', as in Emirbayer and Goodwin (1994).

For the current research, network analysis is applied to input–output relations among branches, and therefore data will show the structure of a social network. To this type of group, the social network, the measures and techniques explained in the next sections will be applied. The objective is to know its structure and that of smaller groups inside it having specific characteristics.

### 3.3.2.1    Data representation and identification of groups inside the social network

The available data, presented in matrix terms, are analysed at first for the study of the most general characteristics, and for the identification of specific groups inside the whole network. These data can be dichotomous (binary) or valued, and they may or may not consider the direction of the relation (directed or undirected). When data are valued they can be transformed into binary through the application of a threshold value, based on the strength of ties in the original valued relation.[30]

In order to represent them, the available sets of nodes and links can be expressed graphically with the broad network concepts turning into graph definitions. Generally speaking, a graph is considered a finite set of nodes, representing actors, plus the set of arrows or lines connecting them, depending on whether relations between actors follow a direction or are undirected. Graphs can acquire several characteristics and names, depending on the specific characteristics of the group under study and of the data, expressed in matrix terms. The main distinction appears among graphs (binary data without considering the direction of the relation), valued graphs (cardinal data) and directed graphs (data including the direction of the relation) labelled 'digraphs' in Iacobucci (1994), among others, although the general term 'graph' is usually applied to both situations, directed and undirected relationships.[31] When relations are valued, and therefore data are weighted, each arrow carries a number in the valued graph. In that case, values may change back into binary according to certain thresholds or filters, as shown in Iacobucci (1994) and Degenne and Forsé (1999).[32]

Although there are several more specific terms, depending on the restrictions considered in the analysis,[33] when only one type of relation is included, and therefore social networks are analysed, the correct term is 'graph'.[34] In this research graphs are analysed as they are applied to social networks.

The name of the graph can also reflect the social network connectivity or cohesiveness. When this is the case, the term 'connected graph' is used when there is a path from every node to every other node, and 'cohesive graph' when there are many short geodesics and small diameters relative to its size.[35] A strongly connected graph is a connected digraph, and a unilaterally connected digraph is a digraph connected in one direction (Borgatti, 1994).[36]

Graphs can be used to show characteristics of the network that cannot be seen in a simple way. In that sense, there are reduced graphs when clusters, instead of actors, are the linked nodes and inside each cluster there are strongly connected components.[37] Once the appropriate graph is chosen to represent groups, sub-groups or social networks, cliques can be identified and their properties studied. A clique is defined as a maximal complete sub-graph of three or more nodes, all of which are interlinked. It implies a very strict definition of cohesive sub-groups and there are other less restrictive terms emerging from it (and more interesting as regards their identification). These terms are cliques at level c for valued data, n-cliques for maximal subgraphs, n-clan, n-club, k-plex, k-core, LS-set and lambda set.[38] Some references explaining, in detail, differences among these terms are Degenne and Forsé (1999) and Wasserman and Faust (1994), the latter referring to Hubbell (1965) as an example applying these concepts to input–output links. The concept of components, already mentioned as a particular type of social network, can also be applied for their identification as regions inside a network.

### 3.3.2.2 Measuring the characteristics of social networks and their groups

All the terms described in this section measure, in network terms, the characteristics of a social network and of the groups that can be identified within it.

*Relational and positional general characteristics*     Measuring the network size, density and distance permits the most general and basic study of its structure and distinguishing nodes that occupy important positions on it. As can be deduced from Degenne and Forsé (1999), among others, the application of this group of measures is usually the first step in the structural analysis of a network.

Network size measures the number of contacts in a network. This simple calculation gives an initial idea about the importance and complexity of the network under study. The order of the network can also be used as a size measure, calculating the number of nodes in a graph.[39] There are other size measures that cannot be considered as general as the two already mentioned; these should be applied in more specific cases, as with the effective size of a node proposed in Borgatti (1997), measuring each node's directed relation minus its redundancy.[40] Redundancy exists to the extent that the contacts of a node are connected among them. Thus, redundancy does not exist if the actors related to the node under study are not interconnected. Low node redundancies can be identified for actors in strategic positions, as they would have access to diverse resources that could not be available for other actors.

Density is the ratio between the number of links, or arrows, in a graph and the arrows in a complete graph with the same number of nodes.[41] It is therefore the number of effective connections related to the total number of possible connections. With $L$ as the number of arrows and $g$ the number of nodes, density is:

$$\Delta = \frac{L}{g(g-1)}, \ 0 \le \Delta \le 1. \tag{3.15}$$

In the case of directed relations, the degree of a network can be calculated as a density measure, as established in Burt (2000), distinguishing between indegree and outdegree. The indegree of a node is the number of arrows converging to a given node, and therefore the number of nodes adjacent to the measured node.[42] The outdegree of a node is its number of outbound arrows and therefore the number of nodes adjacent to the measured node. In directed networks the degree of a node is its indegree plus its outdegree. Whatever technical measures, a social network with high density would show a complex structure with many relationships allowing diverse flows.

Distance between nodes can be measured in several forms, to gain information about the structure of the network.[43] The most general measure of distance is the walk, defined as any sequence of steps of any length, without considering direction, for any group of nodes in the net; nodes and lines can appear more than once. In a directed walk there is a sequence of alternating nodes and arrows, all arrows pointing in the same direction.[44] Other common measures of distance are path and cycle, both of them offering several variants, although other concepts can also be used.[45] Paths, already stated in this chapter, can also be applied to directed data: a directed path is a directed walk in which no node and no arrow is included more than once, with all arrows pointing in the same direction and its length being the number of arrows.[46] A cycle is a closed walk, or directed walk for directed links, of at least three nodes in which all lines are distinct and all nodes, except the beginning and ending, are also different. The two following graphs, taken from Wasserman and Faust (1994, pp. 106, 131), are examples of the defined concepts.

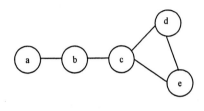
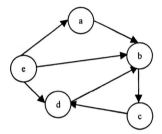

*(a) Undirected social network*          *(b) Directed social network*

*Figure 3.1: Distance in social networks*

In Figure 3.1(a) there are paths such as {b, c, d}, walks like {b, c, d, c}, and the cycle {d, e, c, d} can also be found. In Figure 3.1(b) a directed path is {e, d, b, c}, a directed walk, {e, a, b, c, d, b, c} and a cycle {b, c, d, b}.

The concepts and measures already shown in this section are the most generally used in the structural study of a network, as they make it possible to obtain a wide view of its structure. However, there are more concrete measurements helping to give a deeper analysis of network structures. This is the case of position, studied for the identification of groups of individuals similarly embedded in networks of relations. Such individuals do not need to be in direct or indirect contact, as explained in Wasserman and Faust (1994) where there are some references to works applying these measures to study international trade and the world economic system.[47] When two actors occupy the same position in the network, they have redundant contacts and therefore they are in a situation of structural equivalence.

Following Emirbayer and Goodwin (1994), among others, positional analysis studies the actor's ties to third parties applying structural equivalence and blockmodelling. In a strict sense, two actors are structurally equivalent if they have identical ties to and from all other actors in the network. The collection of equivalent, or approximately equivalent, actors allows for the identification of equivalence classes and, therefore, positions. By applying blockmodelling, the original matrix of relations is permuted to build blocks of equivalent actors in an image matrix that describes the ties between positions and that can be represented in a reduced graph. For the representation of equivalent blocks in an image matrix and a reduced graph, it is necessary to have a criterion to separate the blocks, as perfect structural equivalence is very difficult to find.[48] Two possible measures of structural equivalence are Euclidean distance and correlation.[49] Burkhardt (1994) proposes the application of the measure of structural equivalence – equation (3.16) – appearing in MacEvoy and Freeman (1987), by considering the aggregate dissimilarity or distance between $i$'s and $j$'s relations in a network. Once the index is calculated, and therefore a dissimilarity matrix is obtained, Burkhardt measures the correlation between that matrix and a structurally equivalent matrix:

$$d_{ij} = \frac{\sqrt{\sum_{k=1}^{N}\left(x_{ik} - x_{jk}\right)^2}}{N}. \tag{3.16}$$

Moreover, the position of actors in a network can be affected by the restrictions on it, that is, by the limited access that some agents have to other agents. To consider this question, an index of constraint can be calculated, describing the extent to which a network is concentrated in redundant contacts. The issue is that more constrained networks span fewer structural holes, which means less social capital according to the structural hole argument. Therefore, it is quite important to have a measure of this situation, such as the network constraint index in Burt (2000):[50]

$$NC = \sum_{i} c_{ij} \quad \text{where} \quad c_{ij} = \left(p_{ij} + \sum_{q} p_{iq} p_{qj}\right)^2 \quad \text{and} \quad p_{ij} = \frac{x_{ij}}{\sum_{q} x_{iq}}. \tag{3.17}$$

Having analysed size, density, distance and position, the most interesting calculations to gain greater understanding about the structure of a network are centrality, for actors and groups, and centralization.

High centrality for a node $i$, $C(n_i)$, refers to an actor occupying a central position, highly linked, in relative terms, to all other actors inside the network and then involved in many ties. Centrality can also be measured for groups. The centralization of a group of actors $A$, $C_A$, refers to the group position when it is organized around a focal point. The larger it is, the more likely that a single actor is quite central, with the remaining actors being considerably less so. It measures how variable, or heterogeneous, actor centralities are.

There are three generally recognized measures of centrality, also applied to centralization, known as degree, betweenness and closeness.

Degree centrality can be defined as a test of the existence of high indegree and high outdegree. For undirected data it would be the number of adjacent links to or from an actor, that is, the degree of the node. A general measure can be found in Wasserman and Faust (1994) for undirected data, once values have been transformed into binary to quantify number of links: $d(n_i)$ in (3.18). This measure depends on the network size, and its maximum value is $(g-1)$. It can be standardized to make it independent of the number of nodes in the network, $g$, and therefore comparable with centrality values of networks with different size, in the following way:

$$C_D(n_i) = \frac{d(n_i)}{g-1} = \frac{\sum_j x_{ij}}{g-1} = \frac{\sum_j x_{ji}}{g-1}.$$ (3.18)

For directed data the index is calculated with outdegree instead of degree.[51] Its value is between zero, for an isolated node, and one, for the centre of a network simulating a star, as shown in Figure 3.2.

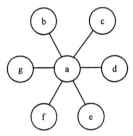

*Figure 3.2: Star network*

Betweenness centrality is defined as the extent to which an actor falls between pairs of other actors on the shortest paths, or geodesics, connecting them. A general measure is similarly found in Brass and Burkhardt (1992), Krackhardt (1992), Wasserman and Faust (1994) and Degenne and Forsé (1999), standardized to allow for comparisons among networks:[52]

$$C_B(n_i) = \frac{\sum_i^n \sum_j^n \left( \frac{g_{ij(i)}}{g_{ij}} \right)}{\frac{(g-1)(g-2)}{2}}, \ j \neq k \neq i, \ j\langle k, \ 0 \leq C_B(n_i) \leq 1. \qquad (3.19)$$

Wasserman and Faust (1994) add that betweenness centrality can be applied to directional data according to Gould (1987), implying the strong assumption that asymmetric dyads are ignored. Directional relations are transformed into non-directional relations, as mutual dyads are considered lines and asymmetric dyads are ignored.[53] An actor with high betweenness is in a position to act as gatekeeper for flows through the network. Betweenness is an indicator of non-redundancy of the source under exchange. There is high betweenness for *i* when without *i* two parts of the network are disconnected.

Closenness centrality is defined as the total graph theoretic distance from the measured node to all others in the network. A general measure, found in Degenne and Forsé (1999) and Wasserman and Faust (1994), is the inverse function of geodesic distances:

$$\left[ \sum_{j=1}^{g} d(n_i, n_j) \right]^{-1}$$

in (3.20).[54] This measure depends on *g*, and its standardization is convenient for comparison purposes, representing the inverse average distance between actor *i* and all others:[55]

$$C_C(n_i) = \frac{g-1}{\sum_{j=1}^{g} d(n_i, n_j)} = (g-1)C_C(n_i), \ 0 \leq C_C' \leq 1. \qquad (3.20)$$

Brass and Burkhardt (1992) propose to count direct links as one step and to give proportionally less weight to indirect links. This would generate a new measure, interpreted as efficiency and also as independence.[56]

The three centrality measures explained above can be compared, as has been done in Wasserman and Faust (1994), concluding that betweenness centrality is the most interesting index, but that it has limitations. One of them is that all geodesics have the same probability of being used, although it seems reasonable that geodesics with actors having large degrees are more likely to be used. Another important limitation is that it only considers geodesic paths, but some actors could have good reasons to choose paths that are longer than the geodesic, mainly in the case of communication flows. Stephenson and Zelen (1989) propose, as an alternative, a weighted betweenness considering every path. In that case, geodesics would be given weights of unity, and longer paths would receive smaller weights, based on the information that they contain.[57] Following this idea, Wasserman and Faust (1994) propose an information centrality measure, for which a new matrix should be obtained from the original data.[58] Then an information centrality index is calculated, measuring how much information is contained in paths that originate, and end, at a specific node.[59] The authors assert that they do not know how to generalize Stephenson and Zelen's theory for information indices to directed links, recommending the use of degree and closeness centrality indices for directed graphs.

In the case of valued data, Degenne and Forsé (1999) propose a flow betweenness measure, and a weighted flow betweenness index for the measurement of centrality.[60] Other, not so general, indices of centrality use the eigenvector measure, or consider the centrality of all actors, as in Bonacich (1987), where an actor's centrality is his summed connections to others, weighted by the centrality of those others. Moreover, for Stephenson and Zelen (1989), centrality is not based on geodesics, but takes into account multiple shared paths between points, as resources do not always flow along the shortest path.

Everett and Borgatti (1999) explain the possibility of calculating centralities for groups, to search for central groups instead of central actors, where a minimal sub-group with maximal group centrality can be looked for. To obtain this information, one possibility is, in the case of closeness or degree group centrality, to find the smallest group of actors within the network. This should be done in such a way that every actor outside the group is adjacent to a member of the group; the size of this group is called the 'domination number' of a graph. Other possibilities are to demand a group centrality greater than a given value, to find a group of fixed size and maximum group centrality, or to find a set of groups that maximize centrality.

Nevertheless, the explained centrality measures can be adapted to groups, obtaining a group degree centrality, measured as the number of non-group nodes that are connected to group members and then considering the number of outsiders tied to at least one group member; a group closeness centrality, as the total distance of the group to all non-members and usually defined as the minimum distance from outsiders to any insider; and a group betweenness centrality, as the number of times that the shortest path between any two outsiders passes through a group member and therefore the proportion of geodesics connecting pairs of non-group members that pass through the group.[61]

In the case of centralization measurements, the position of groups in the net around a focal point, instead of a single actor, is studied. One of the most general centralization calculations is the following:

$$C_A = \frac{\sum_{i=1}^{g}\left[C_A(n^*)-C_A(n_i)\right]}{max\sum_{i=1}^{g}\left[C_A(n^*)-C_A(n_i)\right]}, \ 0 \le C_A \le 1, \qquad (3.21)$$

where $C_A(n^*)$ is the largest value for centrality across the $g$ actors in the $A$ group, and therefore it is $\max_{i} C_A(n_i)$. The denominator in the above measure is the theoretical maximum possible sum of differences in actor centralities. The index takes the value 0 when all actors have the same centrality index and 1 when one actor completely dominates the others. Nevertheless, all the measures explained for the case of a particular actor or node can be adapted to the shape of groups in the network. Therefore, there are also degree, betweenness, closeness and information centralization indices.[62]

The evolution of social network analysis has led to the proposal of more specific tools that should be applied, together with all the measurements explained until now, in a structural analysis. This is the case of cohesion, closure and connectivity, as they help to understand the strength of a network or of groups inside it. Although graphically it is possible to advance the strength of the links, and the existence of key groups, there are several ways to evaluate them more precisely with the application of these specific calculations.

In general terms, social cohesion is understood in Emirbayer and Goodwin (1994) as the presence of a dense network with strong ties among a set of actors. Moreover, Contractor *et al.* (2000) define the existence of group cohesion when there are forces holding group members together. They also argue that it is often measured as the average of each individual member's attraction to the group. In their empirical analysis, studying communication networks in organizations, they consider cohesion through the comparison of the density of the group including nodes $i$ and $j$ with respect to the density of all groups in the network. More specifically, in Wassermand and Faust (1994), a cohesive sub-group is a sub-set of actors among whom there are relatively strong, direct, intense, frequent or positive ties. The general properties of cohesive sub-groups are the mutuality of ties, the closeness or reachability of sub-group members, the frequency of ties among members, and the relative frequency of ties among sub-group members compared to non-members. Following the same authors, a measure of sub-group cohesion is the degree to which strong ties are within rather than outside the sub-group.[63] Another measure, proposed by the same authors, is the probability of observing some $q$ or more lines in a sub-graph.

In order to measure closure, it should be observed that two nodes can be directly or indirectly linked. Indirect links, considering paths of any length connecting two nodes, should be taken into account when looking for the structural properties of a network. According to Degenne and Forsé (1999), a transitivity closure matrix can be obtained from the original one when, in a binary data matrix, a 0 is replaced by a 1 in the case of a path of any length linking the two nodes. Once this matrix is obtained the new rows and columns can be organized by putting together the nodes showing higher connectivity.

Point, or node, connectivity is defined in Iacobucci (1994) as the minimum number of nodes that must be removed to disconnect a graph. A threshold, $k$, value can be decided for that minimum number and then values higher than $k$ would imply superior levels of connectivity. Line, or edge, connectivity is applied according to the minimum number of lines that must be removed to disconnect a graph or make it trivial. More technically, there are specific definitions for different possibilities of connectivities, as is the case of strong connectivity, existing when nodes $i$ and $j$ always share a directed path in each direction, with a sequence of rows from $i$ to $j$ and from $j$ to $i$, for all $i$ and $j$. In a strongly connected sub-graph, nodes are equivalent, all depending equally on each other. Figure 3.3 (taken as an example from Degenne and Forsé, 1999, p. 74) shows the case of a network with strong connectivity. It can be easily checked that all nodes are connected and reachable from every node in the graph following the direction of the arrows.[64]

There is semistrong connectivity when $i$ and $j$ always share a directed path in at least one direction at any time, with a sequence of arrows from $i$ to $j$ and/or from $j$ to $i$, for all $i$ and $j$. Semistrong connectivity implies stratification and a hierarchy of nodes. In a more strict definition, when the sequences are from $i$ to $j$ or from $j$ to $i$ the situation is known as a network unilaterally connected, or $n$-unilaterally connected when the length of the directed paths is considered. Quasistrong connectivity or weakly connected nodes are identified when $i$ and $j$ merely share at least one common predecessor. There is a semipath but there is not a directed path and the direction of the arrows is irrelevant. In this case nodes are incomparable, but they depend on the same nodes.[65]

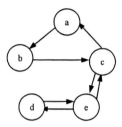

*Figure 3.3: Strongly connected network*

There are several works using the previously mentioned basic measures offered by network analysis, applied to diverse subjects. Examples for the study of international trade and the world economic system include Snyder and Kick (1979), Breiger (1981), Nolan (1983, 1987, 1988), Lenski and Nolan (1984) and Nemeth and Smith (1985). Krackhardt (1992) focuses on the analysis of the strength of strong ties in a firm, and Burkhardt (1994) studies the existence of power and technology attitudes in organizations. Freeman (1997) is focused on the role of hierarchies in organizations, Ahuja and Carley (1998) study the behaviour of a virtual organization, Degenne and Forsé (1999) are dedicated to studying power in organizations and Burt (2000) focuses on social capital.

In the case of regional productive systems, these calculations offer information about the complexity of the productive relations net. The information obtained can be dynamically analysed, to test the relationship between a more complex and dense structure of relations and the regional level of development. Moreover, conclusions about technical changes in productive relations can be deduced from an increase or reduction in the size of the network and the reachability of branches through other branches. Therefore the existence and change of dependency productive relations can also be analysed. In the case of structural equivalence and blockmodelling applied to productive branches, it would be possible to build groups of branches according to their relations, and to study their characterization. These kinds of measures allow simplification of the available information through the group aggregation and the study of their relations.

Another important step in the structural analysis of regional productive systems is the use of centrality measures, after the most basic calculations have been applied to the network as a whole, to get a general idea of its structure, and after specific smaller groups have been identified inside the network. Centrality and centralization indices allow for the identification of key branches according to the number of other branches linked to them, to the distance necessary to reach dependent branches, and to their position in several walks. Moreover, the application of centrality would help to provide information about the structure of a network, made of groups emerging as central or situated around central branches.

Moreover, regions can be identified inside the networks, by imposing some minimum level of cohesion or connectivity among branches; even the already identified groups inside the networks can be characterized. The most interesting situation would be the one where few groups, made of a small number of branches, appear in the structure of a network showing high density and connectivity. These would be key groups for the productive specialization of the area, explaining the effects of technological change and related to growth and development paths in the region.

Nevertheless, the structure and evolution of networks in general, and of productive systems in particular, can be more thoroughly analysed if the general network measures mentioned are used to obtain even more precise calculations. Among the most relevant deduced concepts and measures are core–periphery structures, hierarchy, power and prestige.

The structure of a network can show the existence of a core and a periphery, both made of nodes, or actors, linked in a particular form. In these kinds of networks three different regions can be identified: nodes constituting a core, nodes making a periphery and a third group of nodes occupying a core–periphery region linked to the other two areas. In strict terms, a core is understood as a sub-group of nodes inside a network which are all interrelated. In the periphery, nodes are not linked, but they have connections with the core. An example of this theoretical structure is the star shape of Figure 3.2 or the following Figure 3.4, taken from Borgatti and Everett (1999, p. 4).

The defined structure is a theoretic ideal core–periphery, although there could be other network patterns showing some kind of less restrictive core and periphery structure. An alternative appears when there are ties only among core nodes, and all other nodes are isolates. Another possibility would show that the density of core-to-periphery and periphery-to-core ties is a specific intermediate value between zero (the density of periphery-to-periphery ties) and one (the density of core-to-core ties). In another option the region for core–periphery links is treated as lost data, and a maximum density in the core and a minimum in the periphery are looked for.[66]

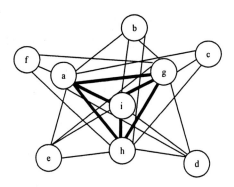

*Figure 3.4: Network with core–periphery structure*

Correlation can be calculated between the original data and an ideal structure, to test whether a network has any of those structures; or even both groups of data can just be compared without applying correlation analysis. Moreover, a structure with a centroid and concentric circles can be looked for, and then a cohesive group would be the core, and the rest of nodes would constitute the periphery, occupying different positions depending on their distance from the core.[67] Therefore, a core–periphery test can be done through correlation, by comparison, applying multidimensional scaling of geodesic distances to obtain groups of concentric circles,[68] or analysing the clique structure of the network.[69] Besides the applied technique, in a tripartite division of the original data there would be the members of the cohesive sub-group as a core, the periphery of that sub-group and the rest of the nodes in the network with some links among them.

There is a clear relationship between coreness and centrality, as actors in a core are necessarily highly central, although not every set of central actors forms a core. Therefore, coreness measures can also be considered centrality measures.

In Barsky (1999) the test for the existence of a core–periphery structure is applied when studying relationships among managers. Moreover, Borgatti and Everett (1999) comment on some references of researchers in international trade looking for the existence of a core and a periphery, by applying network analysis.[70]

In the case of measures to identify hierarchy, power and prestige relations, it should be noted that in every network there could be nodes occupying specific positions, and therefore defining the structure of the network, controlling flows and generating dependency for other nodes. This situation leads to the existence of hierarchies among actors and of nodes with a great influence and therefore power in the network. These are factors strongly linked to centrality and connectivity and help to understand the network structure.

Theoretically, there is hierarchy to the extent to which redundancy can be traced to a single contact in the network. In the extreme case, a network is hierarchical when it is organized around a single contact. Therefore, centrality measures can be applied as hierarchy indices. One of the recommended measures for such a case is betweenness centrality, although there are others which are more specific indices for such a purpose. Burt (2000), in studying social capital, applies a measure of hierarchy depending on redundancy.[71] For Ahuja and Carley (1998), in their application to virtual organizations, there is a degree of hierarchy depending on the level at which relations in a network are directly or indirectly reciprocal, with unreciprocated relationships implying more hierarchical networks.[72] Moreover, there are hierarchical levels depending on the number of levels one must go through in order to obtain information.[73] The degree of hierarchy, hierarchical levels and centralization are indices determining a network dimension and structure.

Power is studied in Brass and Burkhardt (1992) by establishing a relationship between power and centrality, where nodes are organizations. This relationship is not clear, as there could be negatively and positively connected networks. Two nodes are negatively connected when exchange in one diminishes or prohibits exchange in the other. Moreover, to acquire power, actors must decrease their dependence on others, and others' dependence on them must increase. Dependency is considered the basis of power; in graph terms this can be seen when nodes remain linked, necessarily, to other particular nodes, without the possibility of choosing alternative nodes for exchanges. Therefore, power depends on the structural position of each node.

The same idea appears in Degenne and Forsé (1999) and in Monge and Contractor (2004) where power, in terms of exchange theory, is defined as an inverse function of dependence on others in the network.[74] Dependence, in turn, varies with the benefit derived from the exchange and with its relative value when compared with exchanges offered by other sources. There is greater power for an actor when it offers greater access to valued material and informational resources. In positively connected networks power seems to rise with centrality through coordination and therefore measures of centrality reflect different dimensions of power. Following Degenne and Forsé (1999), centrality could be measured as power, by considering the centrality of the actors linked to the one for which centrality is being measured.[75]

Nevertheless, closeness and betweenness are considered correlated with reputational measures of power.[76]

Interorganizational communication and exchange networks are mechanisms by which organizations acquire and disperse scarce resources, creating and perpetuating a system of power relations. Therefore, organizations are dependent upon their positions in the network, influencing their ability to control flows of scarce resources. In that sense, dependency can imply vulnerability when, in graphical terms, the removal of a node in a graph isolates the vulnerable node from all other remaining nodes. Vulnerability decreases with the node proximity to the core or cores. Moreover, vulnerability for nodes will be different depending on whether relations are of cooperation or of competition; consequently the effects of the removal of a node will be diverse.

More egalitarian distributions of power, and therefore less vulnerability, can be found when power is unequally distributed, following two possible strategies – through network extensions, when weaker actors diversify partners, or through network consolidation, when weaker actors unite to restrict the more powerful actors' options. These two possibilities are shown in Figure 3.5.[77]

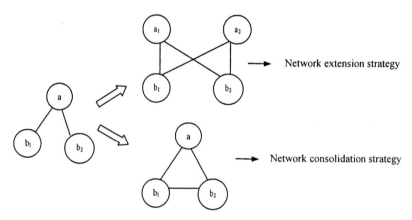

*Figure 3.5: Strategies to reduce vulnerable network positions*

The cases of undirected networks, with measures of power, and directed networks, with measures of prestige, are differentiated in Degenne and Forsé (1999). In that sense, and following Wasserman and Faust (1994), an actor is prominent if his ties make him particularly visible to other actors in the network. There are two types of prominence: centrality and prestige.[78] There is prestige for an actor who is the object of extensive ties, as a recipient of links, with high indegree, only measurable for directional relations. Actor prestige is also called status, deference or popularity. As a measure, the degree prestige is the indegree of each actor.[79] The prestige of actors linked to the one measuring its prestige is also important; therefore, distances should be weighted by prestige measures of the actors in the influence domain. By doing this, the status or rank prestige can be calculated as the prestige of an actor in his net, depending on the prestige of the other actors linked to him in the net.

The measures explained as criteria to value power and prestige can be complemented, following Degenne and Forsé (1999),[80] by the calculation of choice status, extended relations, exclusive relations, power (considering the exclusiveness of the relation) and reflected power as complementary measures.[81]

The offered information, about more precise calculations to study network structures, is useful for analysing productive systems. In looking for regional production systems, the identification of a region inside the whole network with a centre–periphery structure could indicate the existence of a production system. Dependency relations would be identified among branches constituting the core and between the core and the periphery. Moreover, knowing that the core area would have strong cohesion, branches constituting the centre–periphery structure could be taken into account and studied as possible key branches belonging to a regional production system. The emergence of a centre–periphery structure can be considered to be the origin of a production system, where centrality measures offer important information for understanding the network structure. Conclusions can also be obtained from the existence of a hierarchy of branches, according to their dependency relations and therefore to their power and prestige positions and strategies. All this is pretty clear in the case of input–output data, as different centrality and dependency relations always exist among the branches, according to the available technology for their productive processes.

*Embeddedness, weak ties and social capital* It would be of great help to try to test the foundations of social network analysis, developed in the previous chapter, by applying network measures. In that sense, there are studies focused on the empirical analysis of the concept of embeddedness, on proposals to measure weak ties and on techniques to identify social capital. All of these are discussed in this section, because of their relevance for the study of regional productive systems, according to the methodological exposition made in Chapter 2.

The economic performance of organizations is studied in Uzzi (1996), who proposes two related measures of embeddedness. For a better understanding of the proposed measures it is useful to represent, as in Figure 3.6, the situation of two groups of transacting firms.[82]

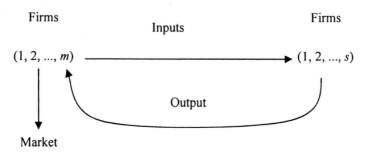

Figure 3.6: Trade links between two groups of firms

*Figure 3.6: Trade links between two groups of firms*

One of the measures, named 'first-order network coupling', captures, according to the author, the idea of embeddednes as a network concept:

$$\sum_{j=1}^{g_m} P_{ij}^2 \text{ where } P_{ij} = \frac{x_{ij}}{x_i}. \qquad (3.22)$$

The above index, where $x$ are outputs, approaches 1 when firms concentrate in few relations; in the opposite case it approaches 0 when there are small trade pieces to many firms and therefore arm's length ties are used to transact.[83] The embeddedness index is near 1 when a contractor has network ties to a limited business group.

The other proposed index is the second-order network coupling, where $x$ are inputs. Its value is 1 when all the work is done by one contracted firm, and 0 if there is a high number of small hired firms:

$$\frac{\sum_{j=1}^{g_m} Q_j}{g_m} \text{ where } Q_j = \sum_{i=1}^{n_s} D_{ji}^2 \text{ and } D_{ji} = \frac{x_{ji}}{x_j}. \qquad (3.23)$$

The second-order network coupling has a low value when the network of $m$ firms with which an $s$ firm transacts uses, on average, arm's length ties. It has a high value when the network of which an $s$ firm is tied is composed of $m$

firms that use embedded ties to transact with *s* firms. It has a medium value when the *s* firm transacts with an integrated network composed of a mix of arm's length and embedded ties. As a conclusion it can be said that high concentration implies more embeddedness.

The generation and maintenance of trust is a key strategy to create an exchange environment, identified with embedded relations. Therefore, the existence of trust ties should be considered, to analyse the possibility of embeddedness more deeply. In Gulati (1995) trust is measured through the proxy of prior alliances between firms. Geography should also be considered, as firms are expected to trust domestic partners more than international or interregional partners. In a domestic context, more and better information about firms is available and the reputation consequences of opportunistic behaviour are greater.

Trust links are of great importance for efficient organizations, but also the use of weak ties with other groups is an efficiency strategy. A test of the strength of the weak ties theory of Granovetter (1973) is proposed in Borgatti and Feld (1994). To apply this test a strength matrix and an overlap matrix should be built from the original data. The strength matrix should measure the strength of ties among all pairs of actors. The overlap matrix includes, for each pair of actors, the number of other actors that both actors are connected to, measuring the extent to which the neighbourhoods of each pair of actors overlap.[84] Finally, for each actor the correlation between the elements of the strength matrix and the overlap matrix is computed. According to Granovetter's theory, if there are strong ties between dyads, then their common elements should overlap. Consequently, there should be a positive correlation between the elements of the strength matrix and the elements of the overlapping matrix.

The whole set of links, with trust relations and weak ties, consists of the network social capital. Therefore, social capital as social structure constitutes a structural resource present in each network. However, it works with different intensity depending on each network structure. Therefore, to value it would be very helpful in order to understand the evolution and performance of the analysed network. There are several possibilities appearing in the literature for social capital measures. In some cases specific indicators are proposed; other authors recommend the visualization of the structure through graphs; and at other times the suggestion is to relate social capital to traditional network measures. All these cases are explained, in summary, in this section.

Burt (2000) asserts that there are two measures of social capital, one counting the bridge relationships and the other a network constraint index, describing the extent to which a person's network is concentrated in redundant contacts. Focusing on the first form through bridge relationships, in Krackhardt (1992), bridges are measured through betweenness centrality. According to the author, betweenness is an attribute of a node in the graph, while local bridge degree is an attribute of a tie. Therefore, both measure the degree to which actors reach disparate and unconnected parts of the network. The higher the degree of the local bridge a person is connected to, the higher that actor's betweenness score will be. The second way to measure social capital, with a network constraint index, has already been presented in this chapter but, in a more extensive analysis, Burt (2000) relates it to size (first term), density (second term) and hierarchy (third term) as follows:

$$NC = \sum_j NC_{ij} = \sum_j \left(P_{ij}\right)^2 + 2\sum_j P_{ij}\left(\sum_q P_{iq}P_{qj}\right) + \sum_j \left(\sum_q P_{iq}P_{qj}\right)^2. \quad (3.24)$$

According to Burt, the social capital level can be identified knowing the constraint of a network, differentiating among diverse possibilities and distinguishing between group relations and links among group and non-group members. Then, network closure within the group, implying internal lack of constraint, can be low (A) or high (B), and non-redundant contacts beyond the group, understood as external lack of constraint, can be high (C) or low (D). The four combinations inferred from these possibilities can be drawn with nodes and lines, as in the examples shown in Burt (2000, p. 88) and reproduced in Figures 3.7 and 3.8. In these examples the group (to represent cases A and B) is made of three members, (a, b and c) and there are six nodes out of the group, (d, e, f, g, h and i) to consider external constraint (cases C and D).

The case with the (A) and (C) situations is identified with a disintegrated group of diverse perspectives, skills and resources. Internal closure does not exist, nodes belonging to the group are not related, but there are external holes that can be exploited as contact among external actors does not exist. This situation is represented in Figure 3.7(a). The situation with (A) and (D), Figure 3.7(b), shows minimum performance from a social capital perspective. An internal net with the profitable closure is not present and externally accessible rich flows are not evidenced; all external actors are related with redundant links as all external actors are related.

The case with (B) and (C), in Figure 3.8(a), shows maximum performance, as there is internal closure (all group members are related), and external holes (actors out of the group are not related) and therefore there are valuable resources to be exploited. The case with (B) and (D), in Figure 3.8(b), represents a cohesive group having access to only one perspective and type of resource, as all actors have access to the same flows.

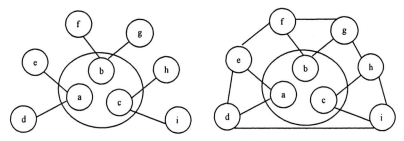

*(a) Non-redundant external contacts*    *(b) Redundant external contacts*

*Figure 3.7: Low internal closure*

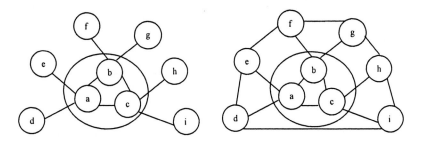

*(a) Non-redundant external contacts*    *(b) Redundant external contacts*

*Figure 3.8: High internal closure*

Although there is social capital in all the above structures, as all of them exhibit a net of relations, the third case, represented in Figure 3.8(a), shows it with the highest intensity.

In Borgatti *et al.* (1998) it is asserted that social capital can be measured with standard network indices, by relating them properly, instead of using specific measures, as above. To explain these relations the authors distinguish between the type of actor (individual or group) and the type of focus (internal or external).

The case of internal and individual is empty, as this is the situation of a node related to itself. Size, degree, heterogeneity, compositional quality and betweenness centrality are positively related to social capital; density, constraint and closeness centrality are negatively related to social capital in the case of external and individual.[85] For the case of internal measures and collective actors, social capital shows a positive relation with density, centralization and core–periphery structure, and negative for average or maximum distance and homophily. In the last case of external measures for collective actors, there are positive relations of social capital with group degree centrality and group betweenness centrality, and negative relations with group closeness centrality.

The same subject is analysed in Lin (1999), who proposes to measure social capital as assets in networks and uses sampling techniques to construct measures of social capital. The author does not offer specific measures of social capital, but he makes it clear that two factors should always be measured: network resources and position. For social capital measured as assets in networks, embedded resources and network location should be considered. Embedded resources, in turn, are analysed by measuring network and contact resources, and network location is measured through bridges or access to bridges and strength of ties; all this is outlined in Figure 3.9. The author specifies the cases of saturation technique, name generator technique and position generator technique to construct measures of social capital with sampling techniques.

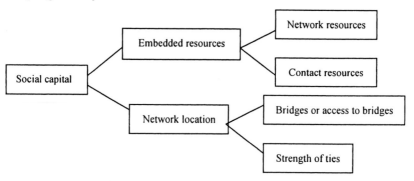

*Figure 3.9: Social capital main factors*

More specifically, and as a final example with a wide application, in Burt (2000) there are three network forms of social capital, focused on the internal structure of economic organizations. More specifically, Burt's research is applied to the study of a particular organization where the central node is a manager (node a) inside the institution. In that sense, the three network forms of social capital are entrepreneurial network, clique network and hierarchical network.

The entrepreneurial network (Figure 3.10) has a sparse and flat structure and there are independent relations sustained by the manager, occupying the central position. There are abundant structural holes and low redundancy, creating information and control benefits. This structure is associated with successful managers, as there is high insiders' performance, and the lowest performance for outsiders. All flows pass through the manager and he is the only contact to relate to the other nodes.

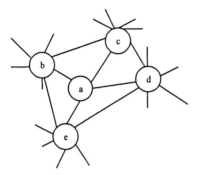

*Figure 3.10: Entrepreneurial network*

The clique network has a dense and flat structure. It has interconnected relations sustaining one another for the central node. There are no structural holes, as all nodes are linked and receive the same flows, and therefore there is high redundancy. This creates social support but minimal information and control benefits. This network is associated with unsuccessful managers, offering low performance for insiders and average performance for outsiders.

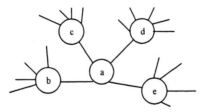

*Figure 3.11: Clique network*

The hierarchical network has a sparse, centre–periphery structure. Its ties are sustained jointly by the manager and there are strategic structural holes, borrowed from strategic partners close to second-hand information and control benefits. It is associated with successful outsiders and unsuccessful insiders.

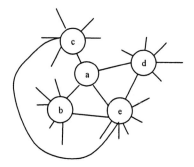

*Figure 3.12: Hierarchical network*

These examples can be applied to other situations, as when the central node is a firm, or a productive branch or sector, in a production system. In these cases, the possibility of potential benefits obtained through structural holes or the change in some actor's position can be studied. Moreover, once links with other institutions have been included in the productive system, the relational structure shows the social capital working in the network more precisely. There are empirical studies analysing those more concrete structures of relations – using 'trust' as a social capital measure and quantifying it through questionnaires. Once the information is obtained in that form, the social capital structure can be studied as shown in this section.

### 3.3.2.3    Correlation analysis and other techniques

In network data, observations are not independent of each other and they do not constitute a random sample, with population distribution of variables unknown and probably not random. In a case such as this, correlation can be applied through the application of permutation matrices in the quadratic assignment procedure (QAP). Some references applying this are Burkhardt (1994), studying technological change, and Kilduff and Krackhardt (1994), analysing reputation in organizations, and generally when analysing centre–periphery structures.

Other techniques applied to the study of networks are qualitative input–output analysis (QIOA) and minimal flow analysis (MFA). Both imply structural analysis of networks, applying algorithms, graphs and some of the measures explained in this chapter. The main difference between these techniques and social network analysis is that they do not offer a methodological framework, and they just apply them for the identification and study of several kinds of networks. Some interesting references are Drejer (1999), for different national systems of innovation, Fontela *et al.* (2000) and Schnabl (2001), studying the input–output structure of several countries and regions, and Aroche-Reyes (2001) for industrial complexes.

### 3.3.3    Overview of the Methods Applied in this Research

This section presents a summary of the methods detailed in this chapter for their application to the cases of Andalusia and the Basque Country in the following chapters. There is also a brief explanation of mechanism causality, as a method to test hypotheses, which will also be used in the applied work of this research. Figure 3.13 shows how the analysed methods will be used in the next chapters to identify regional productive systems, and how mechanism causality will be applied to test hypotheses proposing relations between the systems' structure and evolution and the regional development processes. Figure 3.13, therefore, represents the link between the theoretical research made in Chapters 2 and 3 and the applied work that will be carried out in Chapters 4 and 5.

### 3.3.3.1    Methods summary to identify regional productive systems

Two types of data are used through this research: input–output data and regional qualitative and quantitative information. In the second case, data from individual firms working in the region, and from their more relevant institutions, are included. The historical information is particularly useful for the selection and characterization of the systems, as it makes it possible to consider the specialization and the productive particularities of each region.

The first step in the applied research will be the identification and selection of regional production systems inside the social networks constituted by the available data. For this, network measures and a particular algorithm are used. However, not all the network measures explained in this chapter will be applied to the regional data used; in Chapter 4, some measures have been selected for the systems identification process.

Once the production systems have been obtained, the next step will be to characterize them with input–output indices and with the results obtained from the application of the selected network measures. After the production systems have been identified and characterized, for the two selected regions, institutional information will be added to transform them into regional productive systems. All of this sequence, followed in the methods application for the determination of regional productive systems, is schematized in Figure 3.13.

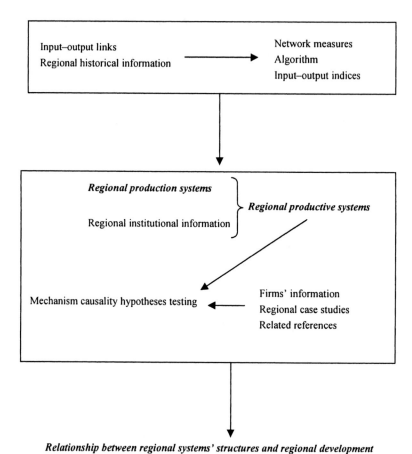

Relationship between regional systems' structures and regional development

*Figure 3.13: Methods application sequence in this research*

### 3.3.3.2    Mechanism causality as the hypotheses testing method

A set of hypotheses will be proposed for testing, once production and productive systems have been studied. Hypotheses will refer to the relationship between the systems' structure and evolution and the regional development paths. Therefore, the units of analysis are production and productive systems and branches. The explanation of phenomena occurring at system level are found in the systems' underlying structure, that is, in the process occurring at an inferior level, which in this analysis is the level of institutions and firms forming the productive branches. The process, which represents firms' actions, is explained in terms of mechanisms, and therefore the analytical perspective considered in this study is mechanism causality.

This is one of the possible types of causality as, according to Doreian (2001, 2002), causal relations working in a process can be presented and studied in four forms, mainly depending on the type of data used, the theoretical perspective adopted and the kind of analysis applied. Table 3.1 presents a brief description of these four different types of causality, as well as some references to works using network data in which they have been applied.

*Table 3.1: Typology of causalities*

| Type of causality | Description | References applied to network data |
|---|---|---|
| System causality | A system of equations is specified to explain changes in the processes | Padulo and Arbib (1974), Fararo (1989) |
| Statistical causality | Estimation of equations and predictions through regression analysis | Wasserman and Pattison (1996), Morgan (1997) |
| Mechanism causality | Looking at social mechanisms and sequences of events to explain the process and to find general mechanisms | Chase (1992), Fararo *et al.* (1994), Morgan (1997) |
| Algorithmic causality | Application of algorithms where rules are encoded to transform input into output values | Hummon and Fararo (1995) |

The four types of causality can be applied to study processes occurring in social and economic networks; more specifically, all of them can be used to analyse their spatial and temporal changes. However, in our view, attending to the type of data used, to the increasing difficulty for the specification of equations, and considering that the objective is to explain a process, the most appropriate analytical approach in this research is mechanism causality.

Mechanism causality is applied to study sequences of events at actor level, with the aim of accounting for them in terms of generalized mechanisms, which can be used for explanatory purposes. In other words, when mechanism causality is applied, the analysis of the processes occurring at the level of the actors that form the network provides the explanation for the processes or facts that are taking place at the macro level of the network. In the mechanism causality approach, social processes are seen as the result of actions of complex intentional agents, taking place in an environment of time and space. In that case, through mechanism – or event – causality, the interaction and action of firms in the two selected regions and systems are the underlying structure explaining the studied changes at branch level.

A set of hypotheses can be proposed to test them when it is observed that certain network ties change, and therefore networks change, in time and space. The observations may suggest that there are general mechanisms explaining the changes. Therefore, to construct general descriptions of mechanisms and event sequences, both specific empirical event sequences and generalised sequences and mechanisms are needed. Table 3.2 presents some examples of the way this has been done in different research areas using network data.

It should be emphasized that the mechanism causality approach should not be confused with a purely descriptive approach. Mechanism causality does not describe – it explains: a purely descriptive approach aims to account for the unique chain of events that leads from one situation or event to another in a particular process; however, the mechanism causality approach looks for general explanatory mechanisms. Clearly, there are many possible mechanisms working at the same time, and not all need to be operative in a given empirical context. Therefore, only some mechanisms are identifiable, but this is a limitation that is present in any kind of causality specification and explanation. Figure 3.13 also includes the stage at which mechanism causality will be used in the applied side of this research.

*Table 3.2: Examples applying mechanism causality and sequences of events*

| Reference | Description |
|---|---|
| Doreian (2002) | Testing the theory of imbalance<br>*Hypotheses*: (H1) Through time, the proportion of balanced triples increases<br>(H2) Through time, the proportion of imbalance triples decreases<br>*Sequences of events*: (1) Relations among a group of monks in three time points, specified in three matrices of relations; experiment in Sampson (1968)<br>(2) Relations among 17 previously unacquainted young men over 15 weeks, specified in 15 matrices of relations; experiment in Newcomb (1961) |
| Doreian (2001) | Testing isomorphic structures of similar schools of social work<br>*Mechanisms*: (1) Coercive: the administration imposes some minimum conditions<br>(2) Mimetic: the less efficient schools try to imitate the more efficient ones<br>(3) Normative: there are general compulsory rules |
| DiMaggio and Powell (1991) | Testing the relations between mental health hospitals and a mental health foundation<br>*Hypothesis*: The greater the dependence of an organization on another organization, the more similar it will become in structure, climate and behavioural focus to yet other organizations that are dependent, in the same fashion, on the same organization<br>*Sequence of events*: Negotiation process between the two types of organizations<br>*Mechanism*: Coercive: the focal organization has the power to impose certain minimum conditions |
| Chase (1992) and Fararo *et al.* (1994) | Testing the formation of hierarchy relations among primates<br>*Sequence of events*: Observation of the behaviour of groups of primates<br>*Mechanisms*: (1) Fighting<br>(2) Bystanders |
| Stinchcombe (1998) | Testing the market process<br>*Mechanism*: Monopolistic competition |
| Abell (1987) | Testing a theory of rational action<br>*Sequence of events*: Individual behaviours in social interactions |
| Abbott and Hrycak (1990) | Testing a typology of musical careers<br>*Sequence of events*: Stages of individual careers of German classical musicians during the Baroque and Classical eras |

## NOTES

1. Nevertheless, total values will be used at some point to complement the analysis for a better understanding of the results obtained.
2. Obtained from Leontief (1986, 2nd ed.).
3. The Leontief model is presented here very briefly as it is very well known and it can be found in many references; for a fuller explanation of it, see Leontief (1951), Dorfman *et al.* (1958) and Leontief (1985).
4. The five matrices are input–output matrix, **A** matrix, **B** matrix, relative to **IS** matrix and relative to **IP** matrix.
5. Nevertheless, the input–output system can be used at current and constant prices, after deciding a year taken as a base. This should be done considering sector price indices; that is, a price index for each branch.
6. Although for time comparisons both kinds of analyses could be more useful; that is, first in current value terms and then translating them into constant price values, using a price index for each branch.
7. Some references maintaining this approach are Bharadwaj (1966), Jones (1976) and Lahr and Dietzenbacher (2001).
8. As an example, when branch *i* sells to branches *j* and *k*, and branch *j* then sells to branch *k*, branches *j* and *k* have a direct relationship, but branches *i* and *k* have a direct and an indirect relationship through *j*.
9. The coefficients in the main diagonal of matrix **B** include a 1, added to other technical coefficients, refering to the flows going to final demand. As an example, in the case of a system made of only two branches: $b_{11} = 1 + a_{11} + a_{11}^2 + a_{11}a_{21} + a_{11}^3 + a_{11}a_{12}a_{21} + \ldots$.
10. They are also indirect, according to the approach followed by the author.
11. This could be the case of services, as the statistical information for such branches is particularly weak. Moreover, for some authors services cannot have the role of key sectors ('Linkages are not confined to industrial sectors, but service sectors have low linkages and would not qualify as key sectors', McGilvray, 1977, p. 32, note 2). Leontief (1951, p. 13), claiming that technical coefficients are largely fixed by technology, asserts, 'Others in the complete matrix of the economy, especially in the trade, services, and household sectors, are established by custom and other institutional factors'. Vivarelli (1997, p. 118) affirms that the dynamics of services do not have any relationship with technological progress: 'In fact, the expansion in services is often completely unrelated to technological progress.'
12. Some references in this respect are McCann and Dewhurst (1998), Harris and Liu (1998) and Flegg and Webber (2000).
13. Yotopoulos and Nugent (1973), distinguishing between developing and underdeveloping countries, calculate indices for 11 countries, and then extrapolate them to 32 countries: 'Our extrapolation was based on the useful observation of Chenery and Watanabe that the structure of production as reflected in the four linkage indices was remarkably similar for one country to another' (Yotopoulos and Nugent, 1973, p. 337). The Chenery and Watanabe linkage indices will be explained further on in this chapter.
14. 'One is not surprised to find that the production of a given commodity requires relatively the same intermediate inputs in the same proportion in one country as it does in another. One would, however, be surprised to learn that the proportion of each input imported or produced domestically is the same across countries' (Riedel, 1976, p. 320).
15. See Hirschman (1959), Bharadwaj (1966) and McGilvray (1977).
16. Although it will be explained in another section of this chapter, it can be said at this stage that the Hirschman idea of linkage effects has the sense of the capacity of a firm to attract other firms to the same location.
17. Detailed information about interviews and questionnaires will be expounded in Chapter 5, where this information is used.
18. Therefore the index of power of dispersion measures the average of backward linkages of branch *j*, considering all the branches selling it intermediate goods, in the numerator and normalized by the denominator. In the same way the index of sensitivity of dispersion

measures the average of forward linkages of branch *i*, considering all the branches buying it intermediate goods, in the numerator and normalized by the denominator.

19. Some Spanish examples of such applications are Segura and Restoy (1986) and López (1995).

20. According to that explanation: $a_{ij}^{\bullet} = \dfrac{\Delta x_{ij}}{\Delta x_j}\dfrac{x_j}{x_i} = a_{ij}\dfrac{x_j}{x_i} = \dfrac{x_{ij}}{x_j}\dfrac{x_j}{x_i} = \dfrac{x_{ij}}{x_i}$ .

21. See Hazari (1970) and Jones (1976).

22. There are some modifications, such as forward linkages measured in relation to production plus net changes in inventories plus imports.

23. McGilvray includes some modifications by weighting them with relative production and considering the minimum economic operative capacity in the supplier sector.

24. This article of Yotopoulos and Nugent received numerous critiques such as those of Jones (1976), Riedel (1976) and Boucher (1976).

25. Rasmussen coefficients are calculated without means or weights.

26. Depending on the level of the research the sub-group can be a dyad (two actors), triad (three actors), or bigger sub-groups, the biggest being the group. When the link has a value associated with it, cohesive sub-groups can be identified for ties with high values according to an imposed threshold.

27. It can be identified at the same levels as sub-groups, that is, for dyads, triads, bigger sub-groups or groups when all actors are considered.

28. There is strong connectivity (strongly linked actors) when there is a path from every node to every other. A path is a sequence of ties, as lines or arrows, in which all nodes and lines are distinct; that is, they are passed through only once.

29. A generally accepted limit is 80 per cent (Emirbayer and Goodwin, 1994).

30. De Mesnard (2001) clarifies Boolean topological methods, that is, the binary transformation of valued matrices, explaining the pros and cons of this type of transformation for input–output data.

31. All those terms are compared and explained in Wasserman and Faust (1994).

32. Values may be 0, 1 and −1, showing positive and hostile relations in signed graphs. Another technical term is block, a sub-graph without cutpoints. A cutpoint is defined as a node whose removal would disconnect the graph (Degenne and Forsé, 1999).

33. The simplest graph concepts refer to a trivial graph, containing only one node, an empty graph, with a finite set of nodes and no lines, and a simple graph, made of undirected relations, without loops, and containing no more than one line between a pair of nodes. When more interesting situations appear, a complete graph can be identified if for any pair of nodes there is at least one arrow. A graph is said to be reflexive when reflexive links are allowed. A reflexive link indicates the relation that a branch has with itself.

34. When more than one relation is considered for the same set of actors, and therefore groups or subgroups are analysed, the chosen term is 'multigraph'. A multigraph is made up of one set of nodes and more than one set of lines. A complex graph is a multigraph containing loops or reflexive links.

35. A geodesic is the shortest path between two nodes. The diameter is the length of the longest geodesic between any pair of nodes. Measures of size are explained in the next section.

36. When, for simplicity reasons, arrows are taken out of the digraph, leaving just lines, the proper term is 'underlying graph'; in this case an underlying connected graph is a weakly connected graph. In Degenne and Forsé (1999) a *P*-graph is the graph in which the maximum number of arrows directed in one way from one node to another is *P*.

37. Moreover, relations can be established among a set of actors and a sub-set of those actors in the case of hypergraphs (Iacobucci, 1994). Another specific case appears when there is a set of actors competing in some events, and a relation indicating superior performance in the competition; this in graphical terms receives the name of 'tournament'.

38. As an example, a clique at level *c* is a sub-graph with ties between all pairs of actors having values higher or equal to a threshold *c*; another condition is that there is no other actor outside the clique with ties of strength equal to or greater than *c*. A complete definition of all these terms can be found in Wasserman and Faust (1994).

39. For a detailed explanation of this measure, see Borgatti (1994), Wasserman and Faust (1994) and Degenne and Forsé (1999).

40. The effective size of node $i$ can be measured as $\sum_j \left[ 1 - \sum_q p_{iq} m_{jq} \right]$, $q \neq i, j$; where

$p_{iq} = \dfrac{\left( x_{iq} + x_{qi} \right)}{\sum_j \left( x_{ij} + x_{ji} \right)}$, $i \neq j$ and $m_{jq} = \dfrac{\left( x_{jq} + x_{qj} \right)}{\max_k \left( x_{jk} + x_{kj} \right)}$, $j \neq k$, in non-valued, undirected

graphs: $p_{iq} = \dfrac{x_{iq}}{\sum_j x_{ij}}$, $i \neq j$ and $m_{jq} = \dfrac{x_{jq}}{\max_k \left( x_{jk} \right)} \Rightarrow m_{jq} = x_{jq}$.

41. Some references explaining it are Borgatti (1994), Iacobucci (1994), Wasserman and Faust (1994) and Degenne and Forsé (1999).
42. Two nodes are adjacent when there is a line linking them.
43. Iacobucci (1994) and Degenne and Forsé (1999) offer detailed information about the several measures of distance.
44. The length of the walk is the number of its lines, and it is the most general kind of sequence of adjacent nodes; the length of a directed walk is the number of instances of arrows in it. Other terms derived from walk and more specific than it are: a 'closed walk', when the walk begins and ends at the same node; a 'semiwalk', when the direction of the arrow is irrelevant and its length is the number of instances; a 'trail' is a walk in which all lines are distinct and the nodes may be included more than once; a 'directed trail' is a directed walk in which no arrow is included more than once; and a 'tour' is a closed walk where each line is used at least once.
45. This is the case of eccentricity, defined as the greatest geodesic distance between the node and any other, summarizing how far a node is from the node most distant in the graph. Another is interaction distance, defined as the number of steps needed to connect two nodes.
46. The notation is not unanimous: in Degenne and Forsé (1994) the definition of path is given to the concept of chain, and our chosen definition of directed path is given to path, therefore, not distinguishing between path and directed path but between chain and path. Path length is understood as the distance between two nodes, that is, the number of arrows connecting the two nodes. A semipath is a path in which the direction of the arrow is irrelevant. Its length is the number of arrows. A semicycle is a closed directed semiwalk where all nodes, except the first and the last, are distinct.
47. Some references are Snyder and Kick (1979), Breiger (1981), Nolan (1983, 1987, 1988), Lenski and Nolan (1984) and Nemeth and Smith (1985).
48. The reduced graph shows that, if there is a link between two blocks, then there is a link among any components of the two blocks. Possible criteria for the separation of blocks are a minimum density within a block, the zero block criterion (the block is zero if all ties on it are zero), the one block criterion (the block is one if all its binary ties are ones), the alfa density for an alfa threshold density value, or through comparison (assigning a density value to each of the three criteria: zero block, alfa density and one block, using a continuum of cutoff values).
49. Euclidean distance is calculated as $d_{ij} = \sqrt{\sum_{k=1}^{g} \left[ \left( x_{ik} - x_{jk} \right)^2 + \left( x_{ki} - x_{kj} \right)^2 \right]}$; for $i \neq k$, $j \neq k$;

its value is 0 when $i$ and $j$ are structurally equivalent. Correlation is obtained with

$r_{ij} = \dfrac{\sum \left( x_{ki} - \overline{x}_{.i} \right)\left( x_{kj} - \overline{x}_{.j} \right) + \sum \left( x_{ik} - \overline{x}_{i.} \right)\left( x_{jk} - \overline{x}_{j.} \right)}{\sqrt{\sum \left( x_{ki} - \overline{x}_{.i} \right)^2 + \sum \left( x_{ik} - \overline{x}_{i.} \right)^2} \sqrt{\sum \left( x_{kj} - \overline{x}_{.j} \right)^2 + \sum \left( x_{jk} - \overline{x}_{j.} \right)^2}}$ ; its value is 1 for two

structurally equivalent actors.
50. Every $c_{ij}$ is 'the proportion of $i$'s relations that are directly or indirectly invested in connection with contact $j$' (Burt, 2000, appendix, p. 4).

51. Both indegree and outdegree can be used, although it is generally accepted that centrality focuses on choices made, and therefore outdegree should be used.

52. $i$ is the actor for which centrality is being measured; $g_{ij}(i)$ is the number of shortest paths, or geodesics, between $i$ and $j$ in the network, including the node $i$; $g_{ij}$ is the number of geodesics without including $i$. Betweenness centrality is standardized by dividing it by its maximum value. Without making it relative, $0 \leq C_B(n_i) \leq \dfrac{(g-1)(g-2)}{2}$ .

53. The index is multiplied by two when relationships are directional.

54. $d(n_i, n_j)$ is the number of lines in the geodesic linking $i$ and $j$. The index is $C_C = (g-1)^{-1}$ when the actor is adjacent to all other actors; $C_C = 0$ whenever one or more actors are not reachable from the actor in question. There could be a problem when applying this index: as all nodes in the network are included in the centrality measure some of them may not be reachable, thus $d$ would be infinite and the index undefined. A possible solution to this problem is to include only reachable pairs of actors (Wasserman and Faust, 1994): $C_C^{\bullet}(n_i) = \dfrac{\dfrac{J_i}{(g-1)}}{\dfrac{\sum d(n_i, n_j)}{J_i}}$ ,

$J_i \in i$ where $J$ includes all the actors in the influence range of $i$. The numerator is a fraction of the reachable actors and the denominator is the average distance of the actors reachable from $i$.

55. The index is the same for directed data.

56. According to this idea, it should be realized that an actor with only a few links may be central.

57. The information of a path is defined as the inverse of its length. The information of a node is the harmonic average of the information for the combined paths from the node to all other nodes.

58. For this new matrix, the diagonal elements are 1 plus the sum of values for all lines incident to $n_i$. For the off-diagonal elements, there is a 1 if nodes $n_i$ and $n_j$ are not adjacent, and 1 minus $x_{ij}$ if nodes $n_i$ and $n_j$ are adjacent. Once this matrix, $\mathbf{A}$, is obtained, its inverse is calculated, obtaining a new matrix, $\mathbf{C}$, for which isolated actors are dropped, and therefore there are no rows or columns of zeros, in order that $\mathbf{A}$ can be inverted. Using the new matrix, the sum of the diagonal is obtained, $\mathbf{T}$, as well as the sum of any one of the rows as all the row sums are equal, $\mathbf{R}$.

59. A relative information index, for comparison purposes, is $C_I'(n_i) = \dfrac{C_I(n_i)}{\sum_i C_I(n_i)}$ , $0 \leq C_I' \leq 1$, where $C_I(n_i) = \dfrac{1}{c_{ii} + \left[ (T - 2R) / g \right]} \geq 0$ , measuring the proportion of total information flow in a graph controlled by an individual actor, $\sum_{i=1}^{g} C_I'(n_i) = 1$ (Wasserman and Faust, 1994).

60. The flow betweenness index is $C_{AFi} = \sum_j^n \sum_k^n f_{jk}(i); i \neq j \neq k; j \langle k$ , where $f_{jk}$ is the maximum flow between $j$ and $k$, and $f_{jk}(i)$ is the flow through $i$. The weighted flow betweenness index is

$$C_{NFi} = \dfrac{\sum_j^n \sum_k^n f_{jk}(i)}{\sum_j^n \sum_k^n f_{jk}} ; i \neq j \neq k; j \langle k .$$

61. Group centralities can be normalized, in the case of degree centrality by dividing it by the number of non-group actors and in the case of closeness centrality by dividing the distance score into the number of non-group members. For degree centrality, multiple ties to the same node are counted only once. For closeness centrality, larger numbers for its index indicate less centrality and, when normalized, larger numbers indicate greater centrality. Group betweenness centrality is calculated, according to Everett and Borgatti (1999), as

$$C_B(C) = \sum_{u<v} \frac{g_{uv}(C)}{g_{u,v}}, u,v \notin C .$$ $C$ is a sub-set of a graph with vertex or node set $V$; $g_{uv}(C)$ is

the number of geodesics connecting $u$ to $v$ passing through $C$; and $g_{uv}$ is the number of geodesics connecting $u$ to $v$. This index can be normalized by dividing each value by the theoretical maximum. All these measures can be found in Wasserman and Faust (1994).

62. Other versions, considering the variance of degrees, betweenness, closeness, standardized indices, the number of paths or information centralization can be found in Wasserman and Faust (1994).

63. When $\dfrac{\sum_{i \in N_s} \sum_{j \in N_s} x_{ij} / g_s(g_s - 1)}{\sum_{i \in N_s} \sum_{j \notin N_s} x_{ij} / g_s(g - g_s)} \rangle 1$ , the ties within the sub-group are more prevalent, on

average, than ties outside the sub-group. For dichotomous relations the numerator is the density of the sub-group; for valued relations the numerator is the average strength of ties within the sub-group.

64. A network is strongly $n$-connected when its directed paths have length $\leq n$. The same nodes will be recursively connected when they are strongly connected and the directed path from $i$ to $j$ uses the same nodes and arrows as from $j$ to $i$. It is recursively $n$-connected when also the lengths of the paths are considered.

65. When the length is considered, there are weakly $n$-connected nodes.

66. A valued network has a core–periphery structure to the extent that the difference in means across blocks is large relative to the variation within blocks.

67. Following Everett and Borgatti (1999) core and periphery can also be defined considering the quantity of ties; therefore a $k$-core is understood as a maximal connected sub-graph where the degree of all nodes is $\geq k$.

68. Where the average distance between points within circles increases monotonically with distance from the centre.

69. Looking for the absence of relatively exclusive cohesive sub-groups and therefore just one core sub-group.

70. Some of these references are Snyder and Kick (1979), Breiger (1981), Nemeth and Smith (1985) and Smith and White (1992).

71. Burt applies the Coleman–Theil inequality, $\dfrac{\sum_j r_j \ln(r_j)}{N \ln(N)}$ , where $r_j = \dfrac{c_{ij}}{NC/N}$ and $NC = \sum_i c_{ij}$

a network constraint index; $N$ is the size, measured as the number of contacts in the network.

72. Degree of hierarchy: $D_H = 1 - \left(\dfrac{V}{\max V}\right)$, $V$ is the number of reciprocated links.

73. Hierarchical level: $H_L = \dfrac{L-1}{N-1}$ , $L$ is the number of levels in a simplified or condensed graph.

74. In Degenne and Forsé (1999) there are comments for other research work focused on relations between organizations, like Levine (1972, 1985, 1987), Mintz and Schwartz (1981a, 1981b), Stokman and Wasseur (1985), Scott (1987), Palmer et al. (1986) and Berkowitz (1988).

75. $C_i = \sum_j r_{ij} C_j$ , where $r_{ij}$ is the value of the relation between $i$ and $j$, which can be defined in different ways.

76. Markovsky *et al.* (1998), focused as well on exchange networks, apply a graph theoretic index of power, measuring each position's potential power.
77. Source: own elaboration.
78. For Degenne and Forsé (1999) centrality implies prestige, because central actors enjoy better access to information and to other resources than marginal actors. Moreover, they are more actively involved in local issues, and they play a decisive role in building coalitions doing early negotiations upstream of actual decision making.
79. Another measure is the proximity prestige, weighting prestige according to closeness or proximity.
80. Mainly when talking about economic organizations or, more widely, about exchange networks.
81. The measures of all these concepts can be found in Degenne and Forsé (1999, p.146).
82. Source of Figure 3.6: own elaboration.
83. The term 'arm's length ties' identifies exchange relations maintained with a high number of small firms and, therefore, corresponding to a situation of market competition.
84. The overlap matrix can be obtained from the strength matrix following this process: transforming the strength matrix into a binary matrix, applying to its values a threshold value and multiplying the new matrix by its transpose.
85. The same equation, but presented somewhat differently, is (3.17).
86. In order to measure them, heterogeneity and compositional quality require attribute data on all nodes in addition to relational data.
87. The aspects that should be considered to measure network resources are the range of resources among ties (distance between the highest- and lowest-valued resource), the best resource (upper reachability in a resource hierarchy), the variety or heterogeneity of resources and the composition of resources (average or typical resources). To measure contact resources, contact's occupation, authority and sector should be considered. Bridges or access to bridges can be calculated through structural holes, structural constraints and betweenness centrality. Strength of ties should be considered through network bridges, intimacy intensity, interaction and reciprocity.
88. The saturation technique should be applied through a complete mapping of the network; data from all nodes are needed; their relationships should be identified and then measurements of network locations can be developed. In the name generator technique a customized content area and an ego-centred network mapping are needed; all ties and locations should be computed; measures such as composition, heterogeneity and upper reachability can be considered. To apply the position generator technique a sample of hierarchical positions should be considered, multiple resources mapped and direct and indirect access computed; network resource indices can be built, such as composition, heterogeneity and upper reachability.
89. Graphs are taken from Burt (2000, p.91).
90. 'Events can be considered actions by a single actor or social interactions between actors' (Aunger, 1995, p.106).
91. According to Aunger (1995, p.105) the constituent events and states of a given structure can be abstracted from historical accounts, observed directly in the field or produced by a computer.
92. According to this theory, individuals relating in a group tend to equilibrate their relations, imbalance creates discomfort, and this generates forces that move triples of individuals towards balance. An example of equilibrated, or balanced, relation in a group formed by three individuals could be 'the friend of my friend is my friend'. However, the triple relation 'I dislike the friend of my friend' constitutes an example of an imbalanced one.

# 4 Regional Productive Structures and Production Systems

## 4.1 INTRODUCTION

Regional production systems will be studied in this chapter for the Spanish regions of Andalusia and the Basque Country and, for some parts of the analysis data, information related to the whole country could be offered as a reference point. The regional productive characteristics will be analysed from a historical perspective as a first step, to get information about the main branches working in the productive fabric of every region. Then, quantitative analyses will be applied to the regional input–output data.

Quantitative analyses are applied to the whole input–output net through descriptive statistics and social network analysis. Deductions from these calculations, and from the application of a specific algorithm, will be used to identify two production systems. Once the regional productive fabric has been studied from a historical, descriptive and network perspective, the identified production systems will be transformed, in the next chapter, into productive systems for their detailed study, by including the necessary information.

The study of the whole net, and the subsequent focus on a sub-group of it (production system), allows us to understand the regional production net from macro and micro perspectives. From a network structure view, the analytical approach for the actor aggregation in a particular unit of analysis may be, according to Burt (1980), actor, multiple actors as a network sub-group, and multiple actors as a structured system. The last two units of analysis are chosen in this part of the research, considering the macro and micro levels. Moreover, the analysis can be approached from a relational or positional perspective; the analytical tools offered by social network analysis allow for the study of both, as will be the case in this chapter.

## 4.2 REGIONAL HISTORICAL CHARACTERISTICS: KEY PRODUCTIVE BRANCHES

Every region inside Spain has its own peculiarities affecting its productive structure and its economic fabric. In the case of the two regions under study in this research, differences in size, population, productive specialization, location, political situation and history are quite important. It is essential to have an earlier picture of their main characteristics for a better understanding of their economic situation at present. This is the purpose of this section.

### 4.2.1   The Basque Country

The Basque Country is one of the 17 regions of Spain, located in the north of the country and bordered by the Cantabrico Sea and the south of France, a more developed area. It has an area of 7234 km$^2$, with a population of 2 115 279 in 2004. It is made up of three provinces: Álava, Vizcaya and Guipúzcoa. Its productive specialization is explained by its economic history, as shown in the first part of this section. There is also a peculiarity of the region that should be taken into account, for a better interpretation of its economic evolution in recent decades – the terrorist actions of ETA, mentioned in passing in the second part of this section.

#### 4.2.1.1   The productive structure of the Basque Country from a historical perspective

Historical studies remark on the specialization of this region ironworks with data from the eighteenth century.[1] Its geographic location with a sea port, its ore resources, its trade tradition, its craftsmanship linked to shipbuilding and to the iron and steel industry, its labour specialization, and its business skills intensified the region's productive concentration throughout the nineteenth and twentieth centuries. Other factors that enhanced the Basque productive tradition were its almost non-existent tax system, international protectionism and its investments in railways. The main factors for regional growth were its location and its ore resources. This led to high urban concentration, higher industrialization and higher railway investment than in other regions.

  In the eighteenth century this region was the main connection between the sea and the national territory of the interior. This implied an important control of exports and the incentive for the creation of a trade culture.[2] These positive factors were applied to the product where the region had its most important comparative advantages: iron ore. The first modern Basque iron and steel factory was established in 1841, while already in 1830 blast furnaces were created in Málaga and Seville (both in Andalusia) working with British iron ore. At the end of the century there was a period of crisis, affected by changes in international trade and the effect of international and national competition (Fernández de Pinedo and Fernández, 2001).

Throughout the nineteenth century there was an industrial process with the transformation of ironworks and foundries into iron and steel firms.[3] Their production was mainly focused on firearms and other ironwork.[4] This other ironwork, in the beginning, consisted of simple products with low value added, while iron products with more technology content were imported, mainly from Sheffield and Birmingham. The Basque Country became the first industrialized region in the country, during a period of growth, with increasing per capita income, population growth, positive migration, increased capital, railway investment, human capital formation, life expectancy increase, new patents and other positive socio-economic factors that intensified the regional specialization. Technological aspects were determinants in the development of the modern Basque specialized industry at the end of the nineteenth century.

From the beginning of the twentieth century the industrialization process continued with the creation of new iron and steel and sea transport firms,[5] and the modernization and enlargement of already existing iron and steel firms. New firms appeared, producing iron and steel products that had been imported up to that time; thus, instead of exporting iron as a raw material and subsequently importing the transformed products, an 'integrated iron industry' was created. One effect was a reduction in the import of iron and steel products within a few years. This was also the case with high-value-added products and intensive technology and skilled labour, leading to import substitution.[6] Later on, a chemical industry emerged in the region, using derivatives from the iron and steel firms.

According to Fernández de Pinedo and Fernández (2001), Basque businessmen were almost alone in the country in having a strategy for growth and not just for surviving. They used substitute imports, taking advantage of protectionist measures, to buy and copy foreign technology and to focus on the national market. The main working links were established between heavy iron and steel production, the chemical industry, shipyards and the agriculture sector and also between the integral iron industry and the basic iron and steel industry. Moreover, the development process, and the expansion of non-perishable consumer goods (white goods), favoured the regional economy.

In the second half of the twentieth century there was a reduction in public subsidies and in protectionism, and an economic depression that led to an industrial rationalization process with firms closing and unemployment rates increasing. The firms most affected were those linked to iron and steel works;

nevertheless, the surviving and new firms focused their production on similar goods but with modern technology and higher productivity. It is not possible to talk about an industrial diversification, because there still was a deep specialization, and the main change was the growing importance of the service sector. At the beginning of the twenty-first century, the Basque Country is considered as belonging to the richest group of regions of Spain, but among the stationary regions, while the rich growing regions are Baleares, Madrid, Navarra and Catalonia.

To conclude, there is a productive concentration in the Basque productive structure, based on historical factors: geographic location (seaport, inland access, navigable rivers and iron ore near the sea), technical and business skills, infrastructure from ironworks (dams, buildings), international and national trade knowledge and absence of manufacturing sector taxes. Together with these factors, other elements drove the creation of iron and steel plants, shipyards and a modern bank. This led to an increase in mining, iron and steel, chemical, banking and sea transport production.

### 4.2.1.2 The role of ETA terrorism in the economic evolution of the Basque Country

The ETA terrorist group was founded in 1959. Since then, and to date, it has committed 817 murders and 77 kidnappings.[7] Although terrorist actions started in 1968, in the middle-1970s they became a major phenomenon. Until then the position of the Basque Country in the national ranking was among the first three regions, considered a place of high growth and intensive industrialization. Since then its economic situation has dramatically changed, with lower rates of growth, less population growth and fewer investments. Nevertheless, there have been other factors taking place in the same period that could have had an even bigger impact in the regional economic evolution, mainly the industrial crisis of the 1970s.

Abadie and Gardeazabal (2001) made a simulation comparing the situation of the region with a hypothetical Basque Country without terrorism. Their main result implies that per capita GDP was 10 per cent less than it could have been without the terrorism problem.[8] Explanations include the abandoning of the region by businessmen victims of extortion and the reduction in foreign direct investment, studied in Enders and Sandler (1996).[9] Their main conclusion is that, on average, terrorism reduced annual net foreign direct investment in Spain by 13.5 per cent, meaning an annual decline of $488.9 million in the period 1975–91, equivalent to 7.6 per cent of annual gross fixed capital formation.[10] Moreover, as foreign direct investment is an important source of revenue for technology transfer, and therefore for economic growth, its decrease would reduce growth. The harm to commercial interest comes, in part, from an extortionist revolutionary tax that could be reducing expected returns and dissuading foreign direct investment, with terrorism having permanent effects on net foreign capital holdings in Spain, through its effect in the temporary decline in investment.

### 4.2.2    Andalusia: Productive Structure from a Historical Perspective

Andalusia is one of the biggest regions in Spain, with an area of 87597 km², located in the south of Spain, bordered by the Mediterranean Sea and the Atlantic Ocean. It is a periphery region in Spain, which is itself a periphery country. It had a population of 7687518 in 2004, distributed over eight provinces: Almería, Cádiz, Córdoba, Granada, Huelva, Jaén, Málaga and Seville. This region is highly specialized in agriculture and agribusiness, explained by history, location and social factors. Nevertheless, there are other sectors with an important industrial history, such as metallurgy, mainly in the past, and services at present (Martínez Rodriguez, 1993).

Natural resources in Andalusia are the key to understanding its productive specialization. It has always had fertile earth and rich subsoil, with its main natural resources linked to agriculture and mining. Moreover, its spatial location privileged international trade relationships, mainly with America until the loss of the colonies.

At the beginning of the twentieth century it was the Spanish region with the most international trade links, most of its production being sent to international markets. Its export structure had a high concentration in transformed agriculture products (mainly wines and liquors in the nineteenth century and olive oil and olives in the twentieth century) and mineral ores. Until the beginning of the twentieth century these two groups accounted for more than 80 per cent of total exports. Throughout the twentieth century other groups with high volumes of regional exports were non-transformed agriculture products, metal and mechanical products and chemicals. The highly traditional productions underwent an industrialization process, focused on sectors where the region had comparative advantages: mining and agribusiness. Moreover, in the development process, service sectors were having an increasing importance in the regional economic structure.

At the beginning of the twenty-first century, Andalusia can be considered a backward region belonging to the poor side of the country. It has, together with Extremadura, the lowest per capita GNP and the highest unemployment rate in Spain. History does much to explain this present situation, with high land property concentrations, unfair tenancy systems with a highly seasonal labour market linked to agriculture, maximum labour exploitation and low productivity with low investment. Together with the important problem of extreme inequality in property and income distribution there was a situation of foreign firms renting and acquiring regional resources and of local traders with no interest in increasing production and regional wealth.

The industrialization process experienced in other regions came to Andalusia more slowly. Economic growth has always been focused on primary specialization and international trade, with the exploitation of mining through the creation of iron and steel production firms and of agriculture with the development of an agribusiness industry.[11] More specifically, the productive structure of Andalusia, from the beginning of the nineteenth century, is focused on the following products: energy (solid fuels and coke, electric energy and gas), non-energetic mineral ores (metal and non-metal ores), basic metal industry (iron, copper, lead and silver transformation), chemical industry (oil and coal, fertilizers and explosives, chemicals for domestic uses), metal and non-metal transformation industry, textiles (cotton, wool), agro-food industry (flour, olive oil, wine, sugar, canned food), lead industry, paper, cork and wood.

In the first half of the nineteenth century the contribution of the olive oil industry to regional industrial production was 16.4 per cent, with 11.8 per cent for pyrites and copper and 10 per cent for lead extraction and metallurgy. In the second half of the nineteenth century the main contributions were 12.6 per cent for pyrites and copper, 10.2 per cent for the olive oil industry and 10.1 per cent for lead extraction and metallurgy. In the first third of the twentieth century the main contribution to industry, 24.3 per cent, was olive oil.[12] Olive oil has been, and still is, crucial for the regional economy. This region is the world's leading producer, and has introduced increasingly innovative techniques to improve its productivity and quality. Moreover, there are other products (derivatives of olive oil and related to olive trees) acquiring benefits from this situation: oil distilled from olive refuse, soap and olives mainly.

In the case of the iron and steel industry there were several problems impeding its evolution. One of the problems was the lack of infrastructure needed for the extraction process and for transportation. Moreover, most of the capital linked to this industry was not regional but the property of Basque or foreign firms. Together with these circumstances, the industrialization process was deeper and faster in the Basque Country; innovations were not adopted in Andalusia, foreign intervention was too high and prices too low. Therefore, the importance of the iron and steel industry of Andalusia to the whole country was decreasing, and the relevant role for regional economic growth was played by the agro-food industry.

To understand the present situation of Andalusia it should be said that the main problems inhibiting its development have been too much inequality of income and property distribution, too much external dependency, and a lack of social and institutional transformations. One of the main consequences is that, in crisis periods, industry has always been the sector suffering most, while agriculture is always trying to maintain its regional economic level. Throughout the twentieth century, agriculture, mining and related sub-sectors occupied the top positions in production, followed by services (mainly basic services). Last place is held by industry. Industry in Andalusia has always been used by other regions and countries for the most basic part of their production processes, impeding its embeddedness in the regional fabric. Moreover, services needed for industry have not been developed in the region, as in other parts of the country; also there is an intense sense of locality (cultural behaviour, affecting their business behaviour, where decisions mainly imply local actors and mistrusting outside people and institutions). The result is a region with a disarticulated and unstructured productive fabric.

### 4.2.3     Deductions from the Historical Comparison between Andalusia and the Basque Country

An important question derived from the historical regional analysis should be made explicit here, as it will explain many of the results appearing in the input–output network analysis. Several authors (Bernal and Parejo, 2001, among others) have identified the disarticulated and unstructured situation of the Andalusia economy as one of the main problems restraining its development. In fact, over long periods, Andalusia has shown quite important growth rates but without development.

The duality of its production structure explains much of the present situation, implying that a part of the production system is focused on agriculture, which is highly traditional, owned by regional producers, with low productivity and low innovation incorporation and appearing as the key sector in crisis periods. The other part of the production system comprises industrial activities, mostly owned by producers from other regions and even countries, with weak links to regional firms, as they are used by other locations to develop part of their production processes. Historically, there were no links among industrial sectors, between industrial and primary sectors, or between industry and service sectors. This situation never arose in the Basque Country, where industry has traditionally been owned by regional producers, the production structure has been highly articulated and natural resources, industry and services have been organized to increase efficiency, productivity and the regional articulation.

As an illustrative example, while in Andalusia services have been focused on restaurants, hotels and trade, in the Basque Country they have been focused on business services and banking. In fact, the first Basque bank, *Banco de Bilbao*, one of the main banks in the country at present, was created in 1857 to finance regional firms in their investments.[13] In Andalusia, in the nineteenth century, there were only a few savings banks (*cajas de ahorros*) belonging to the church, the upper middle class and the aristocracy. The first bank, *Banco de Málaga*, was founded in 1856 and absorbed by the Bank of Spain in 1874. Another illustrative case is the creation of an agribusiness system in Andalusia, dating from the 1980s, following authors such as Delgado Cabeza (1993). Agriculture has always been the main productive sector in the region, but it was not able to develop a system linked to it from the demand and supply sides. In the Basque Country, in contrast, its main sector, focused on metallurgy, was emerging from the beginning.

The regional productive structure of both regions, in the period 1980–95, is analysed in the following sections. This will be done by applying different perspectives and techniques. Therefore, the following section focuses on an explanation of the data and coefficients used for the analysis.

## 4.3   SELECTION OF THE COEFFICIENTS AND DATA USED IN THE EMPIRICAL ANALYSIS

Descriptive and social network analyses have been applied to input–output data in relative terms, once they have been changed into coefficients that, once calculated, showed very low values for some branches. For this reason, threshold values have been selected to eliminate coefficients that are too low. Homogeneous branch classifications have been obtained after eliminating some productive branches with methodological problems.

### 4.3.1   Selection of Coefficients

Most studies applying input–output data for the study of productive structures use technical (*a*) and inverse Leontieff (*b*) coefficients. None of these have been chosen for this research. According to De Mesnard (2001), the use of inverse matrices for their application to network analysis has no sense, for the following reasons:

• The $b$ coefficients include all paths of any length connecting two nodes, therefore the arrow between two nodes does not have any sense. Direct relation coefficients should be used, and paths of length longer than two would show indirect relations.

• After the matrix of links is made binary the inverse loses its sense even more: the $b_{ij}$ coefficient is made 1 when it is higher than or equal to a filter ($w_{ij} = 1$); $b_{jl}$ is made 1 when it is higher than a filter value ($w_{jl} = 1$); and, according to transitivity, the binary value of the relation between $i$ and $l$ is 1 ($w_{il}=1$).[14] But the $b_{il}$ coefficient already includes all possible relations, of every path, between $i$ and $l$, therefore $w_{il}$ has no meaning.

• The Leontief inverse matrix can be decomposed as $B = A^0 + A^1 + A^2 + \dots + A^\infty$. Therefore, $b_{ij}$ coefficients consider paths of any length, even infinite paths, so $b_{ij}b_{jl}$ should be higher than infinite, which has no sense.

To make a first analysis of the whole net, coefficients are calculated with respect to global intermediate sales or purchases, as the object of analysis is inter-sector relationships. Therefore, branches can be classified according to their weight in the whole economy structure, using the following relative intermediate transaction coefficients.[15]

$$\frac{x_{ij}}{IS} = \frac{x_{ij}}{IP} . \tag{4.1}$$

Thus, there are four matrices for each region: 1980 inside and total, 1995 inside and total. Although the analysis will be done with inside values, totals can be used for comparison, as with the data from Spain. Once the whole net has been analysed, the research will focus on the part of the nets constituting production systems. To have more detailed information at this level, the coefficients used are the following relative intermediate sales and relative intermediate purchase coefficients:[16]

$$\frac{x_{ij}}{\sum\limits_{j=1}^{n} x_{ij}} = \frac{x_{ij}}{IS_i}, \qquad \frac{x_{ij}}{\sum\limits_{i=1}^{n} x_{ij}} = \frac{x_{ij}}{IP_j} . \tag{4.2}$$

Both types of coefficients have been calculated after the main diagonal of inter-sector relationships has been eliminated because, as explained in the previous chapter, the main interest of this research is in inter-sector, not intra-sector, relationships. Moreover, the case in which a branch has very high sales to itself and therefore – when calculating the corresponding coefficients – all intermediate sales appear very small, will be avoided in this way.

### 4.3.2 Selection of Threshold Values to Eliminate Trivial Relationships

A frequency statistical analysis has been applied to all coefficients, for total and inside values, to order data according to their trade intensity. Each matrix of coefficients has been divided into percentiles, making 20 groups. As an example, to select approximately 20 per cent of the relationships with highest values, only relations with coefficients equal to or above 1 per cent should be considered.[17] An important deduced piece of information is that, in all cases, the first 35 per cent of potential relationships have coefficients with only zero values. Then, positive values start in the 40 per cent percentile.

### 4.3.3 Final Number of Branches and their Classification

A homogeneity process has been applied to use the same number of branches in both years, 1980 and 1995, for each region. Nevertheless, even after homogeneity had been done, some branches presented methodological problems and, in some cases, they had to be eliminated. Once a final categorization was decided they were classified, again, into bigger groups according to their sector characteristics, technology content and input–output links. It should be remembered that the inter-branch relationships considered only refer to intermediate transactions; therefore, capital transactions are not in the data used.[18]

In the Basque Country, input–output tables include 73 branches in 1980, and 83 in 1995. They have been made homogeneous – leading to a classification with 49 branches; however, three more had to be eliminated owing to methodological problems, leading to a final homogeneous classification with 46 branches. Andalusia includes 64 branches in its input–output tables of 1980, and 89 in 1995. The homogeneous classification would have 47 branches; however, three branches have been eliminated because of methodological problems, and the final classification has 44 productive branches. The input–output table in Spain, in 1980, has 85 branches, and in 1995 there are 70 branches; the final classification, once homogeneity has been done and one of the branches has been eliminated, includes 42 productive branches. In all three places one of the eliminated branches is 'public administration'. The other eliminated branches are, in the Basque Country, 'activities of private households' and 'education' and, in Andalusia, 'health' and 'education'.

For the industrial productive branches there is a particular methodological problem, of high importance in the case of the Basque Country, for 'manufacture of machinery for metallurgy'. It is a key branch in the Basque Country, according to the region's productive specialization; however, in the input–output data, it is a branch with very few links and very low coefficients. Moreover, in 1980, its intermediate sales were zero, indicating that it did not sell to any other branch. The explanation is that its production goes to final demand (investment and exports).[19] The weight of exports on the branch production was 86.6 per cent in 1980 and 74.8 per cent in 1995. The weight of investment on the branch production was 13.5 per cent in 1980 and 20.2 per cent in 1995. This particularity should be considered in the analysis, because of the importance of this branch in the Basque economy.

Once there is a final homogeneous branch categorization, for each of the two regions, they have been classified according to the sector they belong to, their technology content and their input–output links, to elaborate a deeper analysis and to get richer conclusions. It is generally accepted that more developed areas show a specialization in, or a tendency towards, productive branches with high technology content and belonging to the service sector. These conclusions can be tested, for the cases of the Basque Country and Andalusia, by using the proper classifications, when relating the regional structural analyses to the development and growth stage of each region. Moreover, a third classification is offered in this section, as a contribution of this research. While the other two widely known classifications focus on branch attributes, the new proposed classification focuses on branch input–output links. With its complementary application conclusions, about regional development can be explained more thoroughly.

Table 4.1 shows the sector differentiation making the first of the three classifications, indicating the branches belonging to each sector in each region, based on EAS-95 (European Accounting System-95). At a more aggregated level it tries to divide all productive activities into three big groups: agriculture (primary sector), industry (secondary sector) and services (tertiary sector). The version offered in Table 4.1 is more specific, separating the three big sectors into six groups.

Table 4.2 corresponds to a classification focused on the technology content of each productive branch, indicating the branches belonging to each group in each region, after using several sources.[20] The final selected classification combines the intensity of technology content and the characterization of some branches as ICT (information and communication technology) or ICT users. Five groups are obtained; although some branches could belong to two different groups, richer conclusions can be obtained if they are separated, as in the case of 'trade' – considered an ICT branch although just a part of it is recognized as such.[21] Official statistics (OECD, INE – *Instituto Nacional de Estadística* –) usually include 'machinery, equipment and components trade', 'wholesale machinery and office equipment trade', 'wholesale electric and electronic components trade' and 'other retail trade' in the ICT group. As this branch does not belong to any other category there is just one group for it; the intention is to have more information for this analysis.

*Table 4.1: Sector classification*

| Groups | Andalusia | Basque Country |
|---|---|---|
| 1. Agriculture, hunting and fishing | 1–4 (4) | 1–3 (3) |
| 2. Ore industries | 5 (1) | 4,8 (2) |
| 3. Manufacturing industries | 6, 10–36 (28) | 5, 9–33 (26) |
| 4. Electricity, gas and water | 7–9 (3) | 6,7 (2) |
| 5. Construction | 37 (1) | 34 (1) |
| 6. Services | 38–44 (7) | 35–46 (12) |

*Note*: The total number of branches in each group is included in brackets.

*Table 4.2: Technology content classification*

| Group | Andalusia | Basque Country |
|---|---|---|
| 1. Low technology content | 1–12, 15, 16, 22–34, 37, 39, 40 (30) | 1–13, 21–30, 33, 34, 36–40 (30) |
| 2. Medium technology content | 17, 19, 20, 35 (4) | 15, 16, 18, 19, 31, 32 (6) |
| 3. High technology content | 13, 14, 18, 21, 36, 41, 44 (7) | 14, 17, 20, 41, 44 (5) |
| 4. ICT | 38 (1) | 35 (1) |
| 5. Main ICT users | 42, 43 (2) | 42, 43, 45, 46 (4) |

*Note*: Branches selected as both high technology content and ICT (18, 36, 41 and 44 for Andalusia; 17, 41 and 44 for the Basque Country) are included in group 3 of high technology content. ICT: information and communication technology. See note in Table 4.1.

Table 4.3 assembles the conclusion of this research about the third classification, focused on the structural equivalence of the input–output links maintained by all productive branches, indicating the branches belonging to each group in each region.[22] It has been obtained with the application, to every input–output table (Andalusia, the Basque Country and Spain, 1980 and 1995), of the CONCOR algorithm, after applying a sequence of threshold values.[23] CONCOR is based on a positional analysis, by making partitions of actors into sub-sets to find positions of approximately structurally equivalent actors. After the partition is made, productive branches within each sub-set, as a result of the partition, are closer to being structurally equivalent than are branches in different sub-sets. That is, branches in the same sub-set are close to sending and receiving intermediate inputs from the a same other group of branches.

*Table 4.3: Input–output links classification*

| Groups | Andalusia | Basque Country |
|---|---|---|
| 1. Agriculture and hunting | 1, 2, 3 (3) | 1, 2 (2) |
| 2. Fishing and agribusiness | 4, 22–28 (8) | 3, 21–26 (7) |
| 3. Transport machines | 19, 20, 21 (3) | 18, 19, 20 (3) |
| 4. P-S-T | 6–9, 16, 18, 30–38, 41–43 (18) | 5–7, 17, 28–35, 41–43 (15) |
| 5. Transport services | 40 (1) | 37–40 (4) |

*Note*: Group 4 includes branches from the three basic productive sectors (primary, secondary and tertiary), receiving the name of P-S-T, and including sectors like electricity, petroleum, gas, paper industry and construction. See note in Table 4.1.

Groups have been selected after their link structure has been observed. Once the algorithm made groups by applying structural equivalence, the objective was to check with which other groups they related and why (mainly as buyers, as sellers or both; only with one group, with all of them or with some). The five groups in Table 4.3 do not include all productive branches, as some of them are very difficult to assign in a common group. However, in the three analysed places and for the two mentioned years, the common structure presented in Table 4.3 can be generally deduced, although there are some peculiarities that should be clarified:

- Groups 1 and 2 are the only ones appearing in every case as separated groups. Group 1 can be seen as seller and buyer, although its buying and selling links are maintained with a particular group of branches: it sells mainly to itself, to agribusiness, to 'hotels and restaurants' and to 'business services'; it buys mainly from itself, from the P-S-T group, from 'transports' and from 'business services'.
- Group 2 can be characterized as a buying group, because its selling links have importance only for itself and for 'hotels and restaurants'. It includes all the agribusiness branches, together with 'fishing', traditionally considered a primary branch.
- Group 3 is also a buying group, even more evident than group 2, although its sales cannot be considered of importance. Nevertheless, in some cases this is a group difficult to separate from group 4.

• Group 4 is a selling group – selling to all others and buying significant quantities only from itself, from 'metallurgy' and from 'hotels and restaurants'. It is also peculiar because it includes basic fundamental branches for the productive process (petroleum, gas, water, electricity), industry branches (wood, paper, plastic, textiles), construction and services (trade, telecommunications, financing, insurance). It is made up of general inputs, incorporated in most productive processes.

• Group 5 is more difficult to separate from group 4, although it is made of branches always appearing together, and it is a key group for all others.

## 4.4   WHOLE NET ANALYSIS

It is convenient to analyse the whole trade net, before selecting and studying a particular group within it making a production system. This part of the analysis will help to understand the productive structure of the regions under study and, therefore, the context in which the selected production systems work. Going from the macro structure (whole net) to micro structures (production systems), a reference stage is built. Moreover, branches constituting production systems can be studied considering their position and links in their micro system, as well as in the regional structure. The whole net analysis is done descriptively first, and by following the network perspective after, for inside or domestic data. In both cases results are linked to the three classifications offered in the previous section.

### 4.4.1   Descriptive Analysis

The main characteristics of branches and links will be described in this section. In some cases calculus will be done for the whole net, and some other times they will be done once threshold values, or filters, are imposed to inside data

#### 4.4.1.1   Branches analysis

The ten most important branches, according to their intermediate sales (*IS*) and purchases (*IP*) weight on the regional values, are shown in Table 4.4. They have been selected because they have the highest value as intermediate seller or buyers:

$$IS = \frac{IS_i}{IS}, \qquad IP = \frac{IP_i}{IP} . \tag{4.3}$$

Before commenting on the deductions obtained after comparing the data, it is worth noting the increase, between 1980 and 1995, in the cumulative percentage of intermediate sales and purchases, for both regions, of the first ten branches. This shows an increase in the concentration level of both intermediate sales and purchases, although it is more evident from the purchases perspective. The relative cumulative percentage has increased, on average, by 5.47 percentage points. Moreover, in 1995, just five branches accumulated more than half of the regional intermediate sales and purchases in both places, and there is an increase in intermediate transaction concentration for the most important branches in the 1980–1995 period. This process is explained by the regional specialization and by the presence of key branches, as will be explained in this and the following sections.

When comparing Andalusia, the Basque Country and Spain there is a general scheme showing a situation common to developed areas: a) 'trade', 'business services', 'transports' and 'electric power' appear, in both years and in the three places, among the most important intermediate sellers; b) 'construction', 'hotels and restaurants' and 'trade' are always among the most important intermediate purchasers; c) in 1995, 'business services' and 'trade' are selected for both aspects, among the highest values for intermediate sales and purchases, in the three places, showing their character as key branches; d) the common dynamism can also be observed with the evolution of the primary sector reducing its importance in every place. For the branches increasing their participation there is a common path for 'business services', 'trade', 'post and telecommunications', 'construction' and 'hotels and restaurants'. Service sectors appear as the most dynamic economic activities, participating in economic and technological flows and creating productive dependencies. This situation is generally related to growth and development and therefore to the case of Spain and its regions.

There are also regional specifics particular to the specialization, endowments, culture and history of each place. In Andalusia, in both years, among the most outstanding intermediate sellers are 'agriculture' and 'manufacture of wood, cork, metal products and furniture'. For the intermediate purchasers the selected branches in both years are 'agriculture', 'oils and fats' and 'manufacture of other food products'. The key branch in the region, appearing always in 1980 and 1995, according to both aspects – buying and selling –, is 'agriculture', although in 1995 'financial intermediation' is also in both groups.

*Table 4.4: The ten most important branches*

| 1980 | Andalusia | Basque Country |
|---|---|---|
| IS | (1) 'Agriculture': 17.27%<br>(6) 'Coke, P & RO': 10.42%<br>(40) 'Transports': 10.32%<br>(44) 'Business services & other ac.': 7.96%<br>(38) 'R, R & trade': 6.87%<br>(2) 'Farming & H': 4.98%<br>(16) 'Wood, cork & furniture': 4.79%<br>(7) 'Electricity': 4.34%<br>(26) 'Other food ind.': 3.37%<br>(5) 'Mining & quarrying': 2.68%<br>Σ: 73.00% | (5) 'Coke, P & NG': 13.52%<br>(9) 'Metals': 13.24%<br>(35) 'R, R & trade': 10.54%<br>(44) 'Business services': 7.00%<br>(6) 'Electricity': 5.98%<br>(15) 'Metal products & mach.': 5.92%<br>(37) 'Other land tr.': 5.14%<br>(10) 'NFM & Bchem.': 3.21%<br>(2) 'Farming, H & forestry': 3.02%<br>(17) 'Office machinery, P & P': 2.77%<br>Σ: 70.35% |
| IP | (37) 'Construction': 8.76%<br>(26) 'Other food ind.': 8.44%<br>(22) 'Oils & fats': 8.04%<br>(39) 'Hotels & rest.': 7.36%<br>(38) 'R, R & trade': 6.98%<br>(1) 'Agriculture': 5.53%<br>(40) 'Transports': 5.31%<br>(2) 'Farming & H': 4.97%<br>(27) 'Spirits, alcohol & wine': 4.52%<br>(7) 'Electricity': 3.87%<br>Σ: 63.78% | (15) 'Metal products & mach.': 20.15%<br>(9) 'Metals': 13.10%<br>(34) 'Construction': 6.73%<br>(37) 'Other land tr.': 4.14%<br>(17) 'Office machinery, P & P':4.09%<br>(35) 'R, R & trade': 3.58%<br>(6) 'Electricity': 3.45%<br>(36) 'Hotels & rest.': 2.81%<br>(30) 'Paper': 2.67%<br>(39) 'Water & air tr.': 2.46%<br>Σ: 63.18% |
| 1995 | Andalusia | Basque Country |
| IS | (44) 'Business services & other ac.': 16.41%<br>(1) 'Agriculture': 11.96%<br>(40) 'Transports': 10.43%<br>(38) 'R, R & trade': 9.98%<br>(7) 'Electricity': 6.77%<br>(6) 'Coke, P & RO': 5.78%<br>(11) 'Cement': 3.92%<br>(41) 'Post & telecom.': 3.61%<br>(42) 'Financial interm.': 3.15%<br>(16) 'Wood, cork & furniture': 2.46%<br>Σ: 74.47% | (44) 'Business services': 18.66%<br>(35) 'R, R & trade': 11.36%<br>(34) 'Construction': 8.83%<br>(9) 'Metals': 7.32%<br>(15) 'Metal products & mach.': 5.76%<br>(6) 'Electricity': 5.47%<br>(17) 'Office machinery, P & P': 4.59%<br>(5) 'Coke, P & NG': 4.56%<br>(37) 'Other land tr.': 3.82%<br>(41) 'Post & telecom.': 3.05%<br>Σ: 73.42% |
| IP | (38) 'R, R & trade': 16.31%<br>(37) 'Construction': 14.61%<br>(39) 'Hotels & rest.': 9.86%<br>(22) 'Oils & fats': 8.62%<br>(40) 'Transports': 6.10%<br>(44) 'Business services & other ac.': 5.18%<br>(1) 'Agriculture': 3.87%<br>(26) 'Other food ind.': 3.27%<br>(25) 'Fish & vegetable ind.': 2.67%<br>(42) 'Financial interm.': 2.34%<br>Σ: 72.83% | (15) 'Metal products & mach.': 15.66%<br>(34) 'Construction': 11.31%<br>(44) 'Business services': 10.70%<br>(35) 'R, R & trade': 9.02%<br>(9) 'Metals': 6.73%<br>(36) 'Hotels & rest.': 5.43%<br>(17) 'Office machinery, P & P': 3.77%<br>(18) 'Motor vehicles': 3.10%<br>(37) 'Other land tr.': 2.98%<br>(46) 'Social, personal & com. ac.': 2.58%<br>Σ: 71.28% |

*Note*: The names of the branches have been abbreviated; the whole branch names are shown in Annex 4.1.

In the Basque Country the specifics are even more evident as 'metals', 'metal products and machinery' and 'manufacture of office machinery and electrical goods' are in 1980 and 1995 among the branches with highest selling and buying values, demonstrating a permanent key character. The history and culture of Andalusia and the Basque Country, already commented upon, give strength to the explanation of these branches appearing as the core for the productive specialization in either of the two regions. The importance of the agriculture sector and agribusiness in Andalusia and of metals and metal products in the Basque Country is therefore permanent and corroborated.

Although only inside values are shown here, another useful comparison can be established with total values. After comparing, a general conclusion is that, in both regions, there are differences with higher values when using total data. Therefore, some imports are needed for every regional productive process, generating dependency. The distinguished cases are 'mining and quarrying' and 'coke, petroleum and radioactive materials' in Andalusia, and 'non-ferrous metal ores and basic chemicals' in the Basque Country.

Information about each branch's intermediate sales and purchases can also be analysed dynamically, according to the relative changes taking place between 1980 and 1995, as in Figures 4.1 and 4.2, showing the variations in the percentage weight of intermediate sales and purchases. Each figure has been divided into the following areas:

- The $A$ areas are made of branches in expansion from both perspectives, sales and purchases, although in $A_1$ the expansion of sales is higher than that of purchases ($\Delta IS > \Delta IP$) and, in $A_2$, the other way around ($\Delta IS < \Delta IP$). The first sub-area includes branches that can be characterized as 'expansion intensified in sales', and the second as 'expansion intensified in purchases'.
- The $C$ area includes branches in decline, differentiating a group, $C_1$, where decreases are higher for intermediate sales ($\nabla IS > \nabla IP$) and another, $C_2$, where the reductions are higher for intermediate purchases ($\nabla IP > \nabla IS$). The first sub-area will be labelled 'decline intensified in sales' and the second, 'decline intensified in purchases'.
- On the other side, the $B$ area is made up of branches showing an expansion in intermediate purchases but a reduction in intermediate sales ($\Delta IP$, $\nabla IS$). This will be labelled 'purchases expansion area'.
- The $D$ area contains branches showing expansion in intermediate sales but reduction in intermediate purchases ($\nabla IP$, $\Delta IS$). This is a 'sales expansion area'.

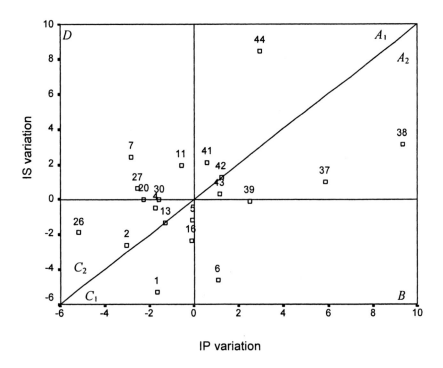

*Note*: Represented values are the difference in percentage points between 1995 and 1980, for relative intermediate sales and purchases. Only branches with changes higher than one percentage point, in absolute terms, in sales or purchases, have been represented. The corresponding numbers and branches are in Annex 4.1.

*Figure 4.1: Branch intermediate trade dynamics, Andalusia, 1980–95*

In the case of Andalusia the situation is similar for total and inside values, having branches with an obvious positive or negative dynamic behaviour. 'Agriculture'(1), 'farming'(2) and 'other food industry'(26) show remarkable decreases in their intermediate sales and purchases. Nevertheless, according to the analysis of Section 4.2, based on the specifics of the regions, and on the links analysis that will be shown next, a strong agro-food system is maintained in Andalusia, but with increasing importance of the agro-food industry and lower importance of the basic primary sector (agriculture, farming, hunting and fishing). On the other hand, with remarkable increases in sales and purchases there are the expected service sectors of 'trade' (38) and 'business services' (44), together with 'construction' (37).

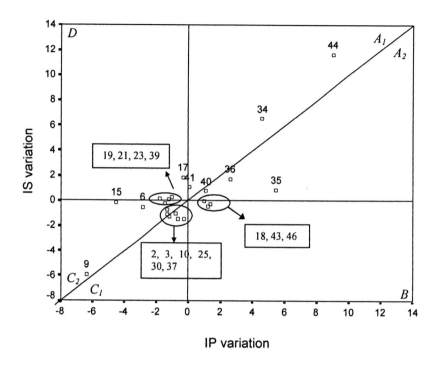

*Note*: See note in Figure 4.1.

*Figure 4.2: Branch intermediate trade dynamics, the Basque Country, 1980–95*

When analysing the situation in the Basque Country, there are important reductions in sales and purchases for 'metals' (9). Services are again the most important branches, with increases in their intermediate sales and purchases, mainly in the cases of 'business services'(44), 'trade' (35) and 'hotels and restaurants' (36). 'Construction' (34) also has high rises, as a sector typically benefiting the Spanish growth path.

### 4.4.1.2　Relationships analysis

The most important regional relationships have been selected by calculating the relative intermediate transaction coefficients presented in Section 4.3.1. After the calculations, the links with a value higher than 1 per cent have been represented for both years, 1980 and 1995, in Tables 4.5 and 4.6.

Figure 4.3 represents links experiencing changes higher than one percentage point, in a positive or negative sense (>|1|). As an example, the link going from branch 44 to 38, in Andalusia, has the highest increase in the analysed period, while the link going from branch 40 to 38 is the second highest, and so on.

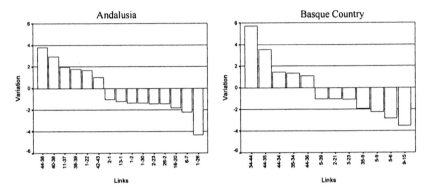

*Figure 4.3: Highest variation links, 1980–95*

*Andalusia*    There are two outstanding relationships in 1980,[24] with values higher than 5 per cent, with the exchanges going from 'agriculture' (1) to 'oils and fats' (22) and to 'manufacture of other food products' (26). In 1995, there are even bigger differences, as trade from 'agriculture' (1) to 'oils and fats' (22) implies more than 7 per cent of the total intermediate transactions. At the same time, Figure 4.3 shows that the variation in one of these relationships (1–22) is among the highest while the other (1–26) has the largest decrease. There is, therefore, evidence of the loss of importance of agriculture and farming of animals as sellers and buyers, which used to be crucial in the agro-food industry; but, as has already been said, the industrial side now has greater importance than the primary sector, focused on olive oil.

Following the agro-food links there are the sales of 'business services' (44) and 'transport' (40) to 'trade' (38) (>6 per cent and >4 per cent, respectively) and 'cement' (11) to 'construction' (37) (>3 per cent), which are also the links with the highest increase in the analysed period (Figure 4.3), showing the regional growth and development process.

To summarize, it can be said that most of the links disappearing in 1995 belong to manufacturing sectors, mainly to 'other food industry'. Nevertheless, an important number of links in the agriculture, hunting and fishing sector are also disappearing. Moreover, most of these branches are of low technology content and, according to the third classification, most of them are in the agriculture group. As for the links appearing in 1995, most of them belong to the service sector, mainly for 'trade' and 'hotels and restaurants'. They are of low technology content, and are in the P-S-T group. The remaining branches are service branches ('trade' and 'transport') with low technology content, and are part of the P-S-T and agribusiness group.

*Table 4.5: The most important links in Andalusia*

| | 1/80 | 1/95 | 2/80 | 7/80 | 20/80 | 22/80 | 22/95 | 23/80 | 23/95 | 24/80 | 25/80 | 25/95 | 26/80 | 30/80 | 37/80 | 37/95 | 38/80 | 38/95 | 39/80 | 39/95 | 40/80 | 40/95 | 42/95 | 43/95 |
|---|---|---|---|---|---|---|---|---|---|---|---|---|---|---|---|---|---|---|---|---|---|---|---|---|
| 1 | | | 2.04 | | | 5.63 | 7.27 | 2.61 | 1.19 | 1.19 | 1.32 | 1.76 | 5.23 | 1.49 | | | | | | | | | | |
| 2 | 1.06 | | | | | | | | | | | | | | | | | | | | | | | |
| 6 | | | | 2.38 | | | | | | | | | | | | | | 1.5 | | 1.03 | 2.27 | 2.41 | | |
| 7 | | | | | | | | | | | | | | | | | | | | | | | | |
| 10 | | | | | | | | | | | | | | | 1.65 | | | | | | | | | |
| 11 | | | | | | | | | | | | | | | 1.91 | 3.88 | | | | | | | | |
| 13 | 1.8 | | | | | | | | | | | | | | | | | | | | | | | |
| 16 | | | | | 1.86 | | | | | | | | | | | 1.82 | | | | | | | | |
| 26 | | | 2.06 | | | | | | | | | | | | | | | | | | | | | |
| 28 | | | | | | | | | | | | | | | | | | | | | | | | |
| 38 | 1.24 | | | | | | | | | | | | | | | 1.43 | | | 1.77 | 1.35 | 1.16 | 1.44 | | |
| 40 | | | | | | | | | | | | | 1.08 | | 1.21 | | 1.22 | 4.16 | | 2.11 | | | | |
| 42 | | | | | | | | | | | | | | | | | | | | | | | | 1.01 |
| 44 | | | | | | | | | | | | | | | 1.39 | | 2.44 | 6.23 | | 1.51 | | | 1.38 | |

*Note:* Intra-branch links have been omitted. There are two columns per branch; the first shows the data for 1980 and the second for 1995. When the percentage is higher than 1 only for one of the two years, just one column appears.

Table 4.6: The most important links in the Basque Country

| | 6 | 6 | 9 | 9 | 15 | 15 | 18 | 21 | 23 | 25 | 34 | 34 | 35 | 36 | 37 | 37 | 39 | 42 | 43 | 44 | 46 |
|---|---|---|---|---|---|---|---|---|---|---|---|---|---|---|---|---|---|---|---|---|---|
| | 80 | 80 | 95 | 80 | 95 | 80 | 95 | 80 | 80 | 80 | 80 | 95 | 95 | 95 | 80 | 95 | 80 | 95 | 95 | 95 | 95 |
| 1 | | | | | | | | | | 0.93 | | | | | | | | | | | |
| 2 | | | | | | | | 1.17 | | | | | | | | | | | | | |
| 3 | | | | | | | | | 1.32 | | | | | | | | | | | | |
| 5 | 2.89 | | 2.81 | | | | | | | | | | | | 1.62 | 1.05 | 1.33 | | | | |
| 6 | | | 2.15 | 1.22 | | | | | | | | | | | | | | | | | |
| 9 | | | | | 9.98 | 5.45 | | | | | 1.09 | | | | | | | | | | |
| 10 | | | | | 1.36 | | | | | | | | | | | | | | | | |
| 13 | | | | | | | | | | | 1.18 | 1.6 | | | | | | | | | |
| 15 | | | 1.01 | 0.86 | | | 0.9 | | | | 1.54 | 1.78 | | | | | | | | | |
| 17 | | | | | | | | | | | | 0.99 | | | | | | | | 1.39 | |
| 29 | | | | | 1.11 | | | | | | | | | | | | | | | | |
| 34 | | | 2.7 | | | | | | | | | | | | | | | | | 6.18 | |
| 35 | | | | | 1.41 | 2.38 | | | | | 1.68 | | | | 1.27 | | | | | | |
| 37 | | | | | | 0.93 | | | | | | | | | | | | | | | |
| 44 | | | 0.84 | | 1.35 | 1.92 | | | | | | 1.63 | 3.92 | 1.14 | | | | 1.27 | 1.16 | | 0.88 |

103

Attention should be paid to 'agriculture', as it is in several links. Its disappearing links are, in both directions, to 'farming of animals', buying 'chemicals' and as a seller for 'other food industry' and 'textiles'. It appears as a buyer from trade. It remains (increasing its percentage) a seller for 'oils and fats' and 'fish and vegetable industry', and it takes part in six of the nine links with the most acute decreases.

Regional specialization and also the growth and development processes are reflected in the data. Andalusia is a region focused on the agro-food system, where the production of olive oil is at the centre of the productive process, showing an important expansion. Another element tested is the role of 'business services', 'trade' and 'transport' in every development path, with the first having a particularly relevant role associated with a development process. Lastly, 'construction' is enjoying a remarkable participation in the whole national economy, with an expansion path.

*The Basque Country* In the Basque Country both processes (specialization and development) emerge again from the link data. In 1980, sales of 'metals' (9) to 'metal products and machinery' (15) had an intermediate trade higher than 9 per cent over the total transactions.[25] In 1995, there were three relationships which should be highlighted: from 'construction' (34) to 'business services' (44) (>6 per cent), from 'metals' (9) to 'metal products and machinery' (15) (>5 per cent) and from 'business services' (44) to 'trade' (35) (>3.5 per cent). Moreover, these are the links (34–44–35) showing the highest increase in the analysed period (Figure 4.3), related to a general process of development as in the case of Andalusia, with the largest decrease (9–15) focused on the regional specialization productive process.

The disappearing branches in 1995 are mainly from manufacturing industries ('metals' and 'metal products and machinery'), with low technology content and belonging to the P-S-T group. The newly appearing branches are from services ('business services' mainly), with high technology content and belonging to the P-S-T group.

As deduced, 'metal products and machinery' has a particular behaviour, disappearing always as a buyer of industrial products, and appearing as a seller for 'motor vehicles', implied in the highest link and in the highest reduction.

Agriculture and agribusiness branches lost their most important links in this 15-year period, while at the same time services, mainly 'business services', emerged with the most outstanding links, sharing their significance with the already recognized importance of 'metals'.

In Spain, changes are much smaller than in Andalusia and the Basque Country, as when comparing the intensity of intermediate branch transactions. The compensation effect occurring, when data are at a more aggregated level, should be considered. With national information, the highest variation is one percentage point.

When comparing inside and total data, in Andalusia, at aggregate level there are two new relations appearing among the most important that did not emerge at inside level. These links are from 'mining and quarrying' (5) to 'coke, petroleum and radioactive materials' (6), reflecting the petroleum dependency of the country, and from 'manufacture of wood, cork, metal products and furniture' (16) to 'construction' (37). These discrepancies with the inside results show the importance of necessary imports of some intermediate goods in different processes. In the case of the Basque Country there is a new important link from 'trade' (35) to 'metals' (9), but only in 1980.

### 4.4.2    Network Analysis

All the regional intermediate transaction nets are analysed in this section, using the most significant network analysis measures and concepts explained in the previous chapter. Relational and positional approaches will be applied in this case to the 'multiple actors/subgroups as a structured system' (Burt, 1980), when the analysis is at the macro whole net level. Results are complementary to the conclusions obtained in the previous section.

#### 4.4.2.1    Net size

The size of the net is the most basic network measure, considering the number of nodes and links; this information is offered in Table 4.7.[26]

*Table 4.7: Net size*

|  | Andalusia | | Basque Country | |
|---|---|---|---|---|
|  | 1980 | 1995 | 1980 | 1995 |
| No. of nodes | 44 | 44 | 46 | 46 |
| No. of directed links | 1150 (60.8%) | 1207 (63.8%) | 1337 (64.6%) | 1286 (62.1%) |

At the beginning of the period, 1980, the relative number of links is higher in the Basque Country than in Andalusia. However, in Andalusia there is an increase of 5 per cent in the number of links, while in the Basque Country the dynamic is just the opposite, with a reduction of 3.8 per cent. In 1995, there are more relative links in Andalusia than in the Basque Country, showing, from this perspective, an approaching or convergence between the two regions. The analysis of this information shows the size, considering the whole net, but it is useful to see the result once several threshold values have been imposed. Moreover, with the branch classifications shown in Section 4.3, a better picture will be obtained.

As the number of branches and links determines the net size, the following analysis focuses on the number of branches disappearing and the number of links staying, when different filters are considered, and classified in groups according to their productive sector, technology content and input–output links.

*Branches disappearing according to several filters*     Tables 4.8 to 4.11 offer information about the branches disappearing, according to their transaction intensity. To observe the disappearing sequence, increasing threshold values have been applied to the net of intermediate relationships, with vanishing branches divided into quartiles. The number of each disappearing branch is included in its corresponding group (sector and technology content) and quartile. In the first quartile there are low-intensity branches, as they are the first to disappear when a filter is imposed. The second quartile is made of medium- to low-intensity branches and the third includes medium- to high-intensity branches. According to the information obtained from these tables, branches with very high intensity in their links can be identified, as they remain, even with very high threshold values; this is the case of branches belonging to the last quartile and called 'high', because of the intensity of their transactions.

In Andalusia, all branches belonging to group 1 in the input–output link classification ('agriculture' and agribusiness), have the most intense links and, as has been remarked before, they are the last in the vanishing sequences. All of them are in the groups 'medium–high' or 'high' in both years. Moreover, in 1980 'agriculture' (1), 'oils and fats' (22) and 'other food industry' (26) have the highest intensity overall.[27] It can also be observed that branches disappearing in the first place have low technology content and belong to the manufacturing sector. Moreover, all branches belonging to group 3 (transport machines) are, in 1995, in the first vanishing group. It is useful to remember that, for the intermediate sales side, only intermediate transactions are considered in the used data, while investment sales should have considerable importance for those goods. Nevertheless, for the intermediate purchases side there is also a loss of importance in the region, and imports should participate more intensively in their productive processes. Another deduction from Tables 4.8 and 4.9 is that all branches moving from 'low' to 'medium–low' in the analysed period, and therefore increasing their link intensity, belong to group 4 (P-S-T). They are basic branches with high presence in most productive processes and with increasing participation in the regional economy.

*Table 4.8: Vanishing sequence, by economic sector, Andalusia*

| Group | N of branches | Low | | Medium–low | | Medium–high | | High | |
|---|---|---|---|---|---|---|---|---|---|
| | | 1980 | 1995 | 1980 | 1995 | 1980 | 1995 | 1980 | 1995 |
| 1 | 4 | 3 | 3 | 4 | 4 | | 2 | 1  2 | 1 |
| 2 | 1 | | | 5 | 5 | | | | |
| 3 | 28 | 14 17; 21 29; 32 34; 35 36 (25.6%) | 14 17; 19 20; 21 29; 30 31; 32 36 (35.8%) | 12 15; 18 19; 31 33 (21.4%) | 13 15; 18 33; 34 35 (25%) | 10 11; 13 16; 20 24; 25 27; 28 30 (35.7%) | 10 23; 24 26; 27 28 (21.4%) | 6 22; 23 26 (14.3%) | 6 11; 16 22; 25 32 (17.9%) |
| 4 | 3 | | 9 | 8 | 8  9 | | 7 | 7 | |
| 5 | 1 | | | | | 37 | | | 37 |
| 6 | 7 | 43 (14.3%) | | 41  42 (28.6%) | | 39 (14.3%) | 41; 42 43 (43%) | 38; 40 44 (42.9%) | 38 39; 40 44 (57%) |

*Note*: First quartile, low: $C_i < 0.27$ (1980), 0.21 (1995); second quartile, medium–low: 0.27 (1980), 0.21 (1995) $\leq C_i < 0.8$; third quartile, medium–high: $0.8 \leq C_i < 2$; fourth quartile, high: $C_i \geq 2.4$. [28]

*Table 4.9: Vanishing sequence, by technology content, Andalusia*

| Group | No. of branches | Low | | Medium–low | | Medium–high | | High | |
|---|---|---|---|---|---|---|---|---|---|
| | | 1980 | 1995 | 1980 | 1995 | 1980 | 1995 | 1980 | 1995 |
| 1 | 30 | 9 29; 32 34 (16.7%) | 3; 29 30; 31 32 (16.7%) | 4; 5 8; 12 15; 31 33 (23.3%) | 4 5; 8 9; 12 15; 33 34 (26.7%) | 10 11; 16 24; 25 27; 28 30; 37 39 (33.3%) | 2 7; 10 23; 24 26; 27 28 (26.7%) | 1 2; 6 7; 22 23; 26 40 (26.7%) | 1 6; 11 16; 22 25; 32 37; 39 40 (30%) |
| 2 | 4 | 17 | 35 | 19 | 17  20 | 19 | 35 | 20 | |
| 3 | 7 | 14; 21 36 (42.9%) | 14; 21 36 (42.9%) | 18  41 (28.6%) | 13  18 (28.6%) | 13 (14.3%) | 41 (14.3%) | 44 (14.3%) | 44 (14.3%) |
| 4 | 1 | | | | | | | 38 | 38 |
| 5 | 2 | 43 | | 42 | | 42  43 | | | |

*Note*: See note in Table 4.8.

*Table 4.10: Vanishing sequence, by economic sector, the Basque Country*

| Group | No. of branches | Low | | Medium–low | | Medium–high | | High | |
|---|---|---|---|---|---|---|---|---|---|
| | | 1980 | 1995 | 1980 | 1995 | 1980 | 1995 | 1980 | 1995 |
| 1 | 3 | | 3 | | | 1  2 | 2 | 3 | |
| 2 | 2 | 4 | 8 | 8 | | | | | |
| 3 | 26 | 12<br>20  24<br>27  28<br>31  33<br>(26.9%) | 1<br>2  19<br>20  23<br>25  27<br>28  33<br>(30.8%) | 16  18<br>19  26<br>(19.2%) | 10  11<br>21  22<br>24  30<br>31  32<br>(30.8%) | 13<br>14  17<br>21  22<br>25  29<br>30  32<br>(34.6%) | 5  14<br>16  18<br>26  29<br>(23.1%) | 5<br>9  10<br>15  23<br>(19.2%) | 5<br>9  13<br>15  17<br>(15.4%) |
| 4 | 2 | | | | | | 7 | 6 | 6 |
| 5 | 1 | | | | | | | 34 | 34 |
| 6 | 12 | 38<br>40  45<br>(25%) | 38  45<br>(16.7%) | 36<br>41  42<br>43  46<br>(41.7%) | 39<br>(8.3%) | | 37  40<br>41  46<br>(33.3%) | 35  37<br>39  44<br>(66.7%) | 35<br>36  42<br>43  44<br>(41.7%) |

*Note*: First low quartile: $C_i < 0.32$ (1980), 0.25 (1995); medium–low quartile: 0.32 (1980), 0.25 (1995) $\leq C_i < 0.72$ (1980), 0.48 (1995); medium–high quartile: 0.72 (1980), 0.48 (1995) $\leq C_i < 1.2$ (1980), 1.1 (1995); high quartile: $C_i \geq 1.4$.

*Table 4.11: Vanishing sequence, by technology content, the Basque Country*

| Group | No. of branches | Low | | Medium–low | | Medium–high | | High | |
|---|---|---|---|---|---|---|---|---|---|
| | | 1980 | 1995 | 1980 | 1995 | 1980 | 1995 | 1980 | 1995 |
| 1 | 30 | 4  12<br>24  27<br>28  33<br>38  40<br>(26.7%) | 3<br>8  12<br>23  25<br>27  28<br>33  38<br>(30%) | 7<br>8  11<br>26  36<br>(16.7%) | 1<br>4  10<br>11  21<br>22  24<br>30  39<br>(30%) | 1  2<br>13  21<br>22  25<br>29  30<br>(26.7%) | 2<br>5  7<br>26  29<br>37  40<br>(23.3%) | 3<br>5  6<br>9  10<br>23  34<br>37  39<br>(30%) | 6<br>9  13<br>34  36<br>(16.7%) |
| 2 | 6 | 31<br>(16.7%) | 19<br>(16.7%) | 16<br>18  19<br>(50%) | 31  32<br>(33.3%) | 32<br>(16.7%) | 16  18<br>(33.3%) | 15<br>(16.7%) | 15<br>(16.7%) |
| 3 | 5 | 20 | 20 | 41 | | 14  17 | 14  41 | 44 | 17  44 |
| 4 | 1 | | | | | | | 35 | 35 |
| 5 | 4 | 45 | 45 | 43 | 42<br>46 | | 46 | 42 | 42  43 |

*Note*: See note in Table 4.10.

In the Basque Country, most branches in the first vanishing group, and considered low-intensity branches, have low technology content. Although this situation was also present in Andalusia, in the Basque Country it is even more evident, 9 out of 12 branches in 1995 in the 'low' group having low technology content and most of them belonging to the manufacturing sector. Primary sector and agribusiness branches are in the 'low' group, too, and also weaken their presence in the regional productive structure. There is the peculiarity that the fishing value chain appears as decreasing its presence in the region: 'fishing' (3), 'fish industry' (23) and 'ships' (19) (see Figure 4.3).[29]

Further conclusions can be obtained from the regional comparison, as tendencies show similarities and differences. Among the similarities there are the intensity increase in 'construction' and the intensity decrease in 'agriculture', although this is more significant in the Basque Country. The remarkable differences appear when comparing the results for technology content groups, because there are higher-intensity branches with high technology content in the case of the Basque Country, and their intensity continuously increases.

The dynamics of the branches can also be observed by combining the threshold and group classifications (by sectors and technology content). 'Decreasing weakness branches' would belong to a group with coefficients <1 but increasing; 'increasing intensity branches' are in the group with increasing coefficients ≥1; 'increasing weakness branches' are in the group with decreasing coefficients <1; and 'decreasing intensity branches' are in the group with decreasing coefficients ≥1. The most outstanding group of branches would be the one of increasing intensity. In the case of Andalusia we find the following in that group:

• Services: 'business services', 'trade', 'transports' and 'hotels and restaurants'. The first three branches not only have intense links but also they are linked to a high number of other branches in the production system. The last, however, is a branch with strong presence for a reduced group of branches, mainly agribusiness branches.
• Coke and petroleum: this is a basic productive branch, with intense presence in a large number of productive processes.
• A group of branches showing the clear productive differentiation of the region: 'agriculture', 'oils and fats' and 'fish and vegetable industry'. These are activities closely related among themselves and with agribusiness branches.
• Two branches of increasing importance in the whole country are 'cement' and 'construction'. The first of these has a very close link with 'construction', while the last appears with many links in the system.

Another important characteristic of Andalusia is the general increase of its coefficients (even if they are in the '<1' group). Nevertheless, branches with a more relevant role in the economy, according to their intensity and evolution, have low technology content, and also are in the increasing weakness group. The main difference is that, in this 'weak' group, branches belong mainly to the manufacturing sector, with the important exception of 'fishing', an activity that has substantially lost its presence in the region.

In the case of the Basque Country the increasing intensity branches ('ceramics and construction materials', 'construction', 'trade' and 'business services') show a situation that can be generalized to every developed region. The first mentioned branch stands out because of its link with the second one, the others because of their general presence in the regional structure. 'Office machinery' is an 'increasing intensity branch' in 1995, important for the region's productive differentiation. For the 'increasing weakness' group, as in the case of Andalusia, most branches show low technology content and belong to the manufacturing group.

According to the regional specialization, in Andalusia, in the agriculture and agribusiness group, all branches but one ('spirits, alcohol and wine') are in the '$\geq 1$' sector. In the Basque Country, however, none of its metallurgy branches, representing its specialization, is in that sector.

There are also some relevant conclusions that can be generalized to both regions: a) there is a tertiary process, with service branches increasing the intensity of their links, according to their maximum coefficient;[30] b) there is an increasing importance of 'construction' leading to a higher relevance of related branches like 'cement', 'ceramics' and 'stone'; c) a process of post-industrialization, or even deindustrialization, as noted by several authors for developed areas, could be identified.[31] Most manufacturing branches decrease their maximum intensity link and only a few manufacturing relations – just one for the Basque Country, 'ceramics', which is a construction-related branch – are 'increasing intensity' branches.

*Links staying according to several filters*     Tables 4.12 and 4.13 offer information about the number of links existing in every group (sector and technology content) for different threshold values, and therefore taking into account also the intensity of the links.[32]

For Andalusia, conclusions are complementary to the results obtained from the branch analysis and the comments made until now. In 1980, most links belong to the manufacturing and low technology groups. But the links staying at the highest threshold value are from groups 1 and 2 in the input–output link classification, implying agro-food branches (1, 22 and 26). In 1995, there is an important change when comparing the above results: with low filters the highest number of links is in the manufacturing and low technology groups, as in 1980; but, when filters increase, the most numerous links are in the service sector group. Nevertheless, the remaining links at the highest filter are again in the agriculture and agribusiness link groups (1–22). Therefore, the productive specialization of the region is proved again, as is the movement towards a tertiary economy, although with the prevalence of low technology activities. At the same time, a reduction in the number of links in the primary sector can be observed in the analysed period, while all other groups increase their links.

*Table 4.12: Number of links, Andalusia*

| Sector groups | 0 | | 0.01 | | 1 | | Technology groups | 0 | | 0.01 | | 1 | |
|---|---|---|---|---|---|---|---|---|---|---|---|---|---|
| | 1980 | 1995 | 1980 | 1995 | 1980 | 1995 | | 1980 | 1995 | 1980 | 1995 | 1980 | 1995 |
| 1 | 160 | 134 | 64 | 67 | 10 | 4 | 1 | 1018 | 1059 | 433 | 456 | 21 | 17 |
| 2 | 49 | 58 | 20 | 23 | 0 | 0 | 2 | 187 | 199 | 63 | 73 | 1 | 0 |
| 3 | 967 | 1027 | 387 | 396 | 17 | 7 | 3 | 378 | 417 | 155 | 175 | 2 | 5 |
| 4 | 182 | 189 | 68 | 77 | 1 | 2 | 4 | 68 | 73 | 54 | 62 | 3 | 8 |
| 5 | 67 | 72 | 36 | 42 | 3 | 5 | 5 | 119 | 117 | 48 | 51 | 0 | 2 |
| 6 | 437 | 454 | 256 | 291 | 7 | 15 | Total | 1170 | 1865 | 756 | 817 | 27 | 32 |

*Note*: Three threshold values are shown, although calculation has been made for a wider group of filters.

*Table 4.13: Number of links, the Basque Country*

| Sector groups | 0 | | 0.01 | | 1 | | Technology groups | 0 | | 0.01 | | 1 | |
|---|---|---|---|---|---|---|---|---|---|---|---|---|---|
| | 1980 | 1995 | 1980 | 1995 | 1980 | 1995 | | 1980 | 1995 | 1980 | 1995 | 1980 | 1995 |
| 1 | 129 | 117 | 40 | 35 | 2 | 0 | 1 | 1171 | 1117 | 499 | 452 | 16 | 9 |
| 2 | 72 | 63 | 18 | 15 | 0 | 0 | 2 | 284 | 283 | 153 | 137 | 7 | 4 |
| 3 | 1051 | 1012 | 471 | 409 | 17 | 8 | 3 | 306 | 305 | 189 | 180 | 1 | 8 |
| 4 | 144 | 138 | 67 | 78 | 2 | 1 | 4 | 75 | 79 | 66 | 64 | 3 | 3 |
| 5 | 76 | 75 | 51 | 55 | 3 | 5 | 5 | 247 | 239 | 103 | 96 | 0 | 2 |
| 6 | 716 | 707 | 354 | 339 | 6 | 11 | Total | 2083 | 2023 | 1010 | 929 | 27 | 26 |

*Note*: See note on Table 4.12.

In the Basque Country the situation is similar to the one in Andalusia. In 1980, manufacturing and low technology are the groups with the highest number of links for all the threshold values. Regional specialization is also shown in the link remaining at the highest filter (9–15). Once again there is a change in 1995: when filters are increased the highest links go from manufacturing to services. In this case, the link from 'construction' (low technology) to 'business services' has the highest intensity (higher than 5.5). Nevertheless, the next highest link (with filters above 1) goes again from 'metal ores' to 'metal products and machinery'. Therefore tertiary and specialization processes are also present in the economic evolution of the Basque Country.

When comparing both regions, in Andalusia, and according to the sector classification, only sector 1 (agriculture, fishing and hunting) decreases its links when the two years are compared; but for the other five sectors the situation is the opposite, with a higher number of links in 1995 continuing in the sequence of threshold values. According to the technology content classification, the number of links is always higher in 1995 than in 1980 (although it is clearer for group 4, ICT branches). Therefore, there is a general situation of a more dense and complex net of relationships with a higher number of links, for all the technology content groups and with the exception of the agriculture sector. In the Basque Country the situation is different. Sectors 1 to 3 (agriculture, ore and manufacturing) decrease their links for all the threshold sequence. Only 'construction' shows a clear increase in its links, although services also show a rise for relatively high, intense links. When the focus is on technology content, again there are important differences from Andalusia, as most groups show reductions in their link number. Nevertheless, it is possible to distinguish the cases of high technology content and ICT users showing a denser presence in the regional system. As has already been remarked upon, these are characteristics that can be generalized to more developed regions.

### 4.4.2.2    Net density

Density is a basic network measure that gives information about the complexity of the net. It calculates, as explained in Chapter 3, the proportion of effective to potential relationships. The threshold values applied in Table 4.14 have been calculated by considering the hypothetical situation of totally homogeneous branches in each region. As the total number of branches is different in each place, that threshold value also varies.[33]

In accordance with the size information, Andalusia shows an increase in its links net in this 15-year period, with a rise in its density net, while in the Basque Country the situation is the opposite. This happens in such a way that, in 1980, the density of the Basque Country is higher than in Andalusia, while in 1995 the situation is reversed.

There could be different hypotheses explaining this situation. These hypotheses will be expounded, as generally in the literature there is the assertion that there is a positive relationship between the level of development and the links density. Therefore, according to this idea, there should be higher density levels in the Basque Country, a highly developed region, when compared with Andalusia, a less developed region. However, the Basque Country shows a reduction in its density, in the direct links of most of its branches and also in the intensity coefficients, except for a few particular branches.[34] Andalusia, on the other hand, follows the expressed general theory of increasing development, associated with higher net density and links intensity.[35] Nevertheless, several authors have shown an inverted-U effect of density on performance, when analysing the effects of social capital and the behaviour of individual firms (Oh, Chung and Labianca, 2004). When using density as a measure, not only should its comparison be considered but also differences in the networks structures, when trying to look for conclusions relative to the actors' outcomes (Johnson, Boster and Palinkas, 2003).

*Table 4.14: Net densities*

| Filters | Values/Regions | | 1980 | 1995 | Variation rate |
|---|---|---|---|---|---|
| 0 | Inside | Andalusia | 0.6089 | 0.6379 | 4.8% |
| | | Basque Country | 0.6459 | 0.6213 | –3.8% |
| | Total | Andalusia | 0.6358 | 0.6443 | 1.3% |
| | | Basque Country | 0.6628 | 0.6512 | –1.7% |
| 0.05285 (An) 0.0483 (BC) | Inside | Andalusia | 0.1231 | 0.1234 | 0.2% |
| | | Basque Country | 0.1328 | 0.1376 | 3.6% |
| | Total | Andalusia | 0.1284 | 0.1321 | 2.9% |
| | | Basque Country | 0.1304 | 0.1492 | 14.4% |

One of the hypotheses under consideration in this research is that the higher development level in the Basque Country corresponds to a more dense net of relationships when considering non-technical links, at formal and informal levels. In the formal sense the effect of the creation of technology parks, research institutes and other institutions will be tested in the next chapter, compiling direct data about these types of formal relationships together with informal relationships. Moreover, it could be that the situation of Andalusia in 1995 was similar to that in the Basque Country in 1980 – that is, still trying to build a solid net of physical links with diversification – while in the Basque Country there is a focus on high technology and ICT productive branches.

Another hypothesis refers to regional specialization. As has already been said, Andalusia is highly specialized in agriculture and agribusiness, that is, in a group made of a relatively high number of branches from every sector: primary (agriculture, fishing and hunting), secondary (agribusiness) and tertiary (hotels and restaurants). In the Basque Country, however, productive specialization is in metallurgy, where only a few secondary branches are implied. Therefore, the number of links derived from the specialization group is higher in Andalusia than in the Basque Country. Moreover, there is a necessity for diversification when growth is based on agriculture, because of the problems coming from having this sector as the economic engine. These problems refer to demand as explained in the Engel Law – that is, the development process shows that higher income levels are associated with lower foodstuffs consumption. There is a demand substitution with higher income percentages expended on service activities and lower percentages for food consumption.

Densities for both regions and years have also been obtained for a sequence of 1400 threshold values, to make spatial and dynamic comparisons.[36] This information is shown in Figure 4.4.

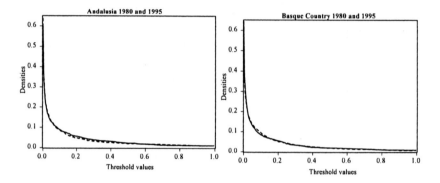

*Figure 4.4: Density sequences*

Figure 4.4 shows the rapid decrease in the number of links, and therefore in density, when the filter value is increased. The sequence is quite similar between both regions and years. Even if for the most general situation, without any threshold value, shown in Table 4.14, there has been an increase in density for Andalusia and a decrease for the Basque Country, when a threshold is imposed there are no such differences, with the situation reversing for a significant filter (approximately 0.07 in Andalusia and 0.02 in the Basque Country).

To highlight the rapid decrease in density, it is observed that for an approximated filter of 0.035, in any case, 75 per cent of links have vanished. Moreover, without any filter, densities are always above 0.6; for a filter of just 0.02 densities fall to 0.2, to 0.1 for approximately 0.075 and to 0.05 for around 0.2. The explanation is that most branches have a very small participation in the regional intermediate transactions, and only a few branches, as shown in Table 4.4, have a significant coefficient weight.

### 4.4.2.3    Net cohesion

The net cohesiveness is calculated in order to know the level at which nodes are linked. When all nodes are directly connected (minimum distance), cohesiveness is at maximum, as explained in Chapter 3. The calculation of a cohesion index[37] based on distance, with values between 0 and 1 (maximum cohesion), shows that all nodes are linked, with a longest path of three steps; therefore all nodes are reachable.

*Table 4.15: Cohesion index*

| Filter | Region | 1980 | 1995 | Variation rate |
|---|---|---|---|---|
| 0 | Andalusia | 0.793 | 0.819 | 3.3% |
| | Basque Country | 0.812 | 0.799 | −1.6% |
| 0.05285 (Andalusia) | Andalusia | 0.384 | 0.421 | 9.6% |
| 0.0483 (Basque C) | Basque Country | 0.387 | 0.431 | 11.4% |

The same explanations expounded as hypotheses in the above section can be applied, to theoretically base the diverse regional evolution observed in Table 4.15. The productive structure of the Basque Country leads to an increasing emphasis towards ICT and high technology branches, and focuses its economic growth on few branches. Nevertheless, all branches are reachable, but not necessarily through direct links – mainly for particular branches (low technology and from primary and secondary sectors). Andalusia, however, with a process of diversification, needs to increase its direct productive links. Moreover, regional specialization in Andalusia, implying a high number of branches, embodies a process of innovation adoption (new processes, synthetic products, chemicals and new containers). Throughout this process both old and new inputs coexist, increasing the number of links. In any of the cases there is high cohesion in the net. In both regions and for both years there is only a weak component, a strong component (including all or almost all branches) and a block.[38] General cohesion has increased in Andalusia, as the number of branches not included in the components reduces, while in the Basque Country it is similar in both years.

At the same time, these cohesive structures are made of sub-groups, some of them showing high cohesion. This has been measured through a lambda-sets analysis (Table 4.16).[39] In Andalusia, in 1980, the group with highest cohesion comprises 18 branches that need to delete 43 branches in order to disconnect them (43-set of 18 branches). The 43-set in 1995 consists of 13 branches. In the Basque Country the highest cohesive group is a 45-set of 19 branches in 1980 and 8 in 1995. The reduction in the number of included branches is obvious in this region, in accordance with the explanations for the different evolution patterns. Moreover, among the remaining branches in the set, there are some of the most important for its productive specialization.

*Table 4.16: Lambda–sets*

| Andalusia: 43-set | Basque Country: 45-set |
|---|---|
| Common branches in 1980 and 1995 | |
| 'Coke, P & RO'<br>'Electricity'<br>'Water'<br>'Wood, cork & furniture'<br>'Machinery'<br>'Paper'<br>'Rubber & plastic'<br>'Construction'<br>'R, R & trade'<br>'Hotels & rest.'<br>'Transports'<br>'Post & telecom.'<br>'Business services & other ac.' | 'Electricity'<br>'Chemicals'<br>'Metal products & mach.'<br>'Office machinery, P & P'<br>'Business services'<br>'R, R & trade'<br>'Other land tr.' |
| Branches disappearing from 1980 | |
| 'O chem.'<br>'Electrical goods'<br>'Clothing & skins'<br>'Leathers & footwear'<br>'P & P' | 'Coke, P & NG'<br>'Auxiliary tr.'<br>'Post & telecom.'<br>'Financial interm.'<br>'Insurance'<br>'Textile ind. & footwear'<br>'Wood & cork'<br>'Other manufacturing'<br>'Construction'<br>'Hotels & rest.'<br>'Tr. railways' |

When threshold values are considered these groups are much smaller, and the highest cohesion in Andalusia appears between 'transports' and 'business services'. In the Basque Country the situation changes between 1980 and 1995, while the most cohesive groups in 1980 were made up of 'petroleum'–'trade' and 'metal products and machinery'–'trade'; in 1995 the latter group stays and there is also, and with highest intensity, the 'trade'–'business services' group.

When measuring the net cohesion there are some cases with peculiar behaviour in the matrix of distance cohesion (number of necessary nodes in the shortest path to reach all other nodes) that should be commented upon. These are branches that do not make any intermediary sale to any other branch and therefore they are not linked as sellers to the others:[40] 'tobacco' in Andalusia (1980)[41] and the Basque Country (1995),[42] and 'machinery for metallurgy' in the Basque Country (1980).

### 4.4.2.4    Centrality and centralization

Several centrality measures have been calculated for each net.[43] Some of them focus on the number of links enjoyed by each branch and others on the length of paths connecting each pair of branches. Only the most interesting cases are shown in this section, for all the values, and also imposing two threshold values of 0.005 and 0.05. These filters allow for 60 per cent of total links in the first case and for 20 per cent in the second.[44]

Table 4.17 shows the network centralization values for normalized in- and out degree. These values can change from 0 (all branches have the same centrality index) to 100 (one branch dominating all other branches, in centrality terms). In other words, centralization measures how heterogeneous branch centralities are and helps to identify strategic branches in the regional production system.

*Table 4.17: Network degree centralizations (%)*

| Filters | Centralizations | Andalusia | | Basque Country | |
|---------|-----------------|-----------|------|----------------|------|
|         |                 | 1980 | 1995 | 1980 | 1995 |
| 0       | Indegree        | 25.8 | 34.7 | 20.3 | 20.5 |
|         | Outdegree       | 40.1 | 37.1 | 36.2 | 38.7 |
| 0.005   | Indegree        | 37.0 | 37.0 | 34.1 | 32.5 |
|         | Outdegree       | 63.2 | 63.2 | 61.4 | 62.0 |
| 0.05    | Indegree        | 34.5 | 31.9 | 34.4 | 36.1 |
|         | Outdegree       | 60.7 | 60.5 | 57.1 | 58.9 |

The first conclusion derived from these data is that outdegree values are always higher than indegrees. Indegree centralization indicates the purchases structure of productive branches; therefore, with low results there is not a key 'purchaser' branch – this structure is dispersed. Outdegree, however, indicates the sales structure of branches. In that case there could be some branches occupying a strategic position, offering their production to most other branches in the system. Outdegree centralization can reach a high value, 60 per cent approximately, when a threshold value is considered. Indegree centralization reaches a maximum value of 37 per cent in Andalusia and 36.1 per cent in the Basque Country, while outdegree indices have higher and increasing values in both cases. There should be a few branches acting strategically, selling relatively high quantities to an important number of other branches.

In order to test these theoretical ideas for the indegree and outdegree centralization evolution, a centrality analysis for every branch has been done with the same filters, for the two regions and both years. Tables 4.18 and 4.19 show the branches with the highest normalized indegree and outdegree centrality values; a group of branches in strategic position in the regional system can then be selected.

*Table 4.18: Highest normalized indegree centralities*

| | | Andalusia | | Basque Country | |
|---|---|---|---|---|---|
| | | 1980 | 1995 | 1980 | 1995 |
| Filter: 0 | | 'Other food ind.' (86) 'Hotels & rest.' (79.1) 'Transports' (79.1) | 'Business serv.' (97.7) 'Hotels & rest.' (93) 'Construction' (67.4) | 'Other food ind.' (84.4) 'Health' (84.4) 'Hotels & rest.' (73.3) 'Metal prod. & mach.' (66.6) | 'Health' (82.2) 'Fishing' (77.8) 'Social, pers. & com. ac.' (77.8) 'Metal prod. & mach.' (73.3) |
| Filter: 0.005 | | 'Other food ind.' (69.8) 'Hotels & rest.' (67.4) 'Business serv.' (60.5) | 'Business serv' (97.7) 'Hotels & rest' (67.4) 'Construction' (58.1) | 'Hotels & rest.' (73.3) 'Metal prod. & mach.' (62.2) 'Health' (57.7) 'Other food ind.' (55.5) | 'Metal prod. & mach.' (66.7) 'Construction' (62.2) 'Social, pers & com. ac.' (62.2) 'Office mach., P & P' (57.8) |
| Filter: 0.05 | | 'Hotels & rest.' (46) 'Other food ind.' (30.2) 'Construction' (37.2) | 'Hotels & rest.' (44.1) 'Construction' (44.1) 'Business serv.' (34.8) | 'Metal prod. & mach.' (46.6) 'Metals' (44.4) 'Hotels & rest.' (37.7) 'Construction' (33.3) | 'Metal prod. & mach.' (48.9) 'Construction' (44.4) 'Trade' (37.8) 'Hotels & rest.' (37.8) |

*Note*: Values in parentheses indicate the branch centrality value for a theoretical minimum of 0 and maximum of 100. In the Basque Country, in 1980, with the 0.05 filter, 'health' has a centrality of 11.1 and 'other food industry', 13.3. In 1995, with a filter of 0.05, 'health' has a value of 17.7.

In Andalusia, in 1980, 'other food industry' has a quite high centrality value, although this is a branch maintaining a high number of links through relatively small quantities. With the 0.05 filter its centrality index is much lower and the only branch emerging, although not in an outstanding form, is 'hotels and restaurants'. In 1995, centrality values are much higher, identified as central 'business services' and 'hotels and restaurants'.

In the Basque Country, with filters, indegree centrality values fall to low values, although the case of 'metal products and machinery', a very important branch in the specialized productive structure of the region, should be highlighted. Its centrality value is relatively high, and also it increases in the 1980–95 period, acquiring intermediate goods from an important number of branches staying in the net.

As has already been assumed, outdegree centralities in Andalusia are quite high, even with restrictive threshold values. There are a high number of branches showing the maximum centrality index without a filter, but with the filter their centrality indices fall a lot. An example is the case of 'clothing and skins', with respective filters' centrality values of 100, 27.9 and 0, which is among the branches selling quite small quantities to all other branches in the system. There are also three branches in the system that can be called 'strategic', because of their high outdegree centrality, increasing in the 1980–95 period, considering the number of outlinks and their intensity. They also appear with the highest centrality for most of the other centrality measures:[45] 'transports', 'business services' and 'trade'.

In the Basque Country there is always an increase in centralization values, showing an even clearer structure with few highly central branches. The increase in the centralization value, between 1980 and 1995, corresponds to a reduction in the number of the most central branches. Most of the branches showing the maximum possible centrality value decrease their index in a very intense way with the filter condition. Therefore, there is a selling structure with a high number of necessary branches for all the others, linked through very low transactions.[46] In this central selling structure a couple of branches can be identified as strategic, also having maximum centrality values for other measures and, in one of the cases ('business services'), its index increasing in the considered period – 'trade', 'business services' and 'electricity'.

*Table 4.19: Highest normalized outdegree centralities*

| | | Andalusia | | Basque Country | |
|---|---|---|---|---|---|
| | | 1980 | 1995 | 1980 | 1995 |
| Filter: 0 | | 'Coke, P & RO' 'Electricity' 'Water' 'Wood & cork' 'Clothing & skins' 'P & P' 'Rubber & plastic' 'Construction' 'R, R & trade' 'Transports' 'Post & telecom.' 'Business services' | 'Coke, P & RO' 'Electricity' 'Water' 'Wood & cork' 'Machinery' 'P & P' 'Rubber & plastic' 'Construction' 'R, R & trade' 'Transports' 'Post & telecom.' 'Business services' | 'Coke, P & NG' 'Electricity' 'Gas & water' 'Metal products & mach.' 'Office machinery' 'Textile & footwear' 'Construction' 'Trade' 'Hotels & rest.' 'Other land tr.' 'Tr. railways' 'Auxiliary tr.' 'Post & telecom.' 'Financial interm.' 'Insurance' 'Business services' | 'Electricity' 'Gas & water' 'Metal pr. & mach.' 'Trade' 'Other land tr.' 'Business services' |
| Filter: 0.005 | | 'Transports' (95.3) 'Business services' (92) 'Trade' (90.6) | 'Transports' (97.7) 'Business services' (97.7) 'Trade' (93) | 'Trade' (97.8) 'Coke, P & RO' (93.3) 'Electricity' (91.1) 'Business services' (91.1) | 'Trade' (95.5) 'Business services' (91.1) 'Other land tr.' (86.7) 'Electricity' (86.7) |
| Filter: 0.05 | | 'Transports' (72) 'Business services' (55.8) 'Trade' (46.5) | 'Transports' (72.1) 'Business services' (72.1) 'Trade' (51.1) | 'Trade' (68.8) 'Business services' (57.7) 'Coke, P & RO' (48.8) 'Electricity' (48.8) | 'Business services' (71.1) 'Trade' (64.4) 'Electricity' (53.3) 'Other land tr.' (37.8) |

*Note*: See note in Table 4.18. All centrality values without filter, have the maximum value of 100

The above results can be complemented by a core–periphery analysis, to test the possibility that the most central branches form a core group, highly differentiated from the other branches, which occupy a periphery position. However, as has already been suggested, a defined core–periphery structure cannot be found in any of the cases. Nevertheless, in both regions, the situation with the 0.005 threshold value in 1995 is the most similar to a core–periphery structure.[47] Branches in the core would be those in Table 4.20, ordered according to their coreness level, as explained in Chapter 3. When comparing the evolution of this structure, in Andalusia the most significant change corresponds to the branch 'basic chemicals', which in 1980 did not belong to the core, but in 1995 it has a significant coreness level; in the Basque Country there is no case as remarkable as this.

*Table 4.20: Branches in the core of a core–periphery structure*

| Coreness level | Andalusia | Basque Country |
|---|---|---|
| 1 | 'Business services & other ac.' | 'R, R & trade' |
| 2 | 'R, R & trade' | 'Business services' |
| 3 | 'Construction'<br>'Transports' | 'Metal products & mach.'<br>'Construction' |
| 4 | 'Hotels & rest.' | 'Office machinery, P & P'<br>'Hotels & rest.' |
| 5 | 'Electricity' | 'Other land tr.' |
| 6 | 'Coke P & RO'<br>'Machinery'<br>'Post & telecom.' | 'Auxiliary tr.' |
| 7 | 'Financial interm.' | 'Coke, P & NG'<br>'Electricity' |
| 8 | 'Wood, cork & furniture' | 'Gas and water'<br>'Chemicals'<br>'Social, personal & com. ac.' |
| 9 | 'B chem.' | 'Paper'<br>'Post & telecom.'<br>'Insurance' |
| 10 | 'Water'<br>'Other food ind.'<br>'Paper' | 'Metals' |
| 11 | 'Electrical goods' | 'NFM & B chem.'<br>'Plastic' |
| 12 | | 'Motor vehicles'<br>'Wood & cork'<br>'Financial interm.' |

### 4.4.2.5   Sub-groups

There are two strategies when trying to find sub-groups inside the whole net: going from the micro towards the macro level (bottom-up) or going from the macro to the micro level (top-down). Both perspectives have been applied, through several measures, to these regional input–output matrices, without a threshold value and with a sequence of filters. The bottom-up is a better perspective to identify branches playing a crucial role when cohesive groups are looked for. This is the perspective adopted in this section, where only the most representative case (cliques identification) is shown.[48] The top-down perspective, however, helps in the characterization of the net from another point view: cohesiveness and highly dense sub-groups.[49]

Remembering the clique definition as a group of nodes all directly linked among themselves, Table 4.21 shows the most important branches in the overlapping sequence of cliques, with a minimum size of five branches (making use of the concepts explained in Chapter 3). These are branches appearing in most of the identified cliques, in all of them in some cases, for different threshold values.

*Table 4.21: The most important branches in the overlapping clique structure*

| | | Andalusia | | Basque Country | |
|---|---|---|---|---|---|
| | | 1980 | 1995 | 1980 | 1995 |
| Filter: 0 | | 'Coke, P & RO' 'Electricity' 'Water' 'O chem.' 'Wood, cork, furn.' 'Machinery' 'Electrical goods' 'Clothing & skins' 'Leathers, footwear' 'Paper' 'P & P' 'Rubber & plastic' 'Construction' 'R, R & trade' 'Hotels & rest.' 'Transports' 'Post & telecom.' 'Business serv.' (59/59) | 'Coke, P & RO' 'Electricity' 'Water' 'Wood, cork, furn.' 'Machinery' 'Paper' 'Rubber & plastic' 'Construction' 'Trade' 'Hotels & rest.' 'Transports' 'Post. & telecom.' 'Business serv. & other ac.' (26/26) | 'Coke, P & NG' 'Electricity' 'Gas & water' 'Chemicals' 'Metal pr. & mach.' 'Office mach.' 'Textiles & footw.' 'Wood & cork' 'O manufacturing' 'Construction' 'R, R & trade' 'Hotels & rest.' 'Other land tr.' 'Tr. railways' 'Auxiliary tr.' 'Post & telecom.' 'Financial interm.' 'Insurance' 'Business serv.' 'Social, person. ac.' (72/72) | 'Electricity' 'Gas & water' 'Chemicals' 'Metal pr. & mach.' 'Office machinery' 'R, R & trade' 'Other land tr.' 'Business serv.' (61/61) |
| Filter: 0.005 | | 'Coke, P & RO' 'Transports' (143/152) | 'Trade' 'Business serv.' (152/157) | 'Coke, P & NG' 'R, R & trade' (88/94) | 'Metal pr. & mach.' 'R, R & trade' (77/80) |
| Filter: 0.01 | | 'Transports' 'Business serv.' (98/103) | 'Trade' 'Transports' (109/114) | 'Coke, P & NG' 'R, R & trade' (74/86) | 'R, R & trade' 'Other land tr.' (81/88) |
| Filter: 0.05 | | 'Trade' 'Transports' (29/49) | 'Trade' 'Transports' (24/29) | 'Metal pr. & mach.' 'R, R & trade' (50/89) | 'R, R & trade' 'Business serv.' (44/45) |

*Note*: Ratios in parentheses indicate the number of cliques including the selected branches over the total number of cliques.

Most branches in Table 4.21 had already been selected in the centrality analysis. From this sub-group view, some of them increase their key character, generating dependency links with a big group of other branches. In Andalusia this is mainly the case for 'trade', 'transports' and 'business services'. In the Basque Country the branches to be selected are 'trade', 'metal products and machinery' and 'business services'.

## 4.5 IDENTIFICATION OF RELEVANT PRODUCTION SYSTEMS

The main objective of this chapter is to study the productive structure of Andalusia and the Basque Country from historical, descriptive and network perspectives to conclude with the identification and characterization of the most relevant production systems in each region. This study is now completed by applying an algorithm, based on Peeters *et al.* (2001), for the systems' identification. Productive branches showing great mutual dependency, by their deliveries and purchases, have been classified in the same system in the following way: a relationship is considered relevant when it is important from the seller or buyer perspective, then branches with links overcoming a filter value, for sale and purchase, are selected. The coefficients used for the algorithm are the relative intermediate sales and the relative intermediate purchases, explained in Section 4.3. With these coefficients, links are selected according to their importance for the involved branches and not for the whole economy, as was the case in the previous analysis. More technically, the selection process is the following one.

In the sequence of the algorithm the most important sale (for every seller) and purchase (for every buyer) is first of all selected, then a filter is applied by rows (in a second step by columns) and another by columns (in a second step by rows). As an illustrative example, the most important sale of a seller is selected only if its relative value is higher than or equal to 0.2 and if its exchange value is higher than or equal to 0.05, when considered as a purchase by the corresponding buyer. The algorithm has been repeated for several threshold values and without considering the maximum criteria.[50]

Other criteria could have been applied, such as the algorithms' employing depth-first search and graph analysis in Aroche-Reyes (2001). According to this author industrial complexes are identified by looking for strongly connected components, that is, groups where there is a chain in both directions between each pair of nodes. This view is not applied in the present research to allow the branches in production systems to be strongly linked in just one direction. Another possibility is to apply factor and cluster analysis, as in Feser and Bergman (2000). Through the application of this technique, similar branches are grouped together according to selected attributes; however, the perspective of the present research does not look for similar branches but for highly linked branches that could show very different characteristics or attributes. Network measures allow for the search of the type of groups looked for in the present research, such as factions.[51] Although this is not the chosen technique it has also been applied to study the network characteristics.

Once the selected algorithm has been applied, there is a net in every region where sub-groups, or production systems, can be identified. Figures 4.5 and 4.6 show the significant production systems for the respective threshold values of 0.2 and 0.05, in 1995. In both regions, among the relevant sub-groups, the agro-food and the metal–mechanical systems have been selected. In Figure 4.5 it can be seen that, in Andalusia, most relevant is the agro-food system, although there is a small metal–mechanical system that will also be studied for comparative purposes. Three further small systems are also found: construction–mining–cement–glass–electricity–transports; business services–public administration–health–financial intermediation–insurance–trade and textiles–clothing–other transport equipment. However, only the agro-food is chosen from this region (and the metal–mechanical for comparison with the Basque Country) as branches in it have already been considered as the most relevant from the historical, descriptive and network analyses made before.

In the Basque Country the agro-food and the metal–mechanical systems are identified. Another two groups can be selected, one of them mainly comprising transport branches and including the fishing value change. There is another round, 'business services', and a third sub-group related to construction activities. Other criteria for selecting the production systems, together with the algorithm rules, are the social and historical characteristics of each territory and branches, considered as relevant in each regional productive structure, and the descriptive and network analysis results. Branches constituting both production systems in both regions are shown in Table 4.22.

There are some particularities in the selected systems that should be commented upon before studying them closely. For the agro-food production system, 'fishing' has a peculiar behaviour. In Andalusia, in 1980, it appears in the system because of its sales to 'fish and vegetable industry' and to 'hotels and restaurants'. However, in 1995, it appears in the system only with very low filters. Moreover, in the Basque Country, this is a branch inserted in a group making a fish chain – 'fishing', 'fish and vegetable industry' and 'ships' – apart from the agro-food system. The metal–mechanical production system is a clearly defined group in the Basque Country but not in Andalusia. Some of its branches have great importance in the productive structure of the region but there is not a consolidated system structure.

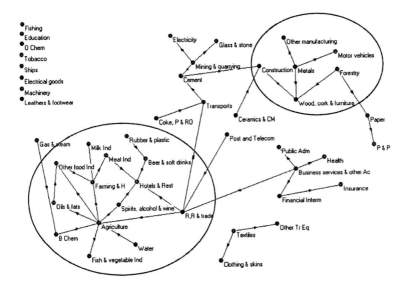

*Figure 4.5: Production systems in Andalusia, 1995*

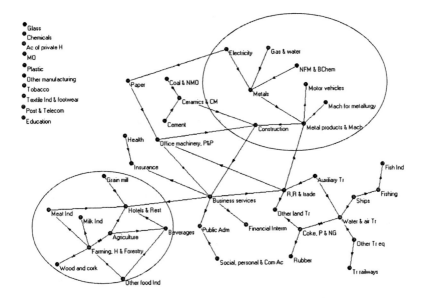

*Figure 4.6: Production systems in the Basque Country, 1995*

*Table 4.22: Agro-food and metal–mechanical production systems*

| | | Andalusia | Basque Country |
|---|---|---|---|
| **Agro-food production system** | | Common branches in 1980 and 1995 | |
| | | 'Agriculture'<br>'Farming & H'<br>'Milk ind.'<br>'Meat ind.'<br>'Other food ind.'<br>'Hotels & rest.'<br>'Spirits, alcohol & wine'<br>'Beer & soft drinks'<br>'Oils & fats'<br>'Fish & vegetable ind.'<br>'B chem.'<br>'R, R & trade' | 'Agriculture'<br>'Farming, H & forestry'<br>'Milk ind.'<br>'Meat ind.'<br>'Other food ind.'<br>'Hotels & rest.'<br>'Beverages'<br>'Grain mill' |
| | | New branches in 1995 | |
| | | 'Water'<br>'Rubber & plastic' | 'Wood & cork' |
| | | Branches disappearing from 1980 | |
| | | 'Textiles'<br>'Fishing'<br>'Coke, O & RO'<br>'Glass & stone'<br>'Paper' | 'Glass'<br>'Paper' |
| **Metal–mechanical production system** | | Common branches in 1980 and 1995 | |
| | | 'Metals'<br>'Construction'<br>'Wood, cork & furniture'<br>'Forestry' | 'Metals'<br>'Construction'<br>'NFM & Bchem.'<br>'Metal products & mach.'<br>'Mach. for metallurgy'<br>'Motor vehicles'<br>'Electricity'<br>'R, R & trade' |
| | | New branches in 1995 | |
| | | 'Other manufacturing'<br>'Motor vehicles' | 'Gas & water' |
| | | Branches disappearing from 1980 | |
| | | 'Mining & quarrying'<br>'Cement'<br>'Glass & stone'<br>'Ships' | 'Coke, P & NG'<br>'Wood & cork'<br>'Plastic'<br>'Ships' |

There are a different number of branches for each region in any of the two production systems, as the number of branches is always higher in the region where the system is more representative (agro-food in Andalusia and metal–mechanical in the Basque Country). One of the reasons for this is the branch aggregation level. Each region has adapted the input–output methodology to its productive characteristics and, therefore, they work with higher specification for branches with more presence in the regional economy. Another explanation is the region specialization emerging from the threshold values selection. In that sense, branches like 'fish industry' or 'basic chemicals' do not appear in the Basque agro-food system, while 'machinery' is not in the metal–mechanical system of Andalusia.

As regards the dynamism of the systems, there is a group of branches disappearing from both regions that could be indicating an import substitution process. This is the case of 'glass and stone', 'paper', 'plastic' and 'petroleum'. There is also another group of branches, which have already been analysed, reducing its presence in the regional economy in a significant way: textile-related branches in Andalusia and the fishing chain value in both places.

The main characteristics of the two production systems, relating to descriptive and network analyses and to the application of the main input–output coefficients, are shown in the next sections.

### 4.5.1    Agro-Food Production System

Tables 4.23 and 4.24 summarize the characterization of the branches in the agro-food system of each region. The first four columns relate to a descriptive analysis; columns five to seven show the results after having applied the three main input–output coefficients considered in Chapter 3; and columns eight to twelve summarize the network analysis results in 1995.

The results summarized in Tables 4.23 and 4.24 verify the remarkable specialization in the agro-food system in Andalusia, while this is not the case in the Basque Country. In Andalusia, seven out of fourteen branches in the production system are among the ten top branches. In the Basque Country just one out of nine is included among the ten most important branches. These are branches with low technology content, working in a highly closed system, as the region has high autonomy and self-sufficiency, both as intermediate seller and for its intermediate inputs.

*Table 4.23: Agro-food production system, Andalusia*

| Branches | 10 | T | Dyn | Dep | CW | S | R | IO | Cen. I | Cen. O | C/P | C | D |
|---|---|---|---|---|---|---|---|---|---|---|---|---|---|
| Milk ind. | – | L | DIP* | A/S | III | M | I | 2 | M | L | P | N | A |
| Meat ind. | – | L | DIP | A/S | II | M | I | 2 | M | M | P | N | A |
| Oils & fats | P | L | EIP* | A/S | III | M | I | 2 | M | M | P | N | B |
| Fish & vegetable ind. | P | L | DIP* | A/S | III | M | I | 2 | H | M | P | N | B |
| Other food ind. | P | L | DIP | A | IV | M | I | 2 | H | M | C10 | N | A |
| Spirits, alcohol & wine | – | L | SE | A/S | III | M | I | 2 | M | L | P | N | A |
| Beers & soft drinks | – | L | PE* | A | II | M | I | 2 | M | L | P | N | A |
| Agriculture | S/P | L | DIS | A/S | II$^a$ | H | IV$^b$ | 1 | M | M | P | N | B |
| Farming & H | S | L | DIP | A | I | M | III | 1 | M | M | P | N | A |
| Hotels & rest. | P | L | PE | A/S | III | L | I | – | H | H | C4 | Y | B |
| B chem. | – | H | DIS | A/S | II | M | II | – | M | M | C9 | N | B |
| R, R & trade | S/P | ICT | EIP | A/S | I$^c$ | L | III$^d$ | 4 | H | H | C2 | Y | B |
| Water | – | L | EIS* | A/S | II | M | I | 4 | M | M | C10 | Y | B |
| Rubber & plastic | – | M | EIS* | – | I | M | III | 4 | M | M | P | Y | B |

*Note*:
10: Ten most important branches (Table 4.4); P, in purchases; S, in sales.
T: Technology content (Table 4.2); L, low technology content; M, medium; H, high and ICT, information and communication technology.
Dyn: Coefficients dynamic (Figures 4.1 and 4.2); DIP, decline intensified in purchases; DIS, decline intensified in sales; EIS, expansion intensified in sales; EIP, expansion intensified in purchases; PE, purchases expansion and SE, sales expansion.
Dep: Regional dependency; A, autonomy, when the percentage of inside intermediate sales on total intermediate sales is higher than 50%; S, self-sufficiency, when the percentage of inside intermediate purchases on total intermediate purchases is higher than 50%.
CW: Chenery–Watanabe coefficients (groups explained in Chapter 3).
S: Streit coefficients; data have been classified in quintiles; H, high, corresponds to the last quintile; M, medium; L, low, corresponds to the first quintile.
R: Rasmussen coefficients (similar groups to those in CW).
IO: input–output classification (Table 4.3).
Cen (Centrality): Indegree (I) and outdegree (O) with a threshold value of 0.005; data have been grouped in quintiles; H, high, last quintile; M, medium; L, low, first quintile.
C/P: P, periphery; C, core level (Table 4.20).
C: According to the overlapping structure of Table 4.21; yes, Y; no, N.
D: Egonetwork density, considering the first indirect link for the ego; A, when density is above the average density; B, when the density is below the average.
a: Sub-branch 'vegetables and fruits crops' is in group IV.
b: Sub-branch 'vine and olive tree crops' is in group III.
c: Sub-branch 'retail trade' is in group IV.
d: Sub-branch 'retail trade' is in group IV.
*: Change is smaller than one percentage point.

Branches in this system are closely linked to other branches,[52] although these links are especially strong in a backward sense (Chenery–Watanabe); that is, intermediate purchases have a high weight in these branches' production, and therefore value added is low in their production processes. There are some differences between the two regions in this sense. In Andalusia there are also five branches with strong forward links and in the Basque Country there are four with low relationships in both directions. This is a system that is highly integrated in Andalusia, while links are weaker in the Basque Country.

*Table 4.24: Agro-food production system, the Basque Country*

| Branches | 10 | T | Dyn | Dep | CW | S | R | IO | Cen I | Cen O | C/P | C | D |
|---|---|---|---|---|---|---|---|---|---|---|---|---|---|
| Meat industry | – | L | DIP | – | II | L | I | 2 | M | M | P | N | A |
| Other food industry | – | L | DIP | – | IV | M | I | 2 | M | M | P | N | S |
| Agriculture | – | L | DIS* | S | II | L | IV | 1 | M | M | P | N | A |
| Farming | – | L | DIS | A/S | II | M | II | 1 | M | M | P | N | A |
| Milk industry | – | L | DIP* | S | III | M | I | 2 | L | M | P | N | A |
| Grain mill | – | L | EIS* | A/S | IV | M | IV | 2 | L | M | P | N | A |
| Beverages | – | L | SE* | – | IV | M | IV | 2 | M | L | P | N | A |
| Wood & cork | – | L | PE* | A/S | II | M | I | 4 | M | M | C12 | N | B |
| Hotels & restaurants | P | L | EIP | A/S | IV | H | III | – | H | M | C4 | N | B |

*Note*: See note in Table 4.23.

In both places these are branches with high diffusion effects in the whole economic system (Rasmussen), mainly through their indirect linkages. Although their direct relationships can be considered at a medium level (Streit), branches belonging to this system are highly interwoven in the system. There are some exceptions to this general situation – 'hotels and restaurants' and 'trade'. These two could be considered as key branches, not only from the descriptive and input–output coefficients' views, showing a differentiated behaviour with high direct linkages, but also attending to their dynamics and to the network results. The evolution of these two branches shows an expansion trend intensified in purchases, while most of the system branches are in decline. Moreover they are highly central and participate in most of the production process, as shown by the overlapping clique information.

Nevertheless, there is a general situation of branches with a medium centrality level, working in the periphery of the system and mainly linked together, without participating directly in other processes. The dynamic evolution of the coefficients shows that the decline is intensified in purchases, in a system where just the main links act in a backward sense; that is, the strongest links (backward) are weakening. This idea is reinforced by the autonomy/self-sufficiency indicators, as inside intermediate purchases fall in the 1980–95 period for all branches, except 'basic chemicals' and 'trade'. The strongest interlinks in the sector, with higher presence in the regional productive structure, show a process of import substitution.

There is high cohesion among the agro-food production system branches in both regions but not when considering their participation in the whole system. This can be demonstrated from Figures 4.5 and 4.6 and with the network indicators in Tables 4.20 and 4.21 showing low overlapping (clique in the tables) and a periphery location (core/periphery in the tables). There are, nevertheless, as shown before, two exceptions to this general situation for the two branches that have been labelled as crucial – 'hotels and restaurants' and 'trade'.

### 4.5.2    Metal–Mechanical Production System

Tables 4.25 and 4.26 show the characterization summary for the branches belonging to the metal–mechanical production system in the Basque Country and Andalusia.

Information in Tables 4.25 and 4.26 verifies the Basque Country's high specialization in the metal–mechanical system, where branches have a medium/low technology content. In Andalusia, this sector is not so developed and it is focused on low technology activities. In general, this is a system highly embedded in the territory (self-sufficiency) even considering only intermediate transactions and knowing the great importance of their destination in final demand as investment, not considered in the used input–output data.

The low importance of this system in Andalusia can also be observed in the input–output coefficients, with most branches showing low backward, forward and indirect links (Chenery–Watanabe and Rasmussen). In the Basque Country, however, these are branches strongly linked through their productive processes (intermediate sales and purchases). Moreover, they have a high diffusion effect in the whole economic system, highly embedded, although not because of their direct links (medium Streit coefficients).

More importantly, in the Basque Country these are highly central branches, mainly according to their out links (outdegree). They are not just central and fundamental branches, in their own production system, as can be seen in Figure 4.6 and in the density column, but also in the whole regional system. Most of them belong to the core of the system and participate in most other processes, as seen in the clique overlapping structure.

'Trade' in the Basque Country, again as in the case of the agro–food system in Andalusia, can be considered a key branch. It is among the top ten branches in the system; it is in expansion, with a high Streit coefficient, high indegree and outdegree centrality, located in the core and overlapping in most of the cliques.

*Table 4.25: Metal–mechanical production system, the Basque Country*

| Branches | 10 | T | Dyn | Dep | CW | S | R | IO | Cen | | C/P | C | D |
|---|---|---|---|---|---|---|---|---|---|---|---|---|---|
| | | | | | | | | | I | O | | | |
| Electricity | S | L | DIP | A/S | II | H | II | 4 | M | H | C7 | Y | B |
| Construction | S | L | EIS | A/S | II | H | II | 4 | H | H | C3 | N | B |
| Metals | S/P | L | DIP | – | II[a] | H | II[b] | – | M | M | C10 | N | A |
| Metal pr. & machinery | S/P | M | DIP | A/S | III[c] | M | I[d] | – | H | H | C3 | Y | B |
| Mach. for metallurgy | – | M | SE* | S | III | M | I | – | M | L | P | N | A |
| Motor vehicles | P | M | PE | A/S | III | M | I | 3 | H | L | C12 | N | A |
| NFM & B chemical | – | L | DIS | – | IV | M | IV | – | M | M | C11 | N | A |
| R, R & trade | S/P | ICT | EIP | A/S | III[e] | H | III[f] | 4 | H | H | C1 | Y | B |
| Gas and water | – | L | EIS* | A/S | I[g] | M | III[h] | 4 | M | H | C8 | Y | B |

*Note*:
For an explanation of the indicators see note in Table 4.23.
a: Sub-branch 'foundries' is in group I.
b: Sub-branch 'foundries' is in group IV.
c: Sub-branch 'mechanical engineering' is in sub-group II.
d: Sub-branches 'mechanical engineering' and 'other machinery' are in group II.
e: Sub-branches 'recycling' and 'vehicles repairing and selling' are in group III and 'retail trade' is in group IV.
f: Sub-branches 'recycling' and 'vehicles repairing and selling' are in group I and 'retail trade' is in group IV.
g: Sub-branch 'water' is in group I.
h: Sub-branch 'water' is in group III.

*Table 4.26: Metal–mechanical production system, Andalusia*

| Branches | 10 | T | Dyn | Dep | CW | S | R | IO | Cen | | C/P | C | D |
|---|---|---|---|---|---|---|---|---|---|---|---|---|---|
| | | | | | | | | | I | O | | | |
| Metals | – | L | SE* | A | IV | M | III | – | M | M | P | N | A |
| Motor vehicles | – | M | SE* | A | IV | M | IV | 3 | M | L | P | N | A |
| Forestry | – | L | PE* | A/S | I | M | IV | 1 | L | L | P | N | A |
| Wood, cork & furniture | S | L | SIS | A | I[a] | M | IV[b] | – | H | M | C8 | Y | B |
| Other manufacturing | – | H | EIP* | – | IV | L | IV | 4 | L | M | P | N | B |
| Construction | P | L | EIP | A/S | III[c] | H | I[d] | 4 | H | H | C3 | Y | B |

*Note*:
a: Sub-branch 'wood and cork' is in group II and 'furniture' in group III.
b: Sub-branches 'wood and cork' and 'furniture' are in group I.
c: Sub-branch 'buildings preparation, installation and finishing' is in group IV.
d: Sub-branch 'buildings preparation, installation and finishing' is in group III.
See note in Table 4.23.

From this analysis further conclusions can be obtained when comparing the productive structure of Andalusia and the Basque Country. There are differences among the two structures that are observed only from the network analysis results, and having important implications for a growth and regional development focus. The high productive specialization in the agro-food system in Andalusia and in the metal–mechanical system in the Basque Country makes the structure of these systems essential in the evolution of the regions analysed, showing that, in Andalusia, the agro-food system has a high cohesion among its branches but not when considering its embeddedness in the whole system, with medium centrality, located in the periphery, and not participating in other cliques. In the Basque Country, however, the metal–mechanical system shows high centrality; it is in the core and participates in most other processes, overlapping in most of the cliques taking place in the net.

It could generally be deduced that the agro–food system is a weakly embedded system. That is also the case for other regions, or even the country as a whole. However, the implications of this deduction for Andalusia are quite relevant as this is a region with a productive and economic structure focused on it. This assertion will be taken up again in the next chapter, where the two selected production systems are complemented by relevant institutional information to treat them as productive systems. Once the new systems are obtained, a set of hypotheses, focused on the relationship between each region's technical and institutional interlinks and the territory growth and development, will be tested.

# ANNEX 4.1   WHOLE BRANCH NAMES AND CORRESPONDING ABBREVIATIONS

**Andalusia**

(1)  Agriculture ⇒ Agriculture
(2)  Farming of animals and hunting ⇒ Farming & H
(3)  Forestry ⇒ Forestry
(4)  Fishing ⇒ Fishing
(5)  Mining and quarrying ⇒ Mining & quarrying
(6)  Production and processing of coke, refined petroleum and radioactive materials and ores ⇒ Coke, P & RO
(7)  Electric power ⇒ Electricity
(8)  Gas and steam ⇒ Gas & steam
(9)  Water ⇒ Water
(10) Ceramic products and building and construction materials ⇒ Ceramics & CM
(11) Cement, lime and plaster ⇒ Cement
(12) Manufacture of glass and stone ⇒ Glass & stone
(13) Manufacture of basic chemicals ⇒ B chem.
(14) Manufacture of other chemical products ⇒ O chem.
(15) Manufacture of basic metals and fabricated metal products ⇒ Metals
(16) Manufacture of wood, cork, metal products and furniture ⇒ Wood, cork & furniture
(17) Manufacture of machinery and equipment ⇒ Machinery
(18) Electrical goods ⇒ Electrical goods
(19) Manufacture of motor vehicles, trailers and semi-trailers ⇒ Motor vehicles
(20) Building and repairing of ships and boats ⇒ Ships
(21) Manufacture of other transport equipment ⇒ Other tr. eq.
(22) Oils and fats ⇒ Oils & fats
(23) Production, processing and preservation of meat ⇒ Meat ind.
(24) Milk and dairy products ⇒ Milk ind.
(25) Fish and vegetable preserves ⇒ Fish & vegetable ind.
(26) Manufacture of other food products ⇒ Other food ind.
(27) Spirits, ethyl alcohol and manufactured wines ⇒ Spirits, alcohol & wine
(28) Beers, malt, soft drinks and mineral waters ⇒ Beer & soft drinks
(29) Tobacco products ⇒ Tobacco

(30)  Manufacture of textiles ⇒ Textiles
(31)  Clothing and skin goods ⇒ Clothing & skins
(32)  Leathers and footwear ⇒ Leathers & footwear
(33)  Manufacture of paper and paper products ⇒ Paper
(34)  Publishing, printing and reproduction of recorded media ⇒ P & P
(35)  Manufacture of rubber and plastic products ⇒ Rubber & plastic
(36)  Other manufacturing products ⇒ Other manufacturing
(37)  Construction ⇒ Construction
(38)  Recycling, repair of motor vehicles, wholesale and retail trade ⇒ R, R & trade
(39)  Hotels and restaurants ⇒ Hotels & rest.
(40)  Transport via railways, other transport, supporting and auxiliary transport activities ⇒ Transports
(41)  Post and telecommunications ⇒ Post & telecom.
(42)  Financial intermediation except insurance and pension funding ⇒ Financial interm.
(43)  Insurance and pension funding ⇒ Insurance
(44)  Business services provided to enterprises, community, social and personal service activities ⇒ Business services & other ac.


## The Basque Country

(45)  Agriculture ⇒ Agriculture
(46)  Farming of animals, hunting and forestry ⇒ Farming, H & forestry
(47)  Fishing and aquaculture ⇒ Fishing
(48)  Mining and processing of coal and non-metal ores ⇒ Coal & NMO
(49)  Mining and processing of coke, crude petroleum and natural gas ⇒ Coke, P & NG
(50)  Electric power ⇒ Electricity
(51)  Gas and water ⇒ Gas & water
(52)  Mining and processing of metal ores ⇒ MO
(53)  Manufacture of basic metals and fabricated metal products ⇒ Metals
(54)  Non-ferrous metal ores and basic chemicals ⇒ NFM & B chem.
(55)  Cement, lime and plaster ⇒ Cement
(56)  Manufacture of glass and glass products ⇒ Glass
(57)  Ceramic products and building and construction materials ⇒ Ceramics & CM
(58)  Chemical products ⇒ Chemicals
(59)  Metal products, domestic appliances, machinery, equipment and furniture ⇒ Metal products & mach.

(60) Manufacture of machinery for metallurgy ⇒ Mach. for metallurgy
(61) Manufacture of office machinery, machinery, electrical goods, publishing and printing ⇒ Office machinery, P & P
(62) Manufacture of motor vehicles, trailers and semi-trailers ⇒ Motor vehicles
(63) Building and repairing of ships and boats ⇒ Ships
(64) Manufacture of other transport equipment ⇒ Other tr. eq.
(65) Production, processing and preservation of meat ⇒ Meat ind.
(66) Milk and dairy products ⇒ Milk ind.
(67) Fish preserves and other sea food ⇒ Fish ind.
(68) Manufacture of grain mill products ⇒ Grain mill
(69) Fruit and vegetable preserves, oils and fats, starches, prepared animal feeds and manufacture of other food products ⇒ Other food ind.
(70) Beverages ⇒ Beverages
(71) Tobacco products ⇒ Tobacco
(72) Textiles, clothes, leathers, skins and footwear ⇒ Textile ind. & footwear
(73) Manufacture of wood and cork ⇒ Wood & cork
(74) Manufacture of paper and paper products ⇒ Paper
(75) Manufacture of rubber products ⇒ Rubber
(76) Manufacture of plastic products ⇒ Plastic
(77) Other manufacturing products ⇒ Other manufacturing
(78) Construction ⇒ Construction
(79) Recycling, repair of motor vehicles, wholesale and retail trade ⇒ R, R & trade
(80) Hotels and restaurants ⇒ Hotels & rest.
(81) Other land transport ⇒ Other land tr.
(82) Transport via railways ⇒ Tr. railways
(83) Water and air transport ⇒ Water & air tr.
(84) Supporting and auxiliary transport activities ⇒ Auxiliary tr.
(85) Post and telecommunications ⇒ Post & telecom.
(86) Financial intermediation except insurance ⇒ Financial interm.
(87) Insurance ⇒ Insurance
(88) Business services provided to enterprises ⇒ Business services
(89) Health ⇒ Health
(90) Social, personal and community activities and social work ⇒ Social, personal & com. ac.

# NOTES

1. Fernández de Pinedo and Fernández (2001) and Domínguez Martín (2002).
2. Additional positive factors were the weather, the orography and the abundant labour force coming from agriculture.
3. Another important sector developed in this period was finance. In 1857, *Banco de Bilbao* (Bilbao bank) was founded. Its creation came from the necessity to finance the regional business investments.
4. The main Basque iron and steel industries, at the end of nineteenth century, were *Santa Ana de Bolueta, Nuestra señora del Carmen, San Pedro de Araya* and *San Martín de Beasaín*.
5. *Altos Hornos de Bilbao, San Francisco, La Vizcaya,* among others.
6. Agriculture machines, engines, copper machinery, wagons, coaches and ships.
7. 547 murders have been committed in the Basque Country.
8. Average for the analysed period, 1968–97.
9. For these authors, the main effects of terrorism are losses from tourist revenues, smaller inflows of investment from abroad, destruction of infrastructure and opportunity costs due to resources used to deter terrorist attacks and to capture terrorists.
10. The simulation made by the authors shows that a particular terrorist action in Spain is estimated to cause a \$23.8 million reduction in net foreign direct investment.
11. The first metallurgy firm in Spain, *La Concepción*, was opened in Andalusia, in the province of Málaga (Bernal and Parejo, 2001).
12. Data obtained from Parejo Barranco (1997).
13. Originally BBVA was BB (*Banco de Bilbao*), changed to BBV (*Banco Bilbao Vizcaya*) after a merger with *Banco de Vizcaya* in 1988. In 1999, a new merger with *Argentaria* led to the present BBVA bank (*Banco Bilbao Vizcaya Argentaria*).
14. The matrix operation to measure transitive links is Boolean sum.
15. *IS*: global intermediate sales; *IP*: global intermediate purchases.
16. An example of studies using that type of coefficient is Peeters *et al.* (2001).
17. In the case of relative intermediate transaction coefficients (equation 4.1), their average value changes between 1.91 and 2.12.
18. The detailed final classifications are in Annex 4.1.
19. The increase, between 1980 and 1995, of its investment was 394 per cent with inside values and 694 per cent with total values. The increase of its exports was 183 per cent. The increase in final demand was, in inside values, 211 per cent and in total values 275 per cent.
20. CNAE-93 (INE), OECD (2001b), Pulido (2000).
21. This branch corresponds to code 38 in Andalusia and 35 in the Basque Country.
22. The concept of structural equivalence has already been explained in Chapter 3.
23. The CONCOR algorithm is expounded in Breiger *et al.* (1975). In this work CONCOR has been used as part of the UCINET package (Borgatti, Everett and Freeman, 2002).
24. Out of 1892 relationships.
25. It has the highest value and therefore it is the most outstanding relation out of 2070 links.
26. The direction of the link is taken into account to measure each relationship, considering directed links.
27. In the lowest intensity links there are the tobacco industry, in both years, and leathers and footwear.
28. $C_i$: Relative intermediate transaction coefficients.
29. The less intense branches are 'tobacco industry' (27) in both years and 'metal ores' (8).
30. The exceptions found are for transports and health in the Basque Country.
31. Bell (1973), Cohen and Zysman (1987) and Tomlinson (1997).
32. All the links, except the relationships maintained by branches belonging to the same group, appear twice. This happens because links are directed, and therefore the sending and receiving branches could belong to different groups. Ten, the sum of links for every threshold value, does not coincide with the real number of links in the net (as an example, Andalusia in 1980 has 1150 directed links but the sum of the links by sectors for a 0 threshold is 1820).

33. Data for Spain, without filter, are 0.6887 (inside 1980), 0.8577 (inside 1995), 24.5 per cent (inside variation rate), 0.6882 (total 1980), 0.8589 (total 1995), 24.8 per cent (total variation rate). The increase in total values could be related to outsourcing and innovation.
34. There is also a reduction in its regional redundancies, a concept measuring the links maintained by the nodes directly linked to each ego, as will be explained later. Exceptions are for 'construction', 'business services' and medium-high technology content branches.
35. This even happens in all groups: agriculture, manufacturing, construction, services; low, medium and high technology content.
36. Threshold values go from 0 to 7 in 0.05 intervals; that is, between the thresholds 0 and 1 there are 200 values.
37. Doreian (1974), Burt (1976).
38. Depending on the year and the filter, Andalusia could not include 'tobacco', 'forestry' or 'skin and footwear'. This is the case in the Basque Country for 'machinery for metallurgy', 'tobacco', 'health' or 'metal ores'. Weak component: nodes are connected, in any form, in at least one direction. Strong component: nodes are connected, in any form, in both directions. Block: sub–group divided by a cut-point.
39. Lambda-set: sub-group where a lambda number of links should be removed to disconnect its nodes.
40. They are not connected through rows, but through columns, as buyers, directly or indirectly.
41. In 1995, 'tobacco' made intermediary sales to 'fishing', 'fish and vegetable industry' and 'water and air trade'.
42. In 1980, 'tobacco' made intermediary sales to 'hotels and restaurants' and 'water and air trade'.
43. Normalised degree centrality (in and out), degree (in and out), closeness (in and out), normalized betweenness, betweenness, normalized flow betweenness, flow betweenness, power and information.
44. The first 0.005 threshold value implies considering transactions of at least 0.7 millions (€) in Andalusia, 1980, and 3.1 mill. (€) in 1995. For the Basque Country it corresponds to 0.4 mill. (€) in 1980 and approximately 2 mill. (€) in 1995. The second 0.05 corresponds to transactions with a minimum value of 2.2 mill. (€) in Andalusia, 1980, 9.4 mill. (€) in Andalusia, 1995, 1.2 mill. (€) in the Basque Country, in 1980, and 5.9 mill. (€) in the Basque Country in 1995.
45. Inclosseness, outcloseness, betweenness, flow betweenness, power and information.
46. The most evident case is 'textile and footwear' with the following centrality values for the three filters: 100, 24.4 and 2.2.
47. The correlation coefficient when compared a perfect core–periphery structure is 0.55 in Andalusia and 0.59 in the Basque Country.
48. The other bottom-up measures that have been applied are n-clique, n-clan, k-plex and k-core.
49. Measures in this case are component, block, lambda-set and faction.
50. The maximum criteria imply to selecting, as the first step, the link with the maximum value.
51. Faction: partition where actors within each sub-group have maximum similarity higher density inside the sub-group than between sub-groups.
52. They have been selected after imposing high threshold values.

# 5 Regional Productive Systems and Development Processes

## 5.1 INTRODUCTION

The economic literature that focuses on the analysis of the processes of development and growth is very wide, attempting to account, among other themes, for the causes explaining the persistence of different development levels between countries and even regions within the same country.[1] Among the main references are Krugman (1995), Porter (1996), Storper (1997), Amin (1999) and Barro and Sala i Martín (1999). Numerous works study the possibility of convergence as the regional dynamic towards per capita income approximation, and its explanation. According to these studies the main explanatory factors for convergence are decreasing capital returns, technological catching-up, migratory movements and intersectoral reallocation of productive factors. Some Spanish analyses in this respect are Dolado *et al.* (1993), Mas *et al.* (1994) and García Milá and Marimon (1999).[2]

This research attempts to highlight the matter of the existence and persistence of development differences among regions in developed countries through a structural analysis, that is, studying the relational structures linking selected components of the regional economic systems, instead of analysing the main components of the systems. This has already been done, partially, in the previous chapter, where only technical links were considered. The deduced regional production systems and their main characteristics implied an initial vision of regional differences and allowed for some development explanations. The analysis will continue in this chapter, focusing on the regional development differences by attending to structural changes, instead of studying the components mentioned above, which are generally considered structural, and instead of analysing the possibility of convergence. This analysis is also regional, while most works studying growth and development differences have a national focus, forgetting the important differences taking place among regions belonging to the same country (Porter, 2003).

In order to do this, a literature review is offered in Section 5.2, considering the relevant research studying structural factors affecting efficiency, growth and development. Then, the empirical work focused on Andalusia and the Basque Country will be continued using additional, non-technical, information to transform the production systems into productive systems, as explained in Chapter 2. The study of these, more complex, systems will be helpful for a better understanding of regional development differences. We proceed by presenting a set of hypotheses that are tested by mechanism causality and are established at the macro level (production structure and productive systems). Following mechanism causality, it will be shown that there is an underlying structure at micro level (firm and institutional), generating the macro situation. Branches, at the same time, are making the production and productive systems at an intermediate level, and these in turn exist in the global complex regional structure of a national and international system, as shown in Figure 5.1.

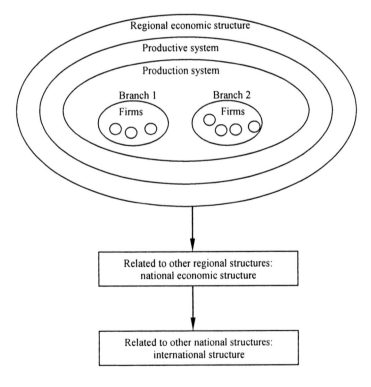

*Figure 5.1: Micro and macro levels and structures*

Inside relations, considering only the intraregional links, allow for a detailed knowledge of the regional systems according to their specialization, historical productive characteristics, labour skills and institutions. The study of productive systems, considering their relationships and changes, should be focused on technical and non-technical relations, regional specialization and technological progress. Among the non-technical explanations the effect of social capital, understood in a wide sense, is the engine maintaining and embedding the productive system in the regional economic structure.

## 5.2   REVIEW OF THE RELEVANT LITERATURE TO STUDY DEVELOPMENT PROCESSES FROM A STRUCTURAL VIEW: SOCIAL CAPITAL AND DEVELOPMENT

There is a fair amount of research explaining, theoretically and empirically, development processes and development differences following a structural view. These studies focus on the relational aspects of regional and national structures, considering their non-technical aspects and the role of social capital, as a whole or as regards their most relevant aspects.

There are books entirely dedicated to the contribution of social capital to economic growth and development, together with the contribution of several researchers, such as the works edited by Evans (1997b), Dasgupta and Serageldin (1999, 2005), Helliwell (2001) and Ramaswamy *et al.* (2002). In all of these one of the analysed subjects is how to measure social capital, in order to relate it to economic growth and development. This is a recurrent theme because the social capital concept is very complex and therefore it is very difficult to measure it. Putnam (2002) defines it as social networks and the norms of reciprocity associated with them, and asserts that it varies systematically across time and space. Putnam also establishes that it can be classified as formal or informal, thick or thin (according to the 'weak tie' concept), inward-looking or outward-looking (the former tends to promote interests of its own members) and bridging or bonding (depending on whether it brings together people who are like or unlike one another). Therefore, it is very difficult to measure it if all these aspects and its continuously changing character have to be considered. Nevertheless, complex indices can be built, as in Putnam (2001), where a social capital index, comprising 13 different variables related to formal membership, participation in many different forms of informal networks, trust and altruism, is proposed.

It can therefore be deduced that the research should focus on particular areas, and then regional quantitative and qualitative information, surveys and questionnaires should be used to consider several social capital aspects (Putnam, 1995; Hjøllund and Svendsen, 2000; Norris, 2003). However, there are several pieces of research comparing country values and generally using trust as a social capital proxy, even knowing that this is a partial social capital aspect or considering that it is not a social capital component but a consequence of it (Nielsen, 2000; Woolcock, 2001; Carter and Castillo, 2002). The World Values Survey (WVS) measures trust as the percentage of respondents in each nation replying 'most people can be trusted', with a mean value of 35.8 in 1991. Some national data are presented in Table 5.1.[3]

*Table 5.1: Trust by countries*

| Countries | Trust | Countries | Trust |
|-----------|-------|-----------|-------|
| Norway (96) | 65.3 | Austria (90) | 31.8 |
| Sweden (96) | 59.7 | UK (96) | 31.0 |
| Denmark (90) | 57.7 | South Korea (96) | 30.3 |
| Netherlands (90) | 55.8 | Czech Republic (90) | 30.3 |
| Canada (90) | 52.4 | Spain (96) | 29.8 |
| Finland (96) | 47.6 | Mexico (96) | 28.1 |
| Ireland (90) | 47.4 | Hungary (90) | 24.6 |
| Japan (96) | 46.0 | France (90) | 22.8 |
| Iceland (90) | 43.6 | Chile (96) | 21.9 |
| Germany (96) | 41.8 | Portugal (90) | 21.4 |
| Switzerland (96) | 41.0 | Nigeria (96) | 19.2 |
| Australia (96) | 39.9 | South Africa (96) | 18.2 |
| India (96) | 37.9 | Argentina (96) | 17.5 |
| USA (96) | 35.6 | Turkey (96) | 6.5 |
| Italy (90) | 35.3 | Brazil (96) | 2.8 |
| Belgium (90) | 33.2 | | |

*Note*: Values in parentheses refer to the year in which the WVS collected the trust data. Source: OECD (2001a).

Table 5.1 shows that Scandinavian countries are at the top of the ranking for trust values, with more developed countries usually showing higher trust values than less developed countries. In every case the time when the data were collected is crucial, and the inclusion in Table 5.1 of values corresponding to a six-year gap should be taken into account, because in that period important socio-political changes took place, leading to clear differences when comparing the values at different times. In this sense, it should be mentioned that, from the comparison of data in Table 5.1 with the data offered in Knack and Keefer (1997), corresponding to years 1980 and 1990 depending on the country, there are significant cases to be noted: the most noteworthy cases increasing their trust levels are Germany (from 29.8 to 41.8), Italy (from 26.3 to 35.3) and Mexico (from 17.7 to 28.1); the notable cases reducing their trust are South Africa (from 30.5 to 18.2), Australia (from 47.8 to 39.9), USA (from 45.4 to 35.6) and Argentina (from 27.0 to 17.5).

Although it is generally used, the WVS trust measure has serious methodological problems, first of all, because it attempts to summarize, in a single aggregated value, the social capital of a country:

> It is even less clear in the case of social capital than it was in the debate of the two Cambridges about physical capital that we can simply 'add up' all these different forms to produce a single, sensible summary of the social capital in a given community; much less an entire nation ... Because social capital is multidimensional, and some of those dimensions themselves are subject to different understandings, we must take care not to frame questions about change solely in terms of more social capital or less social capital. Rather, we must describe the changes in qualitative terms. For example, within a given country one could imagine that the stock of social capital has become more formal but less bridging, more bridging but less intensive, or more intensive but less public-regarding. (Putnam, 2002, pp. 12, 18)

Even more problematic is the use of the question referred in the WVS to measure trust as a social capital proxy. Glaeser *et al.* (2000) argue that the WVS question is vague, abstract and hard to interpret and therefore variation in responses might arise for numerous reasons.[4] Casson and Della Giusta (2004), after collecting social capital information in Mexico through interviews, conclude that their data confirmed the need to approach generalized trust measurements with scepticism as they test whether context matters when analysing trust. Woolcock (2001) asserts that the application of social capital to economic growth analyses should be done by integrating quantitative and qualitative research strategies into the design of comprehensive new instruments, or at least by taking the central ideas underlying the social capital perspective to apply them in innovative ways, instead of simply using 'trust' as a proxy to be entered into macroeconomic growth regressions. Fukuyama (2000) also emphasizes the too-general character of the WVS question to measure trust, leading respondents to vary their answers according to the way the question is phrased by the person who is asking; moreover, there is the problem of the absence of consistent data for many countries and periods. The criticism of Carter and Castillo (2002) follows the Fukuyama argument, defending the study of social capital by focusing on small groups' interactions, mainly because it is not possible to know which aspect of trust is being uncovered with the WVS question. Gibson (2001) analyses social capital in Russia, measuring it directly with interviews and comparing the results with the WVS values, obtaining different results and concluding that they do not rely on that single measure of the social capital concept, and also stressing the necessity of distinguishing among various forms of trust, such as between people and institutions.

For these reasons there are numerous researchers building their own social capital indices, as is the case of Grootaert (1999), Krishna and Uphoff (1999), Yli-Renko *et al.* (1999), Arrighetti *et al.* (2001) and Bjørnskov and Svendsen (2003). Moreover, Ahn and Hemmings (2000) refer to Barro (1991) using political violence frequencies as a government social capital variable to correlate it with growth and private investment, and Grootaert (1998) enumerates several social capital indicators. There are even works, like Glaeser *et al.* (2000), measuring trust through experiments with volunteers.

Knack and Keefer (1997, p. 1256) relate the WVS trust values to economic growth, but even they assert: 'This trust item is somewhat ambiguous with respect to which "people" is general enough that responses should not merely reflect expectations about the behaviour of friends and family.' For this reason they decided to use another complementary variable: the strength of norms of civic cooperation. Moreover, Pérez García (2005) builds a social capital index, made up of 11 variables, to show that there is a positive relationship between social capital and economic growth, when using data for all Spanish regions in the 1983–2001 period, and for 15 OECD countries in 1970–2000.

Knack and Keefer (1997) is among the several works, relating to social capital and growth using the WVS trust data, to find a positive relation between trust and growth. However, while their results are clear for low-income countries, they are not so evident for the analysed OECD countries. In low-income countries trust is assumed to operate as a substitute for formal institutions: 'Trust's relationship to growth in our study is especially large in poorer countries, which may be attributable to their less well-developed financial sectors, insecure property rights, and unreliable enforceability of contracts. Interpersonal trust seems to be more important in facilitating economic activity where formal substitutes are unavailable' (Knack and Keefer, 1997, p. 1284). The analysis was made again in Zak and Knack (2001), including more countries (41), obtaining more robust econometric results and concluding that there is a positive relationship between trust and growth:[5] 'Trust is higher in more ethnically, socially, and economically homogeneous societies, and where legal and social mechanisms for constraining opportunism are better developed, with high-trust societies exhibiting higher rates of investment and growth' (Zak and Knack, 2001, p.297).

Among the research showing a positive link between trust, used as a social capital proxy, and growth, measured as GDP per capita, there are Inglehart and Baker (2000), where the application is made for 65 countries, and Moesen *et al.* (2000) and Whiteley (2000), for 34 countries. In this last case the effect works directly and indirectly by interacting in positive terms with human capital, physical investment and catch-up. Uslaner (2003) analyses 41 countries to conclude that trust leads to greater prosperity, as it is positively related to an open economy index, a foreign policy globalization index, the Internet users as share of population, the real growth rate, the education spending per capita, the transfer spending per capita, a polity democracy score and post-materialist values, while it is negatively related to the Gini index of income inequality and a corruption index.

Among the few works finding a negative impact of social capital on economic results there are Helliwell (1996) and Beugelsdijk and van Schaik (2001). While the first study mentioned shows a negative relationship between trust and productivity growth in 17 OECD countries, the second asserts that social capital, in terms of trust, is not related to economic growth for the 54 analysed European regions, while social capital in terms of active group membership contributes to regional economic growth in Europe. For the authors the different results obtained compared with Knack and Keefer (1997) are because of a sample selection bias; however, Zack and Knack (2001) replicated the results with a wider sample, obtaining even more robust conclusions.

In general terms, the results are clear for low-income countries, while discrepancies can appear for high-income countries when trying to relate trust and economic growth, and the relation between development and trust is evident for the whole set of countries. Knack and Keefer (1997) argue a positive link between trust and civic norms, as social capital proxies, and innovation, human capital and public institutions. They assert that social capital has a positive impact on innovation because it helps in the flow of tacit knowledge and embodied technology. The positive link with human capital comes from the tested positive relation between trust and education, measured by the number of people studying at different levels. They also assert that there is a strong negative correlation between trust and economic inequality, measured by the Gini index. For them, another important factor for trust is the country's formal institutional structure, and they assert that ethnic and linguistic cohesion is positively related to the social capital measures. Similarly, Helliwell and Putnam (1995) reason that Italian regions with a more developed civic community have experienced higher growth rates in the 1950–90 period. Moreover, Putnam (1993) attributes the economic success and government efficiency of regions in the north of Italy, mainly, to their richer associative life. For him social capital can influence growth via its impacts on the quality of regional government, as well as directly by influencing the performance of firms; he concludes that this deduction can be generalized to other countries. Even the different chapters in the wide Helliwell (2001) research, La Porta *et al.* (1997) and Knack (2001) show the positive link between social capital and education, income equality and investment.

The WVS trust values of 17 developed countries are also used in Newton and Norris (2000), to test whether trust leads to effective social and political institutions. In the analysis of six countries made by Osberg and Sharpe (2000) the impact of social capital is clear on well-being, measured by an index including information about consumption flows, wealth stocks, equality and economic security: 'even if social capital had zero impact on per capita GDP, and instead only served to decrease the extent of economic inequality, poverty and insecurity, it would be valuable for economic well-being' (Osberg and Sharpe, 2000, p. 32).

De Clercq (2003) also uses the WVS information to show a positive effect of trust and of associational activity on innovation, when applied to a sample of 59 countries. In La Porta *et al.* (2000) the effect of trust on several performance indicators, including GDP per capita, GDP growth and inflation, efficiency of the judiciary, corruption, bureaucratic quality, tax compliance, and quality and adequacy of infrastructure, is significant and large.

Bjørnskov and Svendsen (2003) use several indicators of social capital (economic freedom,[6] corruption index, generalized trust and civic participation) to show remarkable differences among countries. The authors obtain clusters of countries with different levels of social capital, where the northern European clusters score about twice as much as southern Europe. Among all countries, Switzerland has the highest social capital level, followed by a group comprising the Netherlands, Denmark, Sweden and Norway; a third group would be made up of Finland, with Iceland in fourth place.

There are also studies analysing the economic effects of social capital from a micro perspective, in the case of Yli-Renko *et al.* (1999) for the United Kingdom, in Tsai (2000) for a set of multinationals, in Landry *et al.* (2001) for Montreal, in Burt *et al.* (2000) for France and the USA, in Krishna and Uphoff (1999) for India, in Grootaert (1999) for Indonesia, Evans (1997b) for India, Mexico, Russia, South Korea and Brazil, Carter and

Castillo (2002) for South Africa, and Narayan and Pritchett (1998) for Tanzania. All of them show positive economic effects of social capital on expenditure, livelihood or welfare of households, on development, or on competitive advantages of firms through resource exchanges and learning.

Moreover, Putnam (2001) applies a social capital index including 13 different social capital aspects to the American states, showing a positive effect of the index on education, child welfare, health, tolerance, income equality and civic equality. The analysis also shows negative impacts of social capital on TV watching, murder rates, pugnacious behaviour and tax evasion. Therefore, it can be concluded that, for the analysed states, there is a positive effect of social capital on development.

For the authors referred to so far, the relationship between trust and economic growth was clear for low-income countries and quite clear in general. At the same time, the relationship between trust and a country's institutional structure is evident in any case, and the relation between groups' membership and economic growth was tested for the European regions. For most of the authors there is also a positive relation between trust, civic norms and group membership, social capital indicators, and education, income equality and investment, thus arguing a positive relationship between social capital and development.[7]

Among the arguments explaining the positive effects of a social capital based on trust relationships is that trust avoids opportunism. At a firm level Ouchi (1980), Williamson (1983) and Bolton et al. (1994) explain that opportunistic behaviour, considered a source of market failure, leads to a change from market relationships (outsourcing) to hierarchy or bureaucracy (internalization). This organizational change attenuates opportunism, because the new productive parties belong to a common organization, and internal control and auditing are more effective. Trust, as opposed to opportunism, is necessary for a proper functioning of outsourcing (externalization process), otherwise productive tasks, which could be more effectively outsourced, are internalized by the firm, assuming the efficiency costs derived from this decision. The externalization process, therefore, depends on trust, to a different degree according to the outsourced task.

Ouchi (1980) and Bolton et al. (1994) also assert that relational contracting and clan,[8] as an alternative to markets and bureaucracies, are superior organizational systems. The clan system works under the normative requirements of reciprocity, legitimate authority and common values and beliefs, and the informational requirement of traditions. Thus actors in the clan believe that individual interests can be reached when all of them are embedded in a general interest. Diverse social mechanisms reduce differences between individual and organizational targets, generating a strong community sense. Opportunism is quite unlikely and equity can be reached with relatively low transaction costs. According to the authors conducting both studies, this system is more typical in technologically advanced productive sectors or firms, where teamwork is usual, technological change is continuous and individual results are ambiguous. This system avoids opportunism and therefore monitoring and auditing, and it is helpful for information and innovation diffusion and for the adaptation to continuous market changes. Nevertheless, a particular working tradition and a business culture, which are formed through experience over time, are necessary for a proper functioning of the system.

A similar argument is defended in Dasgupta (2003), arguing that horizontal networks allow for better flows, avoid opportunism and encourage reciprocity norms. Also Putnam (1993) stresses that dense networks of interactions reduce incentives for opportunism and malfeasance. The reduction in transaction costs appears as the main explanation for social capital stimulating growth in Skidmore (2000), Bjørnskov and Svendsen (2003) and Uslaner (2003). For them, trust (general and institutional), reciprocity and collective action generate this reduction in costs. For Fukuyama (2000, p. 6): 'The economic function of social capital is to reduce the transaction costs associated with formal coordination mechanisms like contracts, hierarchies and bureaucratic rules.' Granovetter (2005) uses the term 'loyalty systems' to explain that firms recruit workers within the same existing social networks, as a strategy to facilitate their identification with the firm. In that form, productivity can be increased through the reduction in control and monitoring costs and, therefore, in transaction costs.

Putnam (2002) explains the positive effect of social capital on efficiency through collective action enhancing trust, through embeddedness avoiding opportunism and with trust facilitating reciprocity. For the author, the main driving forces of social capital are technological innovation and entrepreneur culture. Therefore, an adequate social capital of high quality will have a positive impact on development: 'Studies from Tanzania to Sri Lanka have found that economic development under some circumstances can be boosted by adequate stocks of social capital' (Putnam, 2002, p.6). In that situation, the role of organizations with a particular structure, such as clan and relational contracting or horizontal networks, and of particular environments motivating a particular working tradition and a business culture, is crucial for the firms involved, as this will enhance their efficiency and the whole system's.

Therefore, one of the strategies for firms to increase their efficiency is to take advantage of their relationships, both at an internal level and considering their links with other firms and institutions. They look for trust links with all the agents taking part, in all possible forms, in their productive processes. This is why there are business service firms whose product is the identification of their customers' social capital. They claim that a complete knowledge of firms' relationships would have a positive impact on their efficiency and benefits. Some examples of those service firms are Cakehouse, Ecademy, Humax, Knowmentum, Linkedin, Orgnet, Ryze, Typaldos Consulting and Visiblepath.[9] These firms emphasize the role of networking and trust for a firm's results and for personal success at work.[10]

The positive impacts of social capital, trust and coordination relationships have also been analysed in particular contexts, with study cases. In that sense, there are different analyses focused on regions belonging to different countries, studying their regional productive structures and their relationship with development and growth. This is the case of Maillat and Grosjean (1999), analysing the Mittelland area in Switzerland and identifying six territorial production systems, according to the area specialization. The main conclusion of this study is that some systems, mainly based on machine-tooling, automation, watch-making and the micro-technical, had a strong milieu effect attained by both outsourcing and long-term links maintained with other regional firms[11] and research and training institutions, while for other systems this was not the case. For the authors the systems with milieu effects are the ones driving an endogenous development process in the area and come about as a result of learning processes that change over time.

Even more evident are the cases of Baden-Württemberg (Germany) and Emilia-Romagna (Italy), where the keys to their regional development, although with differences among both places,[12] are the structure of intimately linked firms, the networks of cooperation and subcontractors and the dense infrastructure of institutions supporting innovation and information transfer, financing, advising and training. Moreover, the long existence of mutual trust relationships has helped in the creation and maintenance of highly efficient networks and institutions. Cooke and Morgan (2000) also compare the situation of Emilia-Romagna with Calabria, a less developed region in the south of Italy that used to be more developed than the 'industrial districts' northern area in the nineteenth century and at the beginning of the twentieth century. The main implication is that the existence of a cooperative system, localized learning and trust formation taking place in a particular cultural context had clear advantages for growth and development, although there are also other important factors affecting this situation, such as the different location of the two regions.

Another relevant case study refers to Wales, in the UK (Cooke and Morgan, 2000), whose dynamism and development are not at the level of Baden-Württemberg or Emilia-Romagna. The Welsh economy – although the embeddedness of its institutions is more evident than in the rest of the UK –, is based on its public sector, with a lack of private institutions supporting businesses. However, while the Welsh Development Agency (WDA) was until recently the only institution offering the services that firms required, it has realized that this was not the most efficient strategy. Now, the agency is playing the role of *animateur*, enhancing the creation of other institutions where trust and reciprocity are the keys to their successful collaboration.

Moreover, instead of small and medium firm networks, large multinationals' branch plants dominate the productive system in Wales, with the regional economic growth mainly based on foreign direct investment, instead of endogenous development. Nevertheless, there is a process for the creation of firm networks and of regional institutions that have already shown positive effects on efficiency and productivity.

> In contrast to classical British regional policy, the RTP [Regional Technology Plan] is designed to stimulate a collective learning process among the key regional players – the regional state, private firms, public agencies, social partners, and a wide array of intermediary organizations spanning education, training, and technology transfer. Equally important, the RTP exercise is predicated on the notion that the initial impetus for regional renewal must come from within the region and that this turns on the region's networking capacity, that is, the disposition to collaborate to achieve mutually beneficial ends. (Morgan, 1997, p. 153)

Among the regional development strategies are the creation of regional supply chains for the sharing of expertise, the creation of public agencies diffusing innovation and enhancing trust, the creation of horizontal sectoral networks and the promotion of collaborative training programmes.

When adoption of innovations is considered, the regional system shows its lack of dynamism: 'On the SME front, most firms in Wales do not perceive "innovation" as a strategic priority and, when they do engage in product or process innovation, it is often due to customer pressure. For most SMEs, the main source of innovative ideas is the supply chain, while the biggest barriers to innovation are lack of available finance and inadequate technical expertise' (Henderson, 1995).[13]

Public help generally tries to cover the lack of finance, although this does not mean that through financing there is a positive link, acting as one more factor for regional development. Cappellin and Batey (1993, p. 112), studying the situation of lagging European regions, assert: 'Regional authorities and entrepreneurial organisations are currently undergoing conflictual relationships. The entrepreneurs are often looking for financial support from regional authorities but they refuse to share the management and the follow-up of the cooperation projects.'

All the cases mentioned have a clear specialized productive structure, although more concentrated in some cases. The Mittelland area specializes in machinery, vehicles, metallurgy, electronics, optical engineering and jewellery. Baden-Württemberg focuses its productive structure on automotive, electronic and machine-tool industries;[14] Emilia-Romagna focuses on knitwear, ceramics and automotive engineering; Wales historically specialized in coal and steel industries although now most firms work for multinational branches, such as for Sony, Ford, Nissan or General Electric.

There are other cases showing that regional development and dynamism depend on endogenous growth, with cooperation and trust links leading to efficient institutions, outsourcing and firms' efficiency, although at different levels. Some of these cases, each with a particular situation but all showing the importance of specialization, social capital and outsourcing, are the following:

• Avey Valley in Portugal (Garofoli, 1992), specializing in textile, clothing and shoes, is a clear example of close subcontracting relations leading to the introduction of new technologies and high productivity.

• Garofoli (1992) has also studied several Greek regions showing the positive effects of subcontracting: Kastoria, specializing in agriculture, tobacco and cigarette factories; Mesolóngion-Agrinion, focusing on fur processing; and Nàxos, depending on agriculture and tourism. In these Greek areas social capital is still based on informal low-quality links, limiting the path towards a regional productive system that could enhance an endogenous and long-term development process.

• North Doubs (a small subcontracting business depending on the Peugeot plant), Besançon (clock industry), Haut-Doubs (wood, farm, food products and micro-technology), Savoy (aluminium, steel, metalwork, composite materials, electronics and farm and food products) and Upper Savoy (clock-making and mechanical engineering subcontractors) in France have been studied in Garofoli (1992). They are examples of cases showing, with a different degree, the positive effects of outsourcing, based on trust and long-term links, and the necessity of enhancing relationships with customers for the adaptation to technological changes, with training centres and with other firms through collective actions for innovation, technology and knowledge transfers. The systems that appear following this strategy are named 'new production areas' or 'local open systems'. All the measures trying to build 'local open systems' came from public programmes, making it possible to develop a technological environment, an atmosphere for business creation, training for a skilled labour force and support for small business in high technological sectors.

• Silicon Valley (USA) is probably the best known case of economic growth based on firms' and institutions' networks. Although firms in the Valley trade with the whole world, the core of knowledge and production remains local. Among the business institutions acting in the Valley are firms' incubators: 'One way the Valley accomplishes this recombination of knowledge and capital is through spin-offs, which have contributed to the construction of dense social networks of entrepreneurs, inventors, and other institutional actors' (Castilla *et al.* 2000, p. 223). Networks inside and among firms are based on relationships without social distinctions. They depend on a particular institutional configuration comprising financial, commercial and legal institutions and on strong links with University. According to the above authors, only some regions have the proper institutional infrastructure to support such elaborate networks (Route 128 in Boston, 'Third Italy' in Emilia-Romagna) and each has its peculiarities impeding their transfer to other places and implying different results. Different networks are associated with different kinds of outcomes: 'It is our view that these intersectoral flows are what make Silicon Valley unique, and that in the history of the world's economy, the ability to leverage value by shifting resources among previously separated sectors has always provided a vital edge for regions able to do so' (Castilla *et al.* 2000, p. 245).

Other places have been studied to emphasize the importance of their structural links and social capital. This is the case of the Golden Triangle in North Carolina, Silicon Fen in Cambridge, England (Dasgupta, 2003) and Route 128 in the USA (Saxenian, 1994). Also, the positive impact of programmes funded to enhance social capital in Denmark, Ireland and Wales has been analysed in Cooke and Wills (1999).

All the information offered in this review section will be used in Section 5.4, once the relevant productive systems for the two selected regions have been studied, to propose a set of hypotheses that will be tested with direct observations from Andalusia and the Basque Country and making use of other regional information. Nevertheless, this review will also serve as a stronger corroboration of the proposed hypotheses.

## 5.3    REGIONAL PRODUCTIVE SYSTEMS

For the selected regions, Andalusia and the Basque Country, the two systems already identified, agro-food and metal–mechanical, are analysed in this section. First, they will be shown graphically, considering their main components, for a first comparison of the two regional productive systems. The main sub-components will also be illustrated for a better understanding of each system's complexity.

### 5.3.1    The Basque Country

In the Basque Country the metal–mechanical productive system is wider and more complex than the agro-food system, according to the regional specialization. Although the systems are similar when considering their main components, once they are decomposed, in order to know their institutions, the agro-food system is narrower and simpler than the metal–mechanical system. Nevertheless, in general terms, regional productive systems in the Basque Country show great density and complexity, as there are a significant number of institutions working in its productive structure.

#### 5.3.1.1    Metal–mechanical productive system

Figure 5.2 schematizes the Basque metal–mechanical productive system, where the main institutional groups in the region, linked to the production system, have been represented. Some of these groups are quite complex and therefore they are also schematized considering their components, while the relatively less relevant groups have been described in Annex 5.1. The sector production system, deduced in the previous chapter, is at the core of the new system. Then, the main institutional groups related to the firms making the production system are added. In this form eight new components, and their corresponding arrows with double direction connectivity, appear. The links shown are those usually taking place among the system's components.

Figure 5.2 and the following figures, corresponding to the selected regional productive systems, represent the underlying relational structure constituting the base of the system's social capital. Social capital, as discussed in Chapter 2, corresponds to the relational structure of the network, and therefore to networks and norms that facilitate coordination and cooperation for the actors' mutual benefit. Figure 5.2 represents a network showing a particular relational structure, including a set of norms and values and facilitating coordination and cooperation. Moreover, tacit knowledge, skills and organizational culture are among the most important factors that flow, in a different form, in the two analysed regions. In the case of the Basque Country, the structure of the productive system, shaping its social capital generally facilitates these flows in an efficient way. All this will be discussed in detail in the hypotheses-testing section.

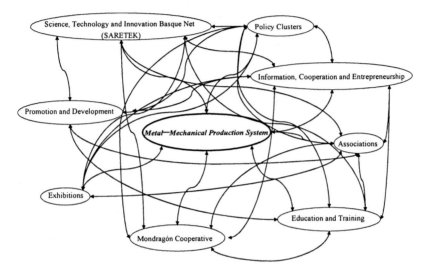

*Figure 5.2: Basque metal–mechanical productive system*[15]

The most important component in the system is the 'science, technology and innovation Basque net' (SARETEK), including most of the institutions with a relevant role in the regional innovation creation and diffusion. It is a private association without lucrative objectives, created in 1997 by the Basque regional government with the main objective of concentrating all public and private efforts to enhance science, technology and innovation incorporation. This would lead to an improvement in competitiveness, and in the regional economic and social development. According to its president, SARETEK represents the scientific, technological and innovator Basque institutions, enhances its associates' relationships, facilitates the links among its members and the public science and technology policy representatives and integrates the science–technology–firm–society system in the Basque Country. The structure of SARETEK is shown in Figure 5.3.

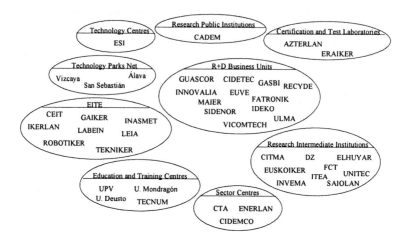

*Figure 5.3: Science, technology and innovation Basque net (SARETEK)[16]*

One of the main components in SARETEK, and also in the Basque productive system, is the Technology Parks Net linking three technology parks, one in each province, with a common general director. Most of the innovation and technology institutions, consitituting a significant number of participant institutions in the regional productive structure, are located in the parks; some of them specialize in particular sectors, mainly related to machines and tools. Most of the relevant centres in the region are associated, as is the case of EITE (Basque association of technology innovation centres), to increase their coordination and take advantage of it.

Another key component in the Basque productive system is the Mondragón Cooperative Corporation, founded in 1956. It is a widely studied institution (Kasmir, 1996; Lutz, 1997) as it is a unique case in Europe comprising a large number of firms (166 firms and 70 884 workers at present), a significant number of them working in a cooperative regime, being part, with training and research centres, of a cooperative group. This is a characteristic institution in the Basque Country, showing in practical terms some of the peculiarities of Basque entrepreneurs and Basque firm culture. Its structure, including training, research centres and firm groups, is represented in Figure 5.4.

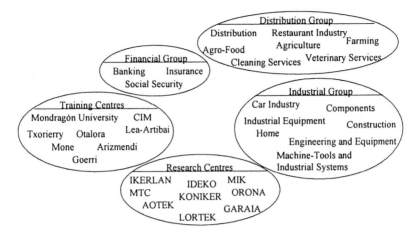

*Figure 5.4: Mondragón Cooperative Corporation*

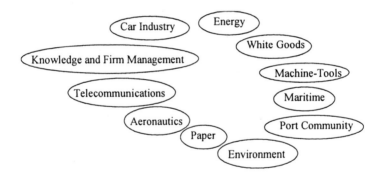

*Figure 5.5: Basque policy clusters*

Figure 5.5 represents a policy instrument created by the Basque government in 1993 to drive the regional growth and development processes. The intention was to create sector clusters comprising firms, technology, innovation and training-specific centres, associations and all the main institutions related to each selected sector that could help its efficiency and growth. The 11 clusters, all of them directly related to the branches forming the metal–mechanical production system, are represented in Figure 5.5.

The main characteristics of the Basque metal–mechanical productive system have been shown in the above figures and explanations. Nevertheless, they will be analysed again, later in the chapter, when compared with the agro-food system and the systems in Andalusia. The next part of this section focuses on the study of the structure and components of the Basque agro-food productive system.

### 5.3.1.2    Agro-food productive system

The Basque agro-food productive system (see Figure 5.6)[17] has a structure quite similar to its metal–mechanical system. However, the institutions making up its main components are less numerous, therefore making a less complex and less dense system. The explanation for this difference is the regional productive specialization, focused on metal–mechanical productions.

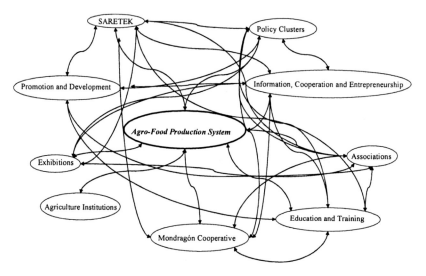

*Figure 5.6: Basque agro-food productive system*

As a consequence of specialization, innovation and training, institutions are less numerous in the agro-food than in the metal–mechanical system. Nevertheless, there are specific agriculture institutions working in the region to enhance information and innovation flows and firms' training and experience. This is the case of innovation institutions like AZTI and NEIKER, or foundations like AZARO, ELIKA and KALIKATEA. There are also other agro-food institutions with an important role in the system, although they are not region-specific, as they can be found in other regions. This is the case of wholesale markets and the trade mark councils. Nevertheless, their regional involvement and efficiency is different in each place, as will be shown in the hypotheses-testing section.

Both selected systems are also schematized and discussed for the case of Andalusia. The two systems will be compared, and they will be compared with the Basque systems, to arrive at conclusions about each regional relational productive structure and their relation to regional development and dynamism.

### 5.3.2 Andalusia

In the case of Andalusia, the agro-food system is more complex than the metal–mechanical. The latter system had important consequences in the regional productive structure in the past, but at present it does not display any involvement in the region. However, it is studied in this part of the research in order to compare it with the Basque system.

### 5.3.2.1 Agro-food productive system

The main productive sectors in Andalusia are agriculture production and transformation, with a wide diversity of agriculture-related products and, at the same time, growing specialization in the production and export of olive oil. The main links in the systems are inside the production system (between primary producers, transformation industry and distribution sector); the region has not developed a machinery sector, not even for agro-food production, and instead machinery is generally imported. Other important links are maintained among the production system, innovation and training centres, associations and specific agriculture institutions such as wholesale markets and trade mark councils. This system is shown in Figure 5.7.

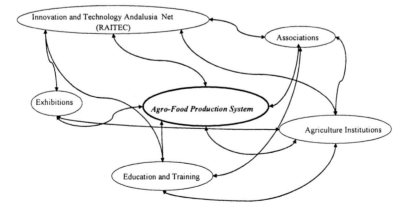

*Figure 5.7: Andalusia's agro-food productive system*

The regional government has driven the creation of an innovation and technology net (RAITEC), similar to SARETEK in the Basque Country. This public institution was created in 2001, as part of the General Plan for Innovation and Technological Development in Andalusia, 2001–3, by the Employment and Technological Development Regional Council. The objective was to generate a tool to articulate the links among technological agents, service suppliers, service customers and the regional productive fabric. More particularly, it was intended to facilitate knowledge and information access to firms in Andalusia. This is the most complex component in the system, whose institutions are shown in Figure 5.8.[18]

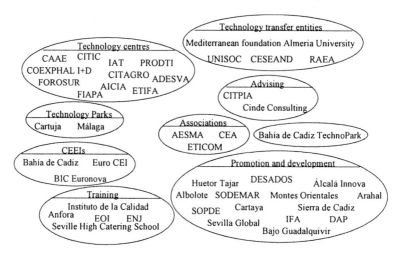

*Figure 5.8: Innovation and technology Andalusia net (RAITEC)*

The institutions focused on agro-food production processes, or directly linked to them, have been included in Figure 5.8. Although there are several innovation and technology institutions in the region, most of them are concentrated in ICT, rarely offering agro-food-pecific services. Therefore, in general terms, there is a lack of links among these institutions and the basic regional productive structure.

In Andalusia there are two technology parks working at the moment and several park projects. Some of these are already under construction, as is the case of the monographic Olive Oil Technology Park in Jaén. However, there is no park net or general coordinator; instead they have very weak relationships.

Relations among provinces are difficult, showing the region locality character (inward-looking culture), and therefore big differences can be found from one province to another, according to institutions and productive development. In fact, most innovation institutions are in Seville, while at the other extreme there is the province of Huelva with almost none of the institutions. Even considering these local disparities, the system shown in Figure 5.7 and the metal–mechanical system, represented in Figure 5.9, are representative of the whole region.

### 5.3.2.2    Metal–mechanical productive system

As in the case of the Basque Country, the two Andalusia systems, in general terms, are very similar. However, when comparing the institutions in the main groups, important differences can be found. In the case of technology centres, only a few develop activities related to metal or mechanical activities. The main differences in favour of the metal–mechanical system relate to specific associations and a training centre. Figure 5.9 represents the structure of this system in Andalusia.

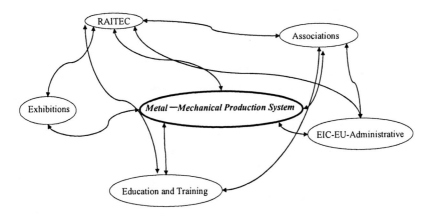

*Figure 5.9: Andalusia metal–mechanical productive system*

All the institutions making up the system components are shown in Annex 5.4. As in the other cases, the most important component is RAITEC, including several technology centres and an important number of promotion and development institutions, most of them depending on the local councils. There is also an association net (redCESEA) connecting province firms' associations and several specific institutions for the construction sector

(CONSTRUCTOR association, and CONSTRUSUR and CONSTRUCOR exhibitions).

The information obtained in the previous chapter, for the regional production systems, and the information of this section, for the regional productive systems, will be used in the next two sections. The objective is to propose and test a set of hypotheses offering an explanation for the regional disparities of these systems' structures, and to relate them to the differing regional development and dynamism. Information has been complemented by face-to-face interviews with firms and other regional case studies explained in the last section.


## 5.4   PROPOSED HYPOTHESES AND GENERAL MECHANISMS TO STUDY THE PERSISTENCE OF REGIONAL DEVELOPMENT DIFFERENCES

Among the purposes of this research already mentioned is the study of structural change patterns in regional productive structures. This analysis will allow for explanations of the persistence of different development levels between more and less dynamic regions, focusing on Andalusia and the Basque Country, through the use of the tools provided by social network analysis, following a network structural methodological view and using the mechanism causality approach.[19] In this framework, the particular set of proposed hypotheses is built in terms of the relationships between development and regional productive structures, institutional development and social capital formation.

### 5.4.1   Hypotheses Proposal

Less developed regions, in an industrialized countries context, enjoy a development stage where the technical side of the regional structure (production system) is experiencing the clearest evolution in their development process. At later stages of economic development technical changes towards diversification and specialization are continuously taking place. The most developed regions, however, have already experienced most of the technical changes of a diversification process, and focus on specialization.

Understood in a wide sense, non-technical links making up the productive system emerge, more or less slowly and with more or less embeddedness in the regional system, depending on the regional institutional dynamism.

Among those non-technical links there are the institutional and formal ones, acting in the region with a different efficiency level also depending on the regional degree of dynamism.[20]

The net of input–output linkages, measuring intermediate transactions and connecting the productive branches according to their trade links, represents the regional production structure. This net changes in time as a result of changes in the number and value of each branch relationship and the position that they occupy in the net, mainly owing to technological changes.[21] As a result, variations in the regional system, generated by the development process, can be observed by looking at branches' links and positions, a timid and weak emergence of non-technical ties, the more efficient participation of formal, non-technical links and a production territorialization process, therefore going from a dense production system to an increasingly complex productive system.

In the system's evolution some productive relations emerge while others disappear, following a general path of an increase in the extent of the branches participating in the structure. Some changes will imply that certain branches become more central and others more peripheral, while in other cases changes will give rise to branches that act as bridges allowing for the connection between groups inside the network. Therefore, there will be a process affecting the considered key branches, according to their extent and position as centres or as bridges linking sub-groups, at the same time as the whole net will be becoming denser and more complex.

It is worth remembering that every productive branch is made up of firms, and therefore the behaviour of branches, although representing mainly technical relations, has a micro foundation in the behaviour of individual purposive firms. Those foundations at firm level will also be analysed as the underlying process explained through mechanisms.

The described progression towards a more complex and denser productive net (including technical and non-technical links) will be faster in more dynamic regions, making them achieve higher positions according to a regional development ranking. There is, therefore, a process in which regions with more efficient decision-taking institutions grow faster.[22] The case studies analysed in this research showed that in these regions innovation is accepted as a key factor, training and education are among the most important objectives and there is a clearer business culture. In general terms, regional institutions are more dynamic. Therefore, there is a process in which this more efficient decision-taking reveals its consequences in growth and development. The dynamism effects have even clearer consequences for development than for growth, as growth is usually understood and measured in very strict economic terms, basically with per capita GDP.

This differentiated process can be observed when comparing Andalusia and the Basque Country. Some facts indicating this have already been explained. Chapter 4 showed the main historical characteristics for the two regions, by which Andalusia has moved from being one of the more outstanding regions of Spain, up to the nineteenth century, to being one of the less developed ones, owing to its lack of dynamism.[23] Nevertheless, looking at the main macroeconomic indicators, the region has experienced growth rates, but without converging to the national averages.

Figure 5.10 shows the growth process of Spanish regions in the period 1955–98, measured in terms of per capita gross domestic product. The Basque Country is in the area with per capita GDP above the national average in both compared years, while the situation for Andalusia is just the opposite, with the differentiated historical process explaining this opposite regional location. Nevertheless, in 1998, the Basque Country was closer to the national average than in 1955, in accordance with the regional convergence hypothesis explained by the neoclassical growth theory. Figure 5.10 shows the evolution of the Basque economy, dropping down the national 'league table', according to its GDP per capita in the whole period 1955–98. There are several factors explaining this change, but first of all the analysed period should be separated into two parts, before and after the year 1975. Until that year the Basque Country occupied the first or second position in the national ranking, being one of the richest regions in Spain. Circumstances changed, mainly owing to the role of ETA, as explained in the previous chapter, and the huge impact of the industrial crisis.

The Basque Country, Asturias and Cantabria were the regions with a more negative impact from the industrial crisis, because they were the regions that specialized more in metal ores and machine-tools, with very low productive diversification. In the period 1975–85, the region even had negative GDP per capita variation rates (Domínguez Martín, 2002). From 1986, however, another intense growth period started in the Basque Country, while the other two most affected regions, Cantabria and Asturias, could not recover in the same way from the crisis. For the Basque Country, however, it can be asserted that there is long-term success owing to its dynamism, as explained throughout this chapter, particularly in terms of investment and R+D.

For Andalusia, however, it is not possible to deduce a convergence process: the data set used in Figure 5.10 shows a similar situation at the beginning and at the end of the period (1955–98). There are also other studies, such as Rodero Cosano *et al.* (2003), analysing the period 1965–99 for regional per capita income, showing that Andalusia has maintained its differences from Spain as a whole (72 per cent per capita income in Andalusia with respect to Spain in 1965, 71 per cent in 1999).

It is even more difficult to accept a convergence process when considering development instead of economic growth, and therefore taking into account additional socio-economic variables. In this sense, the Basque Country is still showing considerable differences with respect to Andalusia. This can be seen by looking at education statistics (mainly for secondary, professional and university studies), life expectancy or public services. Figure 5.11 compares some of these social indicators.

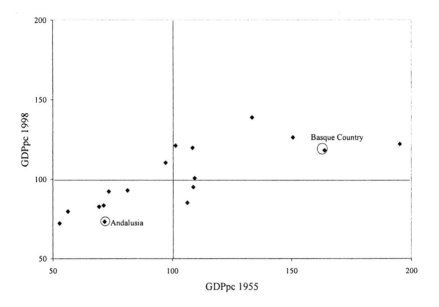

*Data source: Fundación* BBVA (1999).

*Figure 5.10: Spanish regions' GDP$_{pc}$, 1955–98, Spain = 100*

Growth and development differences are explained by historical disparities in regional dynamism; the historical information offered in the previous chapter, and the institutional information in the preceding section, give some important explanatory details. Innovation, training and business culture have played a more crucial role in the Basque Country than in Andalusia. Decision-taking in private firms has generally followed entrepreneurial behaviour in the Basque Country through innovations, cooperation with other firms and institutions, and a tradition of professional education. Andalusia, however, has traditionally shown a lack of this entrepreneur spirit, working at a less well developed stage of innovation, and depending on public initiatives. Some of these differences can be observed in the population and employment dynamism and in the R+D evolution shown in Figures 5.12 and 5.13.

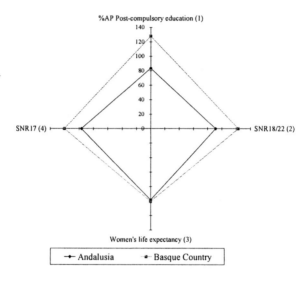

*Note*: (1) % active population that completed post-compulsory education in 2000; (2) net university schooling rate, population age between 18 and 22, 1999–2000; (3) women's life expectancy, 1998; (4) net schooling rate for population at age 17, 1999–2000; in Spain, Education is compulsory until the age of 16. Data source: *Ministerio de educación* (2002) and INE (2002).

*Figure 5.11: Social indicators in Andalusia and the Basque Country, Spain =
100*

Figure 5.12 shows total and working population evolution in all the Spanish regions, compared to the country-average indicators. All the regions with employment variation above the national average (higher than 100) also showed population variations above the country average. Moreover, all regions with relative employment reductions showed a population decrease with respect to the country as a whole.

In the analysed period, 1955–98, the Basque Country experienced higher variation rates than the national average for both population (76 per cent) and employment (43 per cent). The situation is quite different for Andalusia, with positive but lower than the average variation in population (27 per cent) and employment (9 per cent). This is a regional dynamism indicator, with

Andalusia having the highest unemployment rate in the country, together with Extremadura.

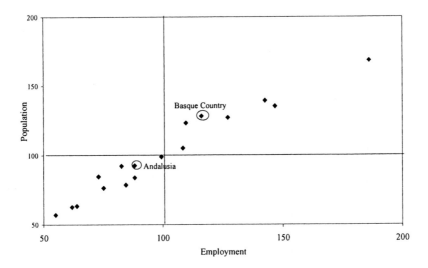

*Data source: Fundación* BBVA (1999).

*Figure 5.12: Population and employment relative-variation rates, 1955–98, Spain = 100*

Figure 5.13 shows that the Basque Country had, in the whole period of 1991–2001, R+D expenditures above the national average and even above most of the regions. Madrid is the only exception, but it is the capital of the country, where the main public and private research centres are located. This circumstance conditions the results, because the capital receives more public and private resources than the other regions. The only regions with R+D expenditures above the national average, Catalonia and Navarra, have also been indicated in the figure, with the corresponding arrows showing their research evolution.

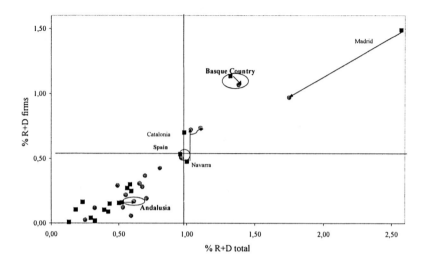

*Note*: The horizontal axis shows the percentage of R+D in regional GDP; the vertical axis shows the R+D expenditure made by private firms as a percentage of regional GDP. Square symbols represent values in 1991 and circles those in 2001. The horizontal and vertical lines represent the average values for Spain as a reference. Data source: INE (1994, 2003).

*Figure 5.13: Regional* R+D, *total and private, 1991–2001*

The country as a whole has hardly changed its position between 1991 and 2001 in either of the two research indicators, where firm R+D expenditure has changed from 0.5 to 0.53, representing approximately half of total R+D expenditure. This value (private out of total R+D expenditure) is for Andalusia one third, and for the Basque Country 86 per cent in 1991 and 77 per cent in 2001, showing the differentiated endogenous effort made by regional firms.

By considering, in a synthetic form, the development and dynamic regional situations, education can be used as a development measure and innovation as a dynamism indicator. Thus, Figure 5.14 summarizes the evolution of development and dynamism in Andalusia, the Basque Country and Spain.

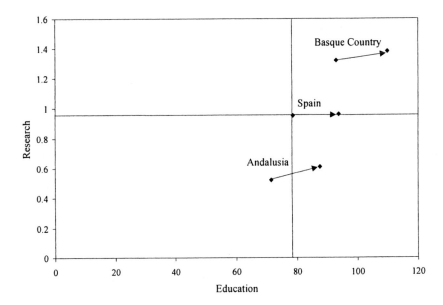

*Note*: Education is measured as the percentage of registered students in secondary and professional education out of the population, with age between 14 and 18. Research is measured as the percentage of total R+D out of regional and national GDP. Arrows indicate the movement from 1991 to 2001. The horizontal and vertical comparative lines have been drawn for the country values in 1991. Data source: INE (1994, 2003).

*Figure 5.14: Education and research in 1991 and 2001*

Figure 5.14 presents a summary of the situation experienced by a more developed and more dynamic region and a less developed and less dynamic region, represented by the regions of the Basque Country and Andalusia, respectively. Education and research have been, over the whole period, above the national average in the Basque Country. Andalusia, however, has lower development and dynamism. Although the region is experiencing a development process it has not reached the country-average position in any of the values.

The above situation, deduced when comparing more or less developed and more or less dynamic regions, can be explained by starting behind in the development process (in a later development stage) for which technical links and social capital are crucial, and can be expressed in hypothesis form for testing, as presented next.

*Hypothesis 1* There is a positive relation between the level of development and the density of the production system structure in a later development stage.

The causation relation in this hypothesis acts in both directions. That is, a higher development situation leads to an increase in the number of links leading to a higher density net, and also a higher density net enhances development. In the process of development – in a context of developed and industrialized countries – there are regions enjoying less advanced development situations than others (this is the case of Andalusia when compared with the Basque Country). In these regions there is a positive relationship between the level of development and the density of the production system. This situation will obtain for some time, with increasing development and density of production systems. When these regions continue their development process, they go beyond or get past that situation, when there is a tendency towards specialization, while non-technical links enjoy increasing importance, building complex and dense productive systems.

The explanation for this double causation will be shown in the next section, where the underlying sequence of events is studied. In general terms, there is a tendency towards increasing degree levels in the case of trade links among branches (outdegrees and indegrees, that is, the number of sent and received relationships) and, therefore, towards more complex and diversified structures of relations. The complexity of the relational net implies also the appearance of more overlapping groups of relations, again positively related to the level of development. At the same time there is the emergence of informal and institutional links, in a second-phase consolidation, shaping a regional productive system. The appearance and the efficiency of these informal and institutional links will be higher the more dynamic the region is.

*Hypothesis 2* There is a positive relation between the level of development and the emergence of service branches as bridges through structural holes. That is, there is a significant and positive relation between the level of development and the role of service branches as bridges.

As in hypothesis 1, the causation relation acts in both directions: some service branches emerge as bridges linking the selected production systems with the rest of the regional production structure as a cause and consequence of the development process. In general terms, the development process always moves from a productive structure focused on industrialization to a structure based on services. Then there is an increase in the intensity of service trade relationships that can be observed by applying different threshold values to the trade values under analysis. Moreover, services have a key role in the evolution of the productive net, acting as bridges and therefore increasing the number of links in the network. This is shown in the specialization and, at the same time, the outsourcing processes of production units, with more positive effects in a more dynamic environment.

The general implication of hypotheses 1 and 2 is that, for less developed regions, in an industrialized countries context and at the macro system level, there is a positive relationship between development and the number and type of technical relations maintained among branches. This can be observed through the change between 1980 and 1995 in the intermediate relations of the production systems. Changes in the technical relations among productive branches are caused by variations in production organization. Changes in the productive processes coming from technical change or from outsourcing decisions are reflected in transformations in the firms' production organizations. This affects the technical relations established among branches. Interactions and dynamic behaviour of the firms forming the system explain the process, caused by events occurring at the micro level, and described later in the next section in terms of events and mechanisms.

These macro changes entail an increase in the number and volume of intermediate relations and also higher complexity and relations density, with new branches appearing as centres (receiving and sending a high number of links) and a clear regional specialization. The intensity of this process changes with the level of development of the particular geographic area, and it is observed dynamically according to the development and growth processes. Regional diversification and specialization are observed, and the system's density will evolve through non-technical links and a focus on specialization. This procedure was observed in the previous chapter and will be analysed in the hypotheses-testing section below. Moreover, more advanced areas benefit from an endogenous development, with the territorialization of their production processes (Garofoli, 1992).

Then there is a stage of higher development positively related to the creation of dense and complex territorial productive systems, owing to the regional endogenous development and social capital. The level of development is higher, more permanent and self-sustained when it is based on local factors. A model of endogenous, as opposed to exogenous, development is focused on a territorialization process through regional complete production value chains, regional production exchanges and the use of regional resources and intermediate inputs. In this case, the economy will be able to achieve autonomous and self-sustained growth processes, avoiding dependency relationships and enhancing the regional society and economy.

Territorialization also enhances the positive effects of social capital on regional productiveness.

The positive link between development and social capital can be split into two separate hypotheses, from the following more general assertion (hypothesis 3a).

*Hypothesis 3a* Formal and informal social capital are economically relevant, and the latter helps in the building up and use of the former. In less developed regions the quality and quantity of informal social capital, when compared with formal social capital, has a greater effect on economic performance than in more developed ones.

When economies enjoy a low development level, their most intense social capital is based on informal links and trust. However, more dynamic regions, *ceteris paribus*, attain faster, higher development levels with the emergence of a social capital focused on formal links with other firms and institutions. The first type of social capital can be considered as more primitive and the second, or the combination of both, as more sophisticated and with clearer effects in economic efficiency and regional development.

Less developed areas focus their social capital on personal links and trust, while, when a significant development stage is attained, the focus is switched towards formal institutional links. This second type has more positive economic effects. There are several cases, some of which will be discussed in this chapter, showing that the combination of both kinds of social capital has led to efficiency improvements. A better quality of informal relationships helps in the creation and maintenance of better-quality formal links.

*Hypothesis 3b* The social capital having greater effects on economic performance in less developed regions, when compared with more developed regions, is based on the set of tacit norms, informal links and informal nets that facilitate collective action. More dynamic regions, *ceteris paribus*, enjoy the high quality of this social capital with positive effects for their development and growth.

The general mechanisms, and therefore the general explanation, of hypothesis 3b is that there is an important role of trust among entrepreneurs and other institutions for the maintenance of social capital and of permanent trade relations (Krackhardt, 1992; Gulati, 1995; Whiteley, 2000). Increasing relations generate trust and this, in turn, raises the level of relations and the social capital. Regional development is intensified and reinforced through relationships and trust, as there are clear externalities derived from high social capital. Even if firms just compete, there are continuous information flows among them, generating social capital. Moreover, when firms have a relationship of competition and cooperation, revealed as a more efficient situation, the social capital is even higher, allowing for a net structure of dense interrelationships, with clear benefits for the whole regional community.[24] Even more, when relations are maintained not only among firms but also between firms and institutions, the social capital increases and regional growth and development improve. The conclusion is that more developed regions show a denser and more solid productive system, owing to its social capital component. This social capital is being built faster and more effectively in more dynamic regions, *ceteris paribus*.

This effect will be tested with the specific literature and through case studies of selected firms in each region. Interviews should offer information about formal and informal relationships of the firms belonging to the regional system. Relationships referred to would be trade, projects, cooperation, training, information and innovation.

*Hypothesis 3c* There is a positive relation, in both causality directions, between the level of development and the quantity and quality of relationships with formal institutions.

These institutions are, mainly, technology parks, universities, innovation, knowledge and training centres. In more dynamic regions, *ceteris paribus*, the most important productive systems evolve by adding and intensifying the links among the branches and the above-mentioned regional institutions. As an effect of this process, the nets representing the systems should be denser and more complex at places and periods of time with higher development levels. The institutional thickness is part of the regional environmental characteristics explaining this economic development. A large number and variety of institutions, with a presence in the regional productive systems through high levels of interaction, implies a higher development level, as complexity in local institutional nets is considered a positive indicator of dynamism and collective initiative, and they express the characteristics of informal institutions (hypothesis 3b).

A correct functioning of informal relationships is helpful for an efficient operation of formal relationships. However, less developed regions depend more on localized informal links and this situation is reinforced when there is a lack of dynamism, *ceteris paribus*.

### 5.4.2    Underlying Structure of Firms' Sequence of Events

In the analysis of the underlying structure of the productive branches, taking place at firm level (micro level), the focus is placed on the idea that firms adapt to continuous market changes, trying to follow a path towards higher efficiency. In the relation between more efficient firms and the proposed hypotheses, there are important factors to consider: the role of innovation, the process of coordination and the path towards higher specialization. All these factors play a more effective role when they are territorially focused, where the productive system is embedded in the regional socio-economic system.

Innovation, considered in a broad sense, includes mainly process and product innovation, new types of industrial organization, opening to new markets, identification of new sources of raw materials and training, and more skilled workers. Even coordination can be considered as innovation, as it implies a change in a firm's organization, which can coordinate with researchers and scientific experts, households, retailers and other producers.[25] Both innovation and coordination allow for a progression towards higher specialization as they facilitate the firm's concentrating on the productive task where it has an advantage.

Every productive branch comprises some firms with entrepreneurs that are able to judge and take decisions to adapt to the continuously changing economic situation. Therefore, there are highly efficient firms adopting innovations, externalizing the productive tasks that can be obtained more cheaply and in more specialized form from other firms, and intensifying coordination with other institutions. At the same time, there are less efficient firms failing to adjust as they should, without adopting innovations, maintaining the whole productive process and disliking coordination. As a result, there is a continuous process in which dynamic firms coexist with less efficient firms. Moreover, as the more dynamic firms generate changes in the productive links, new relations appear in the whole net of intermediate links while old relations are also maintained, and there is a delayed development stage showing an increase in the number of links maintained among productive branches (hypothesis 1).[26] This stage can be observed in the case of Andalusia. The specialization process followed by the more dynamic firms is intensified with the outsourcing of the service side of the productive processes (hypothesis 2).

The continuous search for higher efficiency is strengthened with links that firms maintain with other institutions. A large number of institutions working properly, and highly related to regional firms, will allow for several benefits of positive externalities (hypothesis 3c). These externalities come from the flows of information, innovations and training, the transfer of tacit knowledge, the initiative of joint projects (and therefore firm's coordination) and the permanence of a high credibility and trust in the regional system (hypothesis 3b).

Therefore, there is a positive relation between development and the number and type of relationships the firm maintains with other firms, government and other institutions. This can be inferred when observing the following sequence of events. Firms, in their adaptation process, search for higher efficiency levels, more information (cheaper and better quality) and lower costs, tending to implement strategies that are intended to innovate and to increase their specialization and coordination. The more dynamic firms will incorporate innovations (such as product, process and intra-firm organization), externalize tasks (mainly services) and coordinate with other firms (mainly at local level through trust), giving rise to an increase in the number and type of their relationships with other institutions (technology parks, universities, innovation and training centres) in the process. Moreover, firms acting thus will look for the most efficient supplier for their productive process. This will drive a selection procedure distinguishing the supplier firms that also innovate, externalize and coordinate, reinforcing the efficiency progression and the increase in links.

Then, in a superior, more advanced, stage in the development process, there would be an increase in the number of relations among firms and with other institutions. At the same time, service firms become key branches, as specific services are the generally externalized tasks and, therefore, they increase their relations in number and volume with firms. When the analysis is focused at local or regional level, higher development is positively related to coordination through trust and cooperation. Moreover, the outsourcing process for services also implies a change in the firm's productive structure, moving from a vertical to a horizontal organization. This vertical disintegration process is favoured by trust relationships that firms start establishing with other productive units. A relational structure, made of formal and informal links, of high quality, as is the case of more dynamic regions, facilitates the mentioned organizational change and the path towards higher efficiency and development. At the same time, the development process itself facilitates and enhances the organizational changes and the relationship structure, leading to more efficient productive systems.

Therefore, the intensity of this process will be higher the more developed and dynamic the geographic region is where it takes place, and it is observed dynamically for every place according to a development and growth process.

The observed sequence of events needed to arrive at general conclusions will be obtained from interviews conducted at regional firms, case studies

and the existing literature in this respect. Table 5.2 offers a summary of the
firm's mechanism and its effects.

*Table 5.2: Mechanism at firm level*

| Firm's objective | Firm's actions | Effects |
|---|---|---|
| Efficiency | • Innovation<br>• Specialization ⇒ Outsourcing<br>• Cooperation and trust among firms<br>• Relationships with institutions | • Increase of relationships with firms and other institutions<br>• Services as key branches ⇒ Increase in their number and volume of relationships |

## 5.5   HYPOTHESES TESTING

The three proposed hypotheses are tested by using the structural analysis
conducted in Chapter 4, the information about institutions and their
relationships used to build the productive systems in Section 5.3, personal
interviews at firms in Andalusia and the Basque Country, additional case
studies obtained through questionnaires and publications,[27] and other regional
information.

For the personal interviews and the filling-in of the questionnaires, several
sources have been used to select firms and other institutions in both regions.
In the case of Andalusia, the potential firms and institutions to consider in the
analysis have been found in two relevant directories: the directory of firms
and centres working in the technology park of Málaga, and the directory of
firms in the Agricultural Trade Mark councils. In the case of the Basque
Country, the information on which we have based the selection of firms and
institutions has been taken from the following sources: the directory of firms
and centres in the technology park of Vizcaya, the directory of firms in the
Mondragón Cooperative Corporation and the directory of metal–mechanical
firms in the regional Chambers of Commerce.

For the selection of firms and other institutions a criterion of accessibility
was followed,[28] since they involved recorded semi-structured interviews held
with the general manager of every institution (or a person with a similar
position/job title) and with a duration of no less than three hours. The
objective of the interviews was to collect qualitative information to analyse
particular case studies. Therefore, firms belonging to the sectors in which
each region has focused its productive specialization were sought. In
addition, to confirm the main conclusions obtained from the interviews, one
hundred questionnaires were emailed to randomly selected firms from the

directories already mentioned. This made it possible to add 28 more reports, and to enhance the reliability of the qualitative information used in the analysis.[29]

Making use of the information mentioned above, this section examines and tests each proposed hypothesis in turn, although sometimes explanations refer to more than one hypothesis. The hypotheses have been tested through mechanism causality, having observed a sequence of events, to obtain general conclusions. This method of testing hypotheses, which is a common procedure, mainly in other social sciences, was discussed in Chapter 3, where some examples were also given.

From the information obtained in the empirical analysis made in Chapters 4 and 5 it is established that, while in 1995 in Andalusia the production structure is denser than in the Basque Country, its productive systems are less dense than in the Basque Country. In the previous chapter, we saw that densities increased in the 1980–95 period in the case of Andalusia while they decreased for the Basque Country (Table 4.14). Moreover, the net cohesion analysis (Table 4.15) also explained this situation where in Andalusia, there is a tendency towards diversification, with an increasing number of links and of directly reachable branches, while this is not the case for the Basque Country. The empirical analysis made in Chapter 4 confirms the more patent tendency in Andalusia towards a more complex and diversified production structure.

While this is happening at production system level, in the present chapter it has been shown that, once formal institutional links are added to the system, the productive structure in the Basque Country is denser than in Andalusia (Figures 5.2, 5.6, 5.7 and 5.9). The Basque productive net is made of a higher number of formal institutions than in Andalusia, maintaining solid links with regional firms. Although in both cases an innovation and technology net has been built from the public initiative, the Basque net is more efficient than the one in Andalusia. It is not only made of a higher number of institutions, but also they are more sturdily linked to regional firms and, more importantly, to firms working in the sector in which the region specializes. These assertions were also confirmed by the interviewed firms and institutions in both regions, as will be shown later. Thus, hypothesis 1 is corroborated, explained by the fact that the Basque Country is a more developed region, as discussed in the previous section.

Interviews offered some rich information for the study of the underlying sequence of events, explaining the hypotheses at firm level. This information makes the confirmation of the first hypothesis more evident and helps in the verification of hypothesis 2. In the previous section it was asserted that, at later stages of economic development, there are new relationships appearing while, at the same time, the old relationships are maintained. The main consequence is an increase in the number of links among productive branches. According to the information used, in Andalusia the firm's links sustaining a traditional organizational system are definitely more present than in the Basque Country. When interviewing the olive oil cooperatives in Baena (Córdoba) some of their representatives said that they decided to internalize some tasks that they externalized some time ago, as in the case of transport, while other cooperatives decided to go on with the externalization. In general terms, having interviewed some experts, such as the marketing executive officer in the Málaga technology park and the province coordinator of DAP, which is the most important public agricultural services firm in the region, they agreed that the externalization process is very slow and only being accepted by a section of the firms. In the Basque Country, however, the service externalization process is widely accepted as necessary for the firm's efficiency, even for that of small firms (CEDEMI assistant executive officer) and it has been applied for some considerable time. Nevertheless, there are exceptions, as proved by the interview with LARON, a highly specialized firm maintaining lasting links with University and training centres, but developing the whole production process in house.

These results are in accordance with Ouchi (1980), Williamson (1983) and Bolton *et al.* (1994), arguing that the externalization process depends on trust, to a different degree according to the outsourced task. And, as was stated in hypothesis 3a and confirmed by the related literature (Putnam, 1993; Helliwell and Putnam, 1995; Knack and Keefer, 1997; Zak and Knack, 2001), trust is positively related to higher development and dynamism. Therefore, externalization is also a positive function of these two aspects. According to this, externalization would be more probable in regions such as the Basque Country than in regions like Andalusia.

Also following Ouchi (1980) and Bolton *et al.* (1994), innovation is positively related to the most efficient coordinated organizational system and to regional development and dynamism.[30] Cooperatives in Baena, although big firms with a high export level and in the process of expansion, did not develop innovation themselves. When asked about the incorporation of innovation they asserted that innovations were embodied in the inputs, mainly capital goods, they acquired from their suppliers, when suppliers decided to include some kind of change in their products. They were applying product innovation, mainly in the form of new containers, information to customers and labelling, but always through public institutions like DAP and the Trade Mark Council. Nevertheless, there is an increasing establishment of small firms in the area offering technical advice and machine repairing, once they have learned enough about the capital components that local firms usually buy, from other regions or countries, for their olive oil productive processes. This situation can be compared to that in Wales (Cooke and Morgan, 2000) where the firms' attitude towards innovation is comparable to that of cooperatives in Baena.

In the Basque Country, where firms innovate more than in most of the other Spanish regions, relationships with innovation centres, technology parks and universities is accepted as very useful, and most of the firms studied use them for their innovations and information flows. Thus, continuous information exchange and technology transfers are routine central aspects of institutional relationships. In this situation, relational contracting is the superior alternative organizational arrangement with the most positive effect on efficiency (Teece, 1981; Williamson, 1983; Bolton *et al.* 1994). In relational contracting, although organization outsourcing is a common process, it is more evident for services.

The links maintained with different institutions are crucial for the flow of information and innovation, making use of weak ties. However, less developed areas generally show a lack of weak ties, limiting their access to key resources. This is the situation analysed by Dasgupta (2003) in the case of rural areas in poor countries, where there is a lack of weak ties and instead relationships are mostly intense – narrowing the economic possibilities. Following with the same argument, Fukuyama (2000) analyses the development difficulties of the Chinese parts of East Asia and of much of Latin America, where social capital resides largely in families and in rather narrow circles of friends:

> Traditional social groups are also afflicted with an absence of what Mark Granovetter calls 'weak ties', that is, heterodox individuals at the periphery of the society's various social networks who are able to move between groups and thereby become bearers of new ideas and information. Traditional societies are often segmentary, that is, they are composed of a large number of identical, self-contained social units like villages or tribes. Modern societies, by contrast, consist of a large number of overlapping social groups that permit multiple membership and identities. Traditional societies have fewer opportunities for weak ties among the segments that make them up, and therefore pass on information, innovation, and human resources less easily. (Fukuyama, 2000, p. 3)

According to the increasing importance of services, one general conclusion obtained from the empirical analysis conducted in Chapter 4 was that a post-industrialization process was taking place in both regions, with service branches showing the maximum links intensity and replacing the manufacturing productive presence. This was also proved by the interviews in both regions. Basque and Andalusia firms increasingly use services, in the first region following a faster outsourcing process, in the second using public services very intensively. Although the situation is not the same, hypothesis 2 is corroborated. Differences mainly come from the view that, in the Basque Country, the situation is dominated by high-quality trust in a more dynamic region, and in Andalusia public funding is a key factor for the regional economy. This could have different effects but not for the terms in which hypotheses 2 has been proposed.

From the results of Cooke and Morgan (2000) studying Wales, this region can be compared to Andalusia because of the link between the regional productive structure and the role of public institutions. However, Wales is experiencing an institutional evolution that Andalusia has not reached yet. While in Andalusia public institutions are still acting, generally, in a paternalistic way for regional firms, the WDA in Wales has already realized that this is not the most efficient strategy.

> States can have serious negative impact on social capital when they start to undertake activities that are better left to the private sector or to civil society. The ability to cooperate is based on habit and practice: if the state gets into the business of organizing everything, people will become dependent on it and lose their spontaneous ability to work with one another. (Fukuyama, 2000, p. 11)

As Skidmore (2000, p. 7) asserts, 'strong states need strong societies, particularly at later stages of economic development'; the efficacy of public interventions can be increased by high-quality social networks, because states are limited in their ability to effect economic transformations and to spread information and innovation to society through vertical ties.

The role of public institutions is more important in Andalusia, while private and semi-public institutions are more embedded in the Basque regional system. According to Rodero Cosano *et al.* (2003) the stock of public capital in Andalusia is higher than in the rest of the country. However, per capita income in Andalusia has not approached the national average values in the period analysed in their work (1965–99). The authors ask for reflection about the effectiveness of public investment policies trying to reduce regional disparities. Moreover, *Cámaras de Comercio* (2003) offers some illustrative data to help understand the distinct regional public role and the dissimilar firm's behaviour towards efficiency. According to this publication, the total of R+D workers on regional employment relative to Spain was 83.32 per cent in Andalusia and 128 per cent in the Basque Country. However, when considering only R+D workers in private firms, the percentages are 35.16 per cent in Andalusia and 244.51 per cent in the Basque Country.[31] Further illustrative data concern the number of patents in the region relative to Spain: that for Andalusia is 45.86 per cent and for the Basque Country 153.45 per cent.[32]

Nevertheless, in both regions a net of institutional links works, building the regional social capital and shaping the regional productive structure, but bearing in mind the differences mentioned. In the Basque system, institutions related to the production system spread in an equilibrated form in the territory. An illustrative example is the Basque Technology Parks Net linking three parks (Vizcaya, San Sebastián and Álava), one in each of the three provinces, and with a common general director. In Andalusia, however, there are big differences depending on the area. Most of the institutions are concentrated in one province (Seville), while in others (Huelva being the most extreme case) they are almost non-existent. Andalusia has only two technology parks, Seville and Málaga, in a region with eight provinces, although there are projects to build new ones in Córdoba, Jaén, Granada, Cádiz, Málaga and Almería. The two existing parks are not linked and they even have some kind of rivalry. Another illustrative example could be the case of one of the parks planned, the Olive Oil Technology Park (Jaén), which is close to starting up at the moment. The most important provinces producing olive oil in Andalusia (and also in Spain) are Jaén and Córdoba. However, none of the interviewed firms in Baena (Córdoba) knew anything about the new park, nor could they imagine any benefit from being linked to it – evidence of different regional public policy decisions with diverse effects. Garofoli (1992. p. 192), studying the case of Andalusia, refers to the limitations of policy decision-making for the region:

> The strong administrative dependency of these promotion offices on both the Regional Government and the Local Council Economic Budget, makes them not very flexible in their operations. On the other hand, their location has been following political rather than economic and spatial criteria ... Despite the fact that in their objectives, these policies claim to pursue the territorial articulation through reducing development gaps within the region, the concrete policies do not still follow any spatial strategy discussed previously. So far, they have been implemented on the basis of political reasons.

Firms in Baena have very close personal relationships among themselves, while they do not relate at all to firms in the same sector in Jaén. When asked about this situation they remarked on the 'closed' character of firms in Jaén. The locality aspect can be considered a characteristic of the social capital in Andalusia, working in highly localized terms without being extended to more remote areas in the same region, showing a lack of weak ties as mentioned before. This situation is what Uslaner (2003) identifies as an economy based on particularized trust instead of on generalized trust. This view is also expressed in Buchan *et al.* (2002) as trust behaviour based on direct exchanges, while trust is lower for the indirect exchange conditions. This type of local social capital can be assimilated to the notion of 'bounded social capital', while an efficient open situation will be focused on 'bridging social capital'.[33] For Carter and Castillo (2002) bounded social capital is the type of connection existing in rural areas, meaning highly localized ties based on family and other close relationships. According to Trigilia (2001), this situation, typical of backward areas, offers potential development possibilities by activating their strong and concentrated ties towards the production of an extended social capital favourable to development.

The reality of technology parks and the locality aspects of firms are evidence in favour of hypothesis 3c. For the marketing executive officer of Málaga Technology Park (Andalusia) the main reason why firms decided to be in the park was to have a good image in the market. In the Park of Vizcaya (the Basque Country), however, its director was pretty sure that the main reasons were the innovation benefits obtained through the links created with the innovation centres in the park, and the positive externalities from being close to bigger and more efficient firms working in the same sector.

The links structure maintained with technology and training centres is also in accordance with hypothesis 3c. As has already been said, these centres in the Basque Country have a key role; all the firms interviewed were related, in some form, to them. This was not at all the case for the firms interviewed in Baena. Firms applying any kind of innovation, advice or training obtained it from the regional government through a strong personal link with its local representative. For firms in the Málaga Technology Park there were relationships with the park innovation centres and the university, but not with agribusiness firms. In the park there are only two firms with activities related to agribusiness, in a region where this is the main sector. Generally, firms in the sector are not applying the benefits of information and technology flows that could be acquired in the park context. The director of the park said that there were some hectares in the park that had been reserved for agriculture activities for some time, but no one was interested in them. Most of the organizations in the park are software firms that could offer their services for the agriculture automatization processes and management, as this will be one of the objectives in the Olive Oil Technology Park in Jaén.

In spite of the situation discussed for Andalusia, relationships with institutions were working at the same time as close links among firms. These relationships are crucial in any development process but they take place in a different way in each region, implying clear differences when comparing them. Evans (1997a) and Newton and Norris (2000) discuss this subject, in general terms, by asserting that an appropriate social trust will lead to efficient political and civic institutions, and therefore the key is to be able to 'scale up' the personal and community ties to form developmentally efficient institutions. According to Gibson (2001), more advanced societies do not need to focus on personal trust as people can rely upon institutions. Therefore high-quality informal social capital enhances the creation and maintenance of formal social capital.

In the two studied regions several examples were obtained from the interviews conducted that constitute proof for stronger confirmation of hypothesis 3a, and in particular for 3b. When studying cooperation and coordination inside firms, the regional situation is rather different between the two areas. One of the firms interviewed in the Basque Country was Irizar, a well-known firm in Europe because of its efficient productive system in building luxury coaches, but also because of its peculiar organization system.[34] Its internal organization is based on cooperation and trust; hierarchy does not exist at all in the firm, although hierarchical organization was the firm's system until 1991. This organizational change led to an impressive increase in its productivity and efficiency. When asked about its research and innovation department, the managing director asserted that all workers in the firm are researchers and all of them generate innovation, as information and ideas flow very easily thanks to the horizontal system and the trusting environment.

Irizar is among the numerous firms working in the Basque Country with a cooperative system. The best known case is Mondragón Cooperative Corporation. Attempts have been made in other countries to copy its system, because of its great economic results. Conversely, the cooperatives interviewed in Baeza were not happy at all with their organization system. Information flows and decision making are big problems for these firms: even one of the cooperative presidents asserted that, judging by his experience, cooperative assemblies are 'a nest of ignorance'.

Mondragón Cooperative Corporation is also good evidence of coordination links among firms producing in the same or a similar sector, as is a characteristic of the Basque Country's business culture. Firms belonging to the corporation cooperate and have strong trust links. Group norms include the following: if one of the firms faces financial problems and it needs to make some, or all, workers redundant, they are hired in other firms in the group working in the same or a similar sector; and more advanced firms send their more qualified workers to other firms in the group, working in the same or a similar sector, to train and advise their workers. In Baena, however, there are strong trust relationships among the olive oil firms working in the area – they do not consider each other as competitors – but these strong trust links have disappeared outside Baena though still within the same region (Andalusia).

This indicates the existence of a localized informal social capital in Andalusia, while the analysed firms in the Basque Country make use of a more dispersed, high-quality, informal social capital. Moreover, formal social capital is used more, from an efficiency and economic perspective, in the Basque Country, as evidenced by the situation mentioned in the technology parks, the territorial distribution of formal institutions and the structure of the productive system nets.

Mondragón Cooperative Corporation and firms working in it, with Irizar and Eroski as very clear illustrations, are examples of Ouchi's theory that the most efficient organizational system is based on socialization, trust and coordination. This is reinforced by the examples offered in Granovetter (2005), showing the positive effects of workers having full membership on decision taking, with firms understood as social communities instead of formal organizations. Opportunism is reduced, monitoring and auditing costs are avoided and firms adapt to continuous market changes, making efficient use of the innovation and information diffusion, enhanced by their organizational system. The necessary working tradition and business culture are also embedded in the Basque socio-economic system. The World Value Survey (WVS) reveals that Basques are more egalitarian, less competitive workers and more reluctant to accept hierarchies (Elzo *et al.*, 1992) when compared with other Spanish regions and also with regions in the other European countries. This implies a basic distinctive aspect of the Basque socio-economic system because, as Putnam (2002) argues, the flow of technological innovation and the social and political entrepreneur basis are the driving forces of social capital in development processes. Therefore, the cultural factors of social capital should be seen as productive of wealth (Fukuyama, 2001).

Relationships with customers were completely different when the two regions were compared. In Baena, trust links were not developed at all but reputation was very important. In some cases, insurance contracts were even asked to be signed by the client, just in case they did not meet the agreed conditions. A contrary example was Irizar, in the Basque Country, where reputation is also very important but is attained through personal contacts with the client.

Relations with suppliers in Baeza were maintained with personal contacts through the visits made by providers offering their products. In the Basque Country, however, there are several cases showing the personal involvement of both the buying firm and its supplier. Irizar is a clear case, where contacts with its providers are so continuous and personal that its managing director asserted that, in some cases, the supplier firm had to change its organization system and adapt it to the Irizar one, becoming more similar to it. As an example, any worker in Irizar could phone a supplier asking for any needed information, while usually firms have just one person in charge of provider relationships. Even in the case of Laron, the chief executive officer conceded that trust and personal links with providers were key factors for them. They continuously collaborate in the elaboration of the acquired products. The Caja Laboral marketing executive officer also admitted that trust links make them maintain the same providers without looking for substitutes. This trust generalization avoided opportunism and favoured efficiency.

Trust data are also offered by the WVS at regional level, the last value offered for Andalusia being 31.8 and for the Basque Country 33.6, corresponding to the surveys carried out in the period 1995–6.[35] Although they are quite similar, they are indicators of the existence of higher trust for the more developed Basque region than for Andalusia. However, these data seem more similar than expected.[36] On the other hand, from the fieldwork conducted in both regions, it can be inferred that trust in productive systems works more effectively in the Basque Country than in Andalusia. This apparent contradiction can be explained by the methodological problems appearing from the way in which trust is measured in the survey and commented upon in Section 5.2.[37] Moreover, Pérez García (2005), when applying a social capital index to all Spanish regions, shows higher values in the Basque Country than in Andalusia throughout the 1983–2001 period.

When asked, in general terms, about formal and informal links, cooperation and coordination – social capital in fact – Basque managers had the following opinions. The assistant executive officer in CEDEMI said that it is the 'culture broth' for regional development. The Irizar managing director was very surprised when asked about this, as for him it was pretty clear that it is the most important factor in seeking productivity and efficiency. Caja Laboral and Eroski are cooperatives and both belong to the Mondragón group; for them the social capital benefits are quite obvious, as social capital is part of their organization culture. The director in the Vizcaya Technology Park admitted that one of his main tasks is to promote coordination and personal links inside the park.

In the case of Andalusia neither cooperatives in Baena, the marketing executive officer in Málaga technology park, nor the DAP province coordinator had any opinion. However, they asserted that personal and trust links worked perfectly among closely located firms and with representatives of public institutions.

This social capital comparison between Andalusia and the Basque Country can be seen as similar to the comparison made by Cooke and Morgan (2000) between Emilia-Romagna and Calabria. These Italian regions have changed their development situation as a result of the cooperative system, the localized learning and the trust formation taking place in the northern region, while those factors do not work in the south. According to the authors, these differences explain the development process experienced in Emilia-Romagna and the backward state of Calabria, where the situation used to be the opposite. Nevertheless, their different geographic location should also be considered, among the important factors explaining the disparities experienced in both places.

As has already been said, access to flows of knowledge, information and innovation is a key element in any development process. But access to these flows has to be complemented by an entrepreneurial culture being able to take advantage of them. And this implies one of the main differences in the development processes of the analysed regions when they are compared. Wolfe (2000, p. 9) expresses this fact in the following words: 'Learning depends on the presence of two key factors: a certain degree of business intelligence that serves as the demand trigger for new knowledge and the access to, or availability of, that knowledge.' The entrepreneur culture is considered in Feldman and Assaf (1999) as the micro aspect of social capital that can be labelled 'ethnic entrepreneurship'. The environment necessary in any development process is represented in Casadesus-Masanell and Khanna (2003) in the cases of Mondragón Cooperative Corporation and Irizar. In general terms, as Evans (1997a) establishes, major differences are observed in the existence of synergies combining complementarity and embeddedness taking advantage of the externalities obtained from the interaction among institutions, in general, and in state–society synergies in particular.

The existence of higher trust and higher social capital in the Basque Country, when compared with Andalusia, can be likened to the situation in Scandinavian countries.[38] Table 5.1 shows that the highest trust values correspond to Scandinavian countries and,[39] in several respects, Scandinavian and Basque attitudes are very similar (Johannisson, 2002). Similarities appear in the trust behaviour, according to the fieldwork conducted in the Basque Country, the attitudes toward hierarchies, the cooperation among firms, and also the income equality data and outlook (Osberg, 2003).[40] Case studies have shown that, in Scandinavian countries, their economically successful strategies depend on institutional regimes encouraging participation and association (Bærenholdt and Aarsæther, 2000). Norris (2003) measures associational activism and social trust, concluding that Norway and Sweden are among the countries showing high levels of both factors. This situation is also tested again in the countries clusters obtained in Bjørnskov and Svendsen (2003), where the countries with the highest social capital among the 31 countries analysed, according to several social capital indicators, are

Switzerland, the Netherlands, Denmark, Sweden, Norway, Finland and Iceland.

All arguments in Section 5.2 relating to trust and development can be applied to the comparison between the two selected regions. The specific explanations should be found by looking at the particular character of the regional business culture, institutional relations and region specialization, among other aspects, as has been done in this research. In particular, the Basque region has evidently higher schooling and investment rates,[41] more innovation adoptions and lower Gini indices (more income equality).

All the arguments found in the fieldwork, in the regional data and also in the literature review are in accordance with the hypotheses in this research. In general, social capital is more focused on trust for low-income areas, while high-quality informal social capital enhances formal social capital, and both are positively related to development. At regional level, to have strong trusting relationships with a wide range of institutions is economically very helpful, as compared with the situation where strong trusting relationships are confined to a very limited group of local people.

Trust has been used in several studies as a social capital proxy, because it is one of its main aspects, but also specific and more complex social capital indices have been built and applied in several cases. For any of the social capital measures, the positive social capital effect on development has been found for developed countries, mainly through its decisive impact on investment (Knack, 2001), education (La Porta *et al.*, 1997) and transaction costs (Fukuyama, 2000). One aspect of trust, and of social capital, is the outsourcing process, mainly followed for the service side of the production processes. Services, then, act as bridges over structural holes in the whole net that is hold by the regional social capital. This process of increasing social capital quantity and quality and increasing development is intensified after a first stage in which technical links and diversification are the focus for regional growth and development. The process described has been found in the comparison between Andalusia and the Basque Country by using diverse information that corroborates the proposed hypotheses.

## ANNEX 5.1   COMPONENTS OF GROUPS IN THE BASQUE COUNTRY METAL–MECHANICAL PRODUCTIVE SYSTEM

### Information, Cooperation and Entrepreneurship

- EICs: Basque Country EU-Administrative and Camaranet
- ZAINTEK
- Seed Capital Vizcaya
- CEEIs: BEAZ, CEIA and BIC-BERRILAN
- EUSKALIT
- LANKIDETZA

### Associations

- ASCENE: ARAEX, AUXIN, FASTENEX, MEXIM, COFIEX, PRODESO, BAPCO, INASHMAC, URRKASTING, INCEMIN, COINAMOBEL, DOSYMA, COMTEC, SISCOMP and BEEX
- CONFESBAK: ADEGI, CEBEK and SEA
- ASLE
- CSCE
- ADIDME

### Promotion and Development

- GARAPEN: UGASSA, Active Bidasoa and Álava development agency
- SPRILUR
- SPRI
- CEDEMI

### Education and Training

- HOBETZU
- HETEL
- IKASLAN
- ZABALNET
- U. Deusto

**Exhibitions**

- CINTEX
- FERROFORMA
- SINAVAL
- Subcontratación
- International machinery and technology exhibition

## ANNEX 5.2   COMPONENTS OF GROUPS IN THE BASQUE AGRO-FOOD PRODUCTIVE SYSTEM

### Science, Technology and Innovation Basque Net (SARETEK)

- Technology centres: ESI
- Technology parks net: Vizcaya, San Sebastián and Álava
- EITE: GAIKER, INASMET and LEIA
- Education and training centres: UPV and Mondragón U.
- Technology and innovation institutions: NEIKER
- AZARO Foundation
- CITMA

### Associations

- ASCENE: ARAEX and PRODESO
- CONFESBAK: ADEGI, SEA and CEBEK
- ASLE
- ASCARVE

### Information, Cooperation and Entrepreneurship

- EICs: Basque Country EU-Administrative and CAMARANET
- ZAINTEK
- Seed Kapital Vizcaya
- CEEIs: BEAZ, CEIA and BIC-BERRILAN
- LANKIDETZA

### Policy Clusters

- Knowledge and firm management

### Promotion and Development

- GARAPEN: Álava development agency
- SPRILUR
- SPRI
- CEDEMI

**Mondragón Cooperative Corporation**

- Training centres: Mondragón University, Otalora, Lea-Artibai and Mone
- Research centres: IKERLAN and MIK
- Distribution group: Distribution and Agro-food

**Education and Training**

- IKASLAN
- HOBETZU

**Exhibitions**

- EUROALIMENTACIÓN
- EUROHOSTELERÍA

**Agriculture Institutions**

- Foundations: ELIKA and KALIKATEA
- NEKANET
- Trade mark councils: Idiazabal, Bizkaiko Txakolina and Getariako Txakolina
- Wholesale markets: Mercabilbao

## ANNEX 5.3    COMPONENTS OF GROUPS IN ANDALUSIA AGRO-FOOD PRODUCTIVE SYSTEM

### Associations

- FAECA
- Artesanos de la mar
- AFACA
- Fundación Oliva

### Education and Training

- U. Almería
- U. Cádiz
- U. Córdoba
- U. Seville
- U. Jaén
- U. Huelva
- U. Granada

### Exhibitions

- AGROGANT
- EXPOLIVA
- Feria cinegética

### Agriculture Institutions

- Trade mark regulating councils: Baena, Sierra de Segura, Jerez y Manzanilla, Brandy Jerez, Jamón de Huelva, Málaga and Montilla-Moriles
- Wholesale markets: Mercagranada, Mercasevilla, Mercajerez, Mercamálaga and Mercacórdoba

# ANNEX 5.4   COMPONENTS OF GROUPS IN ANDALUSIA METAL–MECHANICAL PRODUCTIVE SYSTEM

## Innovation and Technology Andalusia Net (RAITEC)

- Technology centres: AICIA, IAT, CITIC and CIT
- Technology parks: Cartuja and Málaga
- CEEIs: Bahía de Cádiz, Euro CEI and BIC Euronova
- Training: Instituto de la calidad, FUECA, EOI and ENJ
- Promotion and development: DESADOS, Huetor Tajar, Alcalá innova, Montes orientales, Arahal, SODEMAR, IFA, SOPDE, Jun, Sevilla global and Bajo Guadalquivir
- Associations: AEPNA, CEMER, CEA and ETICOM
- Advising: CITPIA and Cinde consulting
- Technology transfer entities: Mediterranean foundation, Almería University, UNISOC, CESEAND and COGESUR

## Associations

- RedCESEA: CEJ, CGE, CEM, CEC, CECO, ASEMPAL, FOE and CES
- CONSTRUCTOR

## Education and Training

- U. Cádiz
- U. Córdoba
- U. Seville
- U. Huelva
- U. Granada

## Exhibitions

- FERICOR
- MADEXPO
- CONSTRUCTOR
- CONSTRUSUR

## ANNEX 5.5   BASQUE COUNTRY INSTITUTION'S ACRONYMS

Bidasoa Activa: Bidasoa development agency
ADEGI: Guipúzcoa employers association
ADIMDE: Basque maritime industries association
AOTEK: Automation research centre
ARAEX: Rioja Alavesa exports group
ASCARVE: Dealers, cold-storage plants and cattle quartering plants association
ASCENE: Export consortia association
ASLE: Association of worker-owned companies of the Basque Country
AUXIN: Common export department metallic products
AZARO: Agro-food foundation
AZTERLAN: Metallurgy research centre
AZTI: Fish and agro-food technology institute
BAPCO: Basque paper consortium
BEAZ: Vizcaya innovation and firms centre
BEEX: Bureau of environmental expertise
BIC-BERRILAN: Innovation and firms centre
CADEM: Energy development and saving centre
CAMARANET: Vizcaya Internet access services
CEDEMI: Left bank business development centre
CEBEK: Bizcaya business confederation
CEEI: Firm and innovation European centres
CEIA: Álava innovation and firms centre
CEIT: Guipúzcoa technical research and studies centre
CIDEMCO: Technology research centre
CIDETEC: Electro-chemical technology research centre
CINTEX: Construction exhibition
CITMA: Environment technological innovation foundation
COFIEX: Office furniture export group
COINAMOBEL: Furniture auxiliary industries corporation
CONFESBAK: Basque business confederation
COMTEC: Industrial representatives society
CSCE: Euskadi cooperatives superior council
CTA: Aeronautic technology centre
DOSYMA: Door systems manufacturers
DZ: Design centre
EIC: Advising, orientation and information European centres
EITE: Technology innovation centres Basque association

ELIKA: Basque foundation for food safety
ELHUYAR: Knowledge and culture foundation
ENERLAN: Energy technologies development centre
ERAIKER: Master builders centre
ESI: European Software Institute
EUSKALIT: Quality Basque foundation
EUSKOIKER: University–firm research foundation
EUVE: Virtual engineering technology centre
FASTENEX: Screw export group
FATRONIK: Machinery technology centre
FCT: Technology centres foundation for technology fostering
FERROFORMA: Ironmongery international exhibition
GAIKER: Innovation technology centre
GARAIA: Innovation, science and technology centre
GARAPEN: Basque association development agencies
GASBI: Research and development in biomass gasification
GOIERRI: Teaching foundation
GUASCOR I+D: Research and development centre Guascor group
HETEL: Association of vocational training centres of the Basque Country
HOBETUZ: Basque foundation for continuous professional training
IDEKO: Machine-tool technology centre
IKASLAN: Association of professional technical training institutes
IKERLAN: Technology centre
IKT: Engineering and agriculture consulting
INASHMAC: Construction machinery consortium
INASMET: Technology foundation
INCEMIN: Santa Barbara's crushing components
INNOVALIA: Innovation association
INVEMA: Machine-tool research foundation
ITEA: Steel structure Basque institute
KALIKATEA: Foundation for the enhancement, promotion and development
of quality Basque food products
KONIKER: Assembly technology centre
LABEIN: Technology centre
LANKIDETZA: Firm cooperation
LEIA: Firm technology transformation and environment improvement
foundation
LORTEK: Union technologies research centre
MTC: Maier technology centre
MENDIKOI: Rural training, promotion and development
MEXIM: Engineering export group

Mondragón U.: Mondragón University
NEIKER: Agriculture research and development Basque institute
NEKANET: Basque rural areas information service
ORONA: Lifts research centre
PRODESO: Cumulated knowledge transfer entity
RECYDE: Research, innovation and development business group
ROBOTIKER: Information and communication technology centre
SAIOLAN: Mondragón innovation and firms centre
SEA: Álava businessmen
Seed Kapital Vizcaya: Venture capital fund
SIDENOR I+D: Research and development society
SINAVAL: International naval exhibition
SISCOMP: Subcontracting companies export organization
SPRI: Industrial restructuring and promotion society
SPRILUR: Industrial infrastructures, land and buildings public corporation
SUBCONTRATACIÓN: International subcontracting and firm cooperation exhibition
TECNUN: Navarra University technological campus in San Sebastián.
TEKNIKER: Research, development and innovation technology centre
U. Deusto: Deusto University
U. Mondragón: Mondragón University
UGGASA: Urola Garaia development agency
ULMA: Research and development institution
UNITEC: Technological innovation spreading, development and management association
UPV: Basque Country University
URRKASTING: Specialized workshops subcontracting exports
VICOMTECH: Centre for visual interaction and communication technology
ZABALNET: Virtual professional training centre
ZAINTEK: Competitive intelligence and technology invigilation service

# ANNEX 5.6  ANDALUSIA INSTITUTIONS' ACRONYMS

ADESVA: Association for the development of agriculture productive system in Huelva
AEPNA: Andalusia natural stone business association
AFACA: Association for animal feeding production firms
AGROGANT: Agriculture and hunting exhibition, Málaga
Arahal: Economic and social development in Arahal
AESMA: Andalusia environment firms association
AICIA: Association of research and industrial cooperation of Andalusia
CAAE: Organic agriculture and livestock
CEA: Andalusia firms confederation
CEEI: European centres of firms and innovation
CEMER: Andalusia wood consortia
CESEAND: Link centre for innovation in the south of Europe
CITAGRO: Agro-food innovation and technology centre
CITIC: Technology centre
CITPIA: Centre for technology information and industrial property of Andalusia
COEXPHAL I+D: Innovation and technology centre in Andalusia federation of agriculture cooperative firms
COGESUR: South Geo-technical centre
CONSTRUCOR: Córdoba construction firms association
CONSTRUSUR: Construction exhibition
DAP: Public firm for agricultural and fishing development in Andalusia
DESADOS: Dos Hermanas local economic development society
ENJ: Jerez management school
EOI: Industrial organization school
ETICOM: Information and communication technology firms association
ETIFA: Technology school for agriculture research and training
FAECA: Andalusia federation for agrarian cooperatives
FERICOR: Cork and cork tree exhibition
FIAPA: Foundation for agriculture research in Almería
FOROSUR: Innovation and Technology Forosur Centre
FUECA: Cádiz University–Firm Foundation
IAT: Andalusia technology institute
IFA: Andalusia Foment Institute
Instituto de la calidad: Institute for quality
MADEXPO: Wood exhibition
PRODTI: Foundation for research promotion and industrial technological development

RAEA: Andalusia net for agriculture experimentation
SODEMAR: Society for Marchena development
SOPDE: Planning and development society, Málaga
UNISOC: University–society foundation, University Pablo de Olavide, Seville
U. Cádiz: University of Cádiz
U. Córdoba: University of Córdoba
U. Granada: University of Granada
U. Huelva: University of Huelva
U. Seville: University of Seville

# ANNEX 5.7    FIRMS INTERVIEWED

**Basque Country**

**Irizar S. Coop**

Ormaiztegi, Guipúzcoa, Basque Country
Founded in 1889
Main activity: luxury buses production
Number of workers: 630
Interviewed person job title: managing director

**Eroski Coop**

Elorrio, Vizcaya, Basque Country
Founded in 1969
Main activity: commercial distribution
Number of workers: 29013
Interviewed person job title: communication chief executive officer

**Caja Laboral Popular Coop. de Crédito**

Arrasate-Mondragón, Guipúzcoa, Basque Country
Founded in 1959
Main activity: financial markets
Number of workers: 1550
Interviewed person job title: marketing executive officer

**Larón, S.A.**

Lemona, Vizcaya, Basque Country
Founded in 1973
Main activity: stone crushing machines
Number of workers: 49
Interviewed person job title: chief executive officer

**CEDEMI, S.A.**

Barakaldo, Vizcaya, Basque Country
Founded in 1997
Main activity: business development centre

Number of firms: 27
Interviewed person job title: assistant executive officer

**Vizcaya Technology Park**

Zamudio, Vizcaya, Basque Country
Founded in 1985
Number of firms: 120
Number of workers: 5260
Interviewed person job title: director

**Andalusia**

**DAP, S.A.**

Seville, Andalusia
Founded in 1999
Main activity: public firm for the agricultural and fishing development of
Andalusia
Number of workers: 838
Interviewed person job title: province coordinator

**Andalusia Technology Park**

Málaga, Andalusia
Founded in 1992
Number of firms: 101
Number of workers: 1701
Interviewed person job title: marketing executive officer

**Consejo Regulador de la Denominación de Origen Baena**

Baena, Córdoba, Andalusia
Founded in 1978
Main activity: regulating council for the Baena olive oil trade mark
Number of firms: 29
Interviewed person job title: general secretary

**S.C.A.O. San Isidro**

Baena, Córdoba, Andalusia

Founded in 1944
Main activity: olive oil milling plant
Number of associated members: 830
Interviewed person job title: president

### S.C.A.O. Nuestra Señora de la Consolación

Baena, Córdoba, Andalusia
Founded in 1961
Main activity: extra-virgin olive oil sales
Number of associated members: 862
Interviewed person job title: president

### S.C.A.O. Germán Baena

Baena, Córdoba, Andalusia
Founded in 1972
Main activity: extra-virgin olive oil commercialization
Number of associated members: 725
Interviewed person job title: chief executive officer

### S.C.A.O. Nuestra Señora de Guadalupe

Baena, Córdoba, Andalusia
Founded in 1944
Main activity: olive oil milling plant and extra-virgin olive oil sales
Number of associated members: 900
Interviewed person job title: president

### S.C.A.O. Nuestra Señora del Rosario

Baena, Córdoba, Andalusia
Founded in 1944
Main activity: olive oil milling plant
Number of associated members: 1509
Interviewed person job title: president

**Murcia**

**Duralmond, S.L.**

Lorquí, Murcia
Founded in 1998
Main activity: furniture and roof and wall covers
Number of workers: 14
Interviewed person job title: marketing executive officer

# ANNEX 5.8   INTERVIEW OUTLINE AND QUESTIONNAIRE FORMAT

## INTERVIEWS

### Firms and interviewee data

Institution title/Location/Year of foundation/Main activity/Number of workers–firms

Interviewed person job title/Number of years of the interviewee in the firm

### Interview outline

*Territorialization*
- Situation
  o Benefits derived from the firms' present location.
  o Intermediate consumptions acquisition at local or regional level.
  o Capital resources acquisition at local or regional level.
  o Technology acquisition at local or regional level.
  o Intermediate output sales to local or regional firm's customers.
  o Final product sales to final demand at local/regional/national/international level.
  o Business services acquisition from local firms.
  o Local infrastructure use.
- Evolution
  o Increasing/same/decreasing.
- Results
  o Higher specialization.
  o Higher efficiency.
  o Lower costs.
  o More and better information.
  o Higher profits.

*Innovation*
- Situation
  o Elaboration/adoption/incorporation of innovation.
  o Types of innovations being developed:
    ▪ Process
    ▪ Product
    ▪ Organization

- Opening to new markets
- New raw-materials resources identification
- Workers' training
- Exhibitions participation
- Evolution
  o Increasing/same/decreasing.
- Results
  o Higher specialization.
  o Higher efficiency.
  o Lower costs.
  o More and better information.
  o Higher profits.

*Coordination*
- Situation
  o Coordination with other local/regional/national/international firms by making use of trust.
  o Confident or suspicious about coordination with other firms.
  o Coordination tasks with:
    - Customers
      □ Other firms as customers through market impersonal relationships.
      □ Final demand through market impersonal relationships.
      □ Retail sellers through market impersonal relationships.
      □ Obtaining relevant information from the customer through personal relationships, when compared to a pure market relation.
      □ Sales through Internet.
      □ Access to new customers allowed by the relationships with existing customers.
    - Suppliers
      □ Formal or informal relationships.
      □ Collaboration in the development process of the acquired product.
      □ Trying to avoid behaviours that could damage each other or take advantage of the partner/fulfilment of promises/sharing the same objectives/accepting and understanding the partner's objectives.
    - Competitors
      □ Type of relationship with them.
      □ Formal or informal relationships.

       □   Pure impersonal competition.
       □   Collaboration in marketing/R+D.
       □   Outsourcing.
       □   Importance of personal relationships for the firm's success.
       □   Learning from each other/copying ideas from each other.
       □   Sharing or facilitating the local business services hiring.
       □   Sharing technical information.
       □   Taking advantage/sharing/preparing local training courses.
       □   Creating/taking advantage of opportunities for cooperative sales or purchases.
       □   Creating opportunities for cooperative marketing.
       □   Relying on the competitors for problem solving.
- Scientific experts from outside the firm (such as university)
       □   Collaboration in the design of innovations.
- Researchers from outside the firm
       □   Joint participation with the research centre.
- Evolution
  o Increasing/same/decreasing.
- Results
  o Higher specialization.
  o Higher efficiency.
  o Lower costs.
  o More and better information.
  o Higher profits.

*Outsourcing*
- Situation
  o Outsourcing of productive tasks that could be obtained, cheaper and more specialized, or developing the whole productive process at home.
    - Services
    - Some parts of the whole previous productive process
  o Changing towards a concentration on specific tasks of a particular part of the productive process where the firm has competitive advantages.
  o New relationships or maintaining the same links after the outsourcing.
- Evolution
  o Increasing/same/decreasing.
- Results
  o Higher specialization.
  o Higher efficiency.
  o Lower costs.

o  More and better information.
o  Higher profits.

*Relationships with regional institutions*
- Situation
  o  Relationships with other institutions:
     ▪  Technological parks
     ▪  Universities
     ▪  Innovation centres
     ▪  Advising centres and industry organizations
  o  Membership of any association: firms/exporters/sector cluster.
  o  Increasing exploitation of information flows thanks to institutional links.
  o  Access to more innovations.
  o  Participation in training activities.
  o  Participation in joint projects with other firms.
  o  Increasing the firm's credibility and trust with other institutions/firms in the regional productive system.
- Evolution
  o  Increasing/same/decreasing.
- Results
  o  Higher specialization.
  o  Higher efficiency.
  o  Lower costs.
  o  More and better information.
  o  Higher profits.

*Suppliers*
- Are they innovative?
- Do they outsource?
- Are they specialized?
- Replacing suppliers and looking for the most innovative, also outsourcing, and specialized.
- Coordination.

*Social capital*
- Using contacts to hire new workers.
- Using contacts to get strategic information.
- Relationships inside the firm: helping in knowledge creation and diffusion.
- Informal relationships and particular environment inside the firm.

- Events allowing for socialization inside the firm.
- General feeling about trust with suppliers/customers/competitors.
- Evolution, within the last few years, of the trust relationships maintained with suppliers/customers/competitors/other institutions.
- Unpleasant and conflictive or pleasant and problem-free relationships with customers/suppliers/competitors.
- Explicit consideration of the importance of social capital for the firm. Specific or strategic activities in the firm to maintain it and increase it.

*Technological parks' specific questions*
- Relative number of research/training/technology/advising centres. Evolution of this number.
- What firms in the park look for and find.
- Park working properly; evolution.
- Relative number of firms relating with the centres on the park; evolution and satisfaction.
- Importance of informal and trust relationships.
- Effects on the efficiency of the firms; effects from a positive externalities view.
- Evaluation of the effect of belonging to the park for the firms and of area's success.

# QUESTIONNAIRE

**Name of the firm:**
**Main activity:**
**Job title for the person filling in the questionnaire:**

*Questions 1 to 7 refer to the firm's location and to the geographical scope of its commercial relationships*

**1. Most of your intermediate consumptions and capital resources are acquired at the following level:**

Local☐      Regional☐      National☐      International☐

**2. How has the acquisition of intermediate consumptions and capital resources evolved, in each of the following levels?** (1 decreasing, 2 same, 3 increasing)

| | | | |
|---|---|---|---|
| Local | 1☐ | 2☐ | 3☐ |
| Regional | 1☐ | 2☐ | 3☐ |
| National | 1☐ | 2☐ | 3☐ |
| International | 1☐ | 2☐ | 3☐ |

**3. Your customers are mainly located at the following level:**

Local☐      Regional☐      National☐      International☐

**4. The geographical location of your customers (market) has been evolving at every level:** (1 decreasing, 2 same, 3 increasing)

| | | | |
|---|---|---|---|
| Local | 1☐ | 2☐ | 3☐ |
| Regional | 1☐ | 2☐ | 3☐ |
| National | 1☐ | 2☐ | 3☐ |
| International | 1☐ | 2☐ | 3☐ |

**5. The business services that you hire are mainly acquired at the following level:**

Local☐      Regional☐      National☐      International☐

**6. How has the acquisition of business services for your firm evolved?**
(1 decreasing, 2 same, 3 increasing)

| | | | |
|---|---|---|---|
| Local | 1□ | 2□ | 3□ |
| Regional | 1□ | 2□ | 3□ |
| National | 1□ | 2□ | 3□ |
| International | 1□ | 2□ | 3□ |

**7. Give a value to the positive consequences of your present location for the efficiency of your firm:** (0 none − 4 high)

0□     1□     2□     3□     4□

*Question 8 refers to innovation activities made by your firm*

**8. Does your firm undertake any of the following types of innovation?**
(0 never, 1 decreasing, 2 same, 3 increasing)

| | | | | |
|---|---|---|---|---|
| Process | 0□ | 1□ | 2□ | 3□ |
| Product | 0□ | 1□ | 2□ | 3□ |
| Organization | 0□ | 1□ | 2□ | 3□ |
| Opening to new markets | 0□ | 1□ | 2□ | 3□ |
| Identification of new resources | 0□ | 1□ | 2□ | 3□ |
| Workers' training | 0□ | 1□ | 2□ | 3□ |
| Exhibitions participation | 0□ | 1□ | 2□ | 3□ |

*Questions 9 to 24 refer to the coordination in the firm, competitors, customers and suppliers*

**9. Which is the dominant structure of your firm?**

Hierarchical□     Horizontal coordination□

**10. Give a value to the weight of relationships inside your firm based on trust:** (0 none − 4 high)

0□     1□     2□     3□     4□

**11. Does your firm coordinate with other firms in the same sector by using <u>trust</u>?** (0 never, 1 decreasing, 2 same, 3 increasing)

0□        1□        2□        3□

**12. Give a value to the weight of relationships maintained with other firms of the same sector based on <u>trust</u>:** (0 none − 4 high)

0□        1□        2□        3□        4□

**13. Which type of relationship do you have with the other firms working in the same productive sector as yours?**

Formal personal relationships    □
Informal personal                □
Impersonal competition           □

**14. Does your firm collaborate, through joint projects, with firms working in the same productive sector, in any of the following aspects?**

Marketing□   R+D□   Publicity□   Subcontracting□      None□

**15. Give a value to the importance of personal relationships for the success of your firm:** (0 none − 4 high)

0□        1□        2□        3□        4□

**16. According to the relationships that your firm has with other firms working in the same productive sector, to what degree do the following apply?** (0 none, 1 decreasing, 2 same, 3 increasing)

You learn from each other
0□  1□  2□  3□
You copy ideas from each other
0□  1□  2□  3□
The hiring of local business services is more efficient
0□  1□  2□  3□
You share technical information
0□  1□  2□  3□
You collaborate in the elaboration and participation of training courses
0□  1□  2□  3□

Opportunities for cooperative sales or purchases are created or used
0□  1□  2□  3□
Opportunities for cooperative marketing are created
0□  1□  2□  3□

**17. If you have to face a new problem, can you rely on any other firm of the same productive sector to help you in solving it?**

Yes□        No□

**18. Which type of relationship do you have with your customers?**

We coordinate in the product development process        □
Market impersonal relationships                         □

**19. Do you get relevant information from the direct relationship that you maintain with your customers?**

Yes□        No□

**20. Have the relationships you have with your existing customers allowed you to access new customers?**

Yes□        No□

**21. Give a value to the weight of relationships with your customers based on <u>trust</u>: (0 none − 4 high)**

0□        1□        2□        3□        4□

**22. Which type of relationship do you have with your suppliers?**

Formal□     Informal□        Both□

**23. Do you participate, in any form, in the development of the products that you acquire from your suppliers?**

Yes□        No□

**24. Give a value to the weight of relationships with your suppliers based on <u>trust</u>:** (0 none − 4 high)

0□      1□      2□      3□      4□

*Questions 25 to 27 refer to the outsourcing process in your firm*

**25. Do you hire other firms for productive tasks that your firm used to handle itself?**

Service tasks□      Some parts of the productive process□      No□

**26. If you have outsourced productive tasks, you have done it with firms which the following best describes:**

That already had a trade link with my firm□      New firms□      Both□

**27. Has the outsourcing had a positive effect on the efficiency and the profits of your firm?**

Yes□      No□      Do not know□

*Questions 28 to 32 refer to the institutional relationships maintained by your firm*

**28. Does your firm maintain any relationship with any of the following institutions?**

Technology parks      □
Universities      □
Innovation centres □
Advising centres      □

**29. Is your firm a member of any association? (Industry organizations, exporters, sector policy cluster):**

Yes□      No□

**30. Institutional relationships and associations have allowed you to:**

Improve information-flows exploitation      □

Increase access to innovations        □
Increase participation in training activities    □
Develop joint projects with other firms      □

### 31. Has the use of these institutional relationships been increasing?

Yes□       No□

### 32. Have your institutional relationships had a positive effect on the efficiency and profits of your firm?

Yes□       No□       Do not know□

## NOTES

1. According to Florax *et al.* (2002, p.1), making a review of the empirical economic growth literature: 'the empirics are geared towards determining the significance of institutions, catch-up and convergence, and knowledge accumulation for economic growth differentials'.
2. Some other basic references for regional growth and development theory are Hirschman (1958), Arrow (1962), Romer (1994) and Nelson (1995).
3. The survey also offers some regional data that will be discussed, in the cases of Andalusia and the Basque Country, in the hypotheses-testing section.
4. Among these reasons the authors describe the following: differences in beliefs about the trustworthiness of a common set of people; differences in interpretation of who comprises 'most people'; differences in interpretation of what it means to be able to trust someone; differences in the ability to elicit trustworthy behaviour from other people; and some respondents might not even be willing to answer truthfully when asked such a question on a survey.
5. According to Beugelsdijk *et al.* (2004) the improvement in robustness is caused by the inclusion of countries with relatively low scores on trust, most notably the Philippines and Peru.
6. This includes political rights and civil liberties by country.
7. The World Bank also dedicates resources to study social capital in poor countries, trying to enhance it as a development initiative; see 'Social capital for development' (http://www1.worldbank.org/prem/poverty/scapital).
8. Relational contracting is an intermediate form of governance between market and vertical integration. It can also be understood as an inter-firm network (Thorelli, 1986), where outsourcing is common with durable trade relationships among firms based on trust.
9. Detailed information about these firms can be found in their web pages: www.cakehouse.co.uk, www.ecademy.com, www.humax.net, www.itsnotwhatyouknow.com, www.linkedin.com, www.orgnet.com, www.ryze.com, www.typaldos.com and www.visiblepath.com. There are also publications offering wider information about these kinds of firms, such as *Network Moves* ('The Monthly Newsletter for Business Networking & Opportunities').
10. This is an online publication available at www.networkmoves.com.
11. The authors define 'milieu' as 'a territorialised entity ruled by norms, rules, values which are so many guidelines for the behaviour of the players and the relations between them' (Maillat and Grosjean, 1999, p. 3). The milieu is based on 'cohesion' and is made up of five basic

aspects: 1) spatial entity, 2) group of players, 3) specific material elements, 4) organizational logic and 5) learning logic.

12. The Baden-Württemberg economy is based on 'mittelstands', groups of SMEs linked to large firms through supply chains and with some degree of lateral networking with other small firms. The Emilia-Romagna structure is based on 'industrial districts' made up of small firms making networks of cooperation and based on competing subcontractors.

13. Taken from Cooke and Morgan (2000, p. 150).

14. This is an area with big firms such as Mercedes-Benz, Bosch, DASA, Daimler and Porsche, but generally maintaining the same business culture as the SMEs.

15. The source of this and the following figures is my own elaboration based on fieldwork.

16. The meaning of each Basque institution's acronyms is shown in Annex 5.5.

17. All the institutions making up the nine components around the Basque agro-food production system are listed in Annex 5.2.

18. The meaning of the Andalusia institutions' acronyms is shown in Annex 5.6.

19. Chapter 3 explained mechanism causality as one way to test hypotheses. This should not be confused with the more quantitative approach used in econometrics, although the same terminology is used. Table 3.1 shows the different types of causality and Table 3.2 shows several examples testing hypotheses with mechanism causality.

20. Moreover, regional production processes depend on external relations, with other regions in the country and with other countries.

21. Peeters *et al.* (2001, p. 6), mentioning Lundvall (1992), De Bresson *et al.* (1994) and Edquist (1997), assert: 'economic (supplier–user) linkages between industries – as reflected in the I/O tables (intermediary flows of goods and services between industries) – are the main "carriers" of technology diffusion in an economy; through interactive learning processes'.

22. These institutions include firms and other private and public institutions.

23. In some economic aspects, such as exports, the region was still considered among the most successful Spanish regions until the beginning of the twentieth century.

24. Brandenburger and Nalebuff (1997) use the term 'co-opetition' referring to a firm strategy based, at the same time, on cooperation and competition.

25. 'A coordination plan that is novel in some respect qualifies as an innovation' (Casson, 1997, p. 73).

26. Considering a dynamic process instead of a comparative static analysis where the situation should show the substitution, and not the coexistence, of relations.

27. Information about the interviewed firms is in Annex 5.7. Other Basque and Andalusia study cases, reinforcing the hypotheses, are based on the following firms: Asle, Copreci, Fagor, Gasnalsa, AYD, IMH, ITP, Microdeco, TVA, Batz, Bultzaki, Gamesa, Goizper, Ibermática, Orkli, Grupo Ulma, Neionnova, Aucore, Plaza and Björm, Actividades Químicas Andaluzas, Mercaempresas SA, Permasa, NSN Sistemas SAL, Placinor SL, Wide World Geographic Services SL, PRLSfot, HIS Weiglling SL and Infobasa Agencia de Comunicación SL.

28. For a definition and justification of the use of this criterion, see Kvale (1996) and Judd *et al.* (2001).

29. The main details about the 15 interviewed firms and institutions are provided in Annex 5.7; the outline followed in the interviews is included in Annex 5.8. The detailed questionnaire is provided in Annex 5.8.

30. The most efficient organizational systems are, for the authors cited, clan and relational contracting.

31. That is, in relative terms, in the Basque Country the number of R+D workers multiplies by 2.4 the national average R+D workforce.

32. The R+D workers and patents data mentioned refer to year 1999.

33. These terms have been defined in Section 5.2.

34. Research that has analysed the Irizar case includes: *Fundación Vasca para la Calidad* (2001) and Casadesus-Masanell and Khanna (2003); its high efficiency has also been commented on by The Economist Intelligence Unit (2000).

35. These regional data have been obtained from Moesen *et al.* (2000).

36. The country average value, corresponding to the year 1996, shown in Table 5.1, is 29.8.

37. It should be remembered that trust data have been obtained from the answers to the following question: 'Generally speaking, would you say that most people can be trusted or that you can't be too careful in dealing with people?'
38. The Scandinavian countries group includes Norway, Denmark, Sweden, Finland and Iceland.
39. Zak and Knack (2001) show some anecdotes comparing the high trust level in Scandinavian cities with the low trust of New York. Uslaner (2003) remarks as the most trusting countries the Nordic nations and the Netherlands, while on the opposite side there are Brazil, the Philippines, Peru, Colombia and Turkey.
40. The Gini indices are, for the period 1973–74, in Andalusia 0.3235 and in the Basque Country 0.2856, and in 1990–91, Andalusia 0.2919 and Basque Country 0.2565 (Goerlich and Mas, 1999).
41. Schooling rates after the compulsory period.

# 6   Conclusions

This work has analysed productive systems from a structural relational perspective. This has been done theoretically and also empirically, discussing the adoption of the network perspective and relating the structure and evolution of productive systems to economic growth and development.

In the first two core chapters, the network perspective has been discussed as being the most appropriate approach to analyse economic systems, and therefore to analyse groups of interrelated firms and institutions at a micro level and productive branches at a more macro level. The distinctive character of this methodology is in its structural and relational nature, focused on the relationships maintained among the actors under study.

Economic organizations, acting as purposive actors, are embedded in wider social structures and therefore the approach and concepts offered by the network perspective are available for their study. In fact, there is a part of the network analysis which focuses on the study of economic organizations and proposes exchange theories. However, the works in this respect are very limited and they have mainly been applied to study the internal structure of firms where information is being exchanged; in some cases, their links with other firms are also considered.

The application of the network perspective to analyse socio-economic systems has been examined, to study the whole set of actors constituting them. In this form, relationships – instead of attributes – and purposive relational actors – instead of independent agents – are considered. Moreover, the application of this perspective benefits from the contributions of economics and sociology, recovering the social character of economics and the importance of the historical and geographical contexts. Therefore, this is an interdisciplinary analysis.

When studying economic systems, there appear several concepts in the relevant literature to define them. All the definitions refer to sets of exchanging firms and some of them include other institutions. Of all of them the productive system concept considers the widest collection of institutions, including formal and informal relationships and, therefore, reflecting the system's structure in a more realistic form. The productive system concept has been related to a particular geographical context so as to account for the area's specificities, explaining its structure and evolution. Therefore, regional productive systems have been selected for analysis them in the empirical part of the research.

Regional productive systems and their relationship with differentiated development paths have been studied from a network perspective. The data used in the empirical part are at a regional level and correspond to input–output links, institutional information, economic history, interviews conducted at selected firms, and other quantitative and qualitative information. The main methods that have been applied to these data for the study of regional productive systems, according to the adopted methodological perspective, is social network analysis focused on the structure of relational systems. The most important measures and concepts have been explained in Chapter 3, dedicated to the data and methods explanation, while input–output indices also have been discussed, as they have been applied in a complementary form. These indices have usually been used to study trade relationships among productive branches. However, in this research the proposition that an alternative method is necessary to study transacting actors, from a relational structural point of view, is defended. Therefore, social network analysis is the main method and input–output indices have been used complementarily.

To test the proposed hypotheses in the empirical part, mechanism causality has been the adopted perspective, because the micro units making productive systems are firms and institutions. Therefore, it is necessary to explain the behaviour at system level in the sequence of events taking place at firm, and therefore more micro, level. For this reason, direct observations have been obtained from interviews carried out at a set of selected firms.

The methodological discussion offered in the first two core chapters has been applied in a second empirical part, made of the two following chapters, to analyse the relationship taking place between productive systems' structures and evolution and development at a regional level. Therefore, before establishing and contrasting these relations, regional productive systems have been identified. Two Spanish regions have been selected for this purpose, Andalusia and the Basque Country. The first is a very extensive region in the south of Spain, considered to be among the less developed regions of the country. The second is a small northern region, included among the most developed and dynamic Spanish regions.

The first step in the study of regional productive systems has been the identification of their technical part: regional production systems. With the use of historical information, descriptive statistics, social network analysis, input–output indices and a specific algorithm, two regional production systems, comprising input–output branches, have been selected in each region: the agro-food and the metal–mechanical production system. In a regional historical context, the agro-food system has always been a key element in the socio-economic fabric of Andalusia. The metal–mechanical branches also had a relevant role for the region in the past, although at present they are not clearly inserted in the economic structure of the region. Both systems have, nevertheless, been studied for comparative purposes. In the case of the Basque Country its economy is clearly concentrated, historically and also at present, in branches belonging to the metal–mechanical system. Nevertheless, an agro-food system can also be identified and therefore compared with the system in Andalusia, although its importance for the regional economy is less evident.

The structures of the identified agro-food system in Andalusia and of the metal–mechanical system in the Basque Country are essential for the regions' development and growth, owing to their high productive specialization. The characterization of the systems shows that the agro-food system in Andalusia has a very cohesive structure, but when considering its embedding in the whole productive net, it is not solidly inserted because of its weak and sparse links with other branches and systems. The metal–mechanical system in the Basque Country, however, shows a clear cohesion with the whole regional productive structure. These conclusions are of great importance because they have consequences for the differentiated regional development processes. Nevertheless, additional relevant implications appear once institutional information and links are added to constitute regional productive systems.

There are institutions in both regions maintaining constant links with the firms forming the branches included in the two selected production systems. Some of these institutions have a public character while others are private. However, the Basque systems are denser and more complex than the systems in Andalusia. The main differences appear from the quantity of innovation and training institutions linked to the productive branches in which the regions specialize. Another important difference emerges from the cooperative and associative culture of the Basque Country, which has led to the creation of a cooperative corporation, innovation centres groups and a technology parks net.

Once the productive systems have been built, a set of hypotheses has been proposed for testing through mechanism causality. Hypotheses refer to the systems' structure and evolution in regions belonging to developed countries, but with different dynamism and development. They are tested with observations from Andalusia, a less developed and less dynamic region, and the Basque Country, a more developed and more dynamic region. The different development and dynamism have been proved with indicators referring to GDP per capita variations, employment and population evolution, post-compulsory education rates, life expectancy and total and private R+D expenditures.

After the hypotheses testing it can be asserted that, in the development process, regions at a less advanced development stage focus their economic growth on the diversification of their production structure. Therefore, there is an increase in the complexity and density of their production structures. The development process focuses on technological links, with innovations embodied in the productive processes. As regions continue their development process, attaining more advanced development stages, the increasing quantity and quality of non-technical links augment the complexity of their regional systems, through institutional relationships. Therefore, more developed and dynamic regions, with higher specialization, have denser and more complex productive systems. At the same time, service branches appear as strategic branches constituting bridges across structural holes in the whole structure, enhancing a post-industrial economy. The main firms' behaviour, leading to an increase in the number of links with services, is the outsourcing of the services' tasks from their productive processes.

The set of relationships constituting the regional productive systems, sustained by the regional social capital, has a different impact on the regional economic performance, depending on its formal and informal aspects. In less developed regions, when compared with more developed regions, the social capital having a greater impact on their economy is its informal institutional links side, but the situation changes with regional progress and dynamism, in the sense that high-quality informal social capital enhances high-quality formal social capital. More dynamic regions, *ceteris paribus*, attain high-quality informal social capital that enhances the creation of formal social capital. At the same time, more developed regions, *ceteris paribus*, enjoy higher levels of social capital, with its formal part having greater effects on economic performance than in less developed regions. Causality goes in both directions: higher development implies more high-quality social capital and vice versa.

The most developed regions have an economy affected more by the social capital side made of formal institutional links, when compared with less developed regions. Therefore, in less advanced stages, the main aspect of social capital working in the region is tacit norms, informal cooperation and trust. The development process makes that trust, and durable relationships drive the creation of stable links with formal institutions.

This is the situation observed when comparing Andalusia and the Basque Country. There is a development process in which, at the beginning, productive systems focus on diversification and technical links, as observed in Andalusia, maintaining the productive specialization of the region. Thus, specialization is more intense, with service branches occupying strategic positions linking different sub-systems, the most efficient firms facilitating this part of the process by outsourcing services, as most of the analysed firms have been doing in the Basque Country. As development goes on, non-technical links appear with greater importance, constituting increasingly solid productive systems. The non-technical links having a greater impact on the region's economy are informal links based on trust, in a first step, but they enhance the creation of formal links with institutions.

In Andalusia, formal institutional relationships are mainly maintained with public institutions having a very important presence in the regional economic structure. Cooperation and trust links work, but with a marked local character where reputation is also very important. In the Basque Country, informal trust links have led to the creation and maintenance of formal institutional relationships, where cooperation is very important for the efficiency of productive processes. In the search for this efficiency, firms are highly specialized, outsourcing most of the service tasks, and establishing solid links with regional institutions such as technology parks and innovation and training centres. The cooperative organizational system is also much extended according to the regional business culture. Therefore, cooperation through formal and informal relationships is present in the efficiency path.

After the fieldwork, the study of other significant case studies, and the relevant literature review, it can be deduced that there is a positive relationship between the density of the regional production structure and development in less advanced development stages, and also with the appearance of services as key branches. There is also a positive relationship between development and social capital that, in less developed regions, depends more on its informal side, and in regions where a higher level of development has been attained these informal links, if they are of high quality, enhance the creation of formal institutional links. More dynamic regions, *ceteris paribus*, facilitate the transformation of informal social capital into formal social capital, enhancing the regions' development.

Regions with institutional networks based on cooperation, with solid high-quality social capital, will help the flow of information, tacit knowledge and disembodied technology, and in the maintenance of reputation and long-term trade links. These regions will enjoy endogenous development, where the territory has a crucial role. These regions will experience a development path allowing them to attain more sustained, durable and successful development and growth.

# Bibliography

Abadie, A. and Gardeazabal, J. (2001), 'The economic cost of conflict: a case–control study for the Basque Country', *Faculty Research Working Papers Series RWP01–048*, October, John F. Kennedy School of Government, Harvard University.

Abaunz, J. L., Aguirre, A. and Valle, J. J. (1998), 'Grupo Ulma. Los valores corporativos como clave del desarrollo del proyecto empresarial', País Vasco: Cluster del Conocimiento.

Abbott, A. and Hrycak, A. (1990), 'Measuring resemblance in sequence data: an optimal matching analysis of musicians' careers', *American Journal of Sociology*, 96, pp. 144–85.

Abell, P. (1987), *The Syntax of Social Life: The Theory and Method of Comparative Narratives*, Oxford: Oxford University Press.

Abrahamson, E. and Rosenkopf, L. (1997), 'Social network effects on the extent of innovation diffusion: a computer simulation', *Organization Science*, vol. 8, no. 3, May–June, pp. 289–309.

Ahn, S. and Hemmings, P. (2000), 'Policy influences on economic growth in OECD countries: an evaluation of the evidence', *Economics Department Working Papers* no. 246, ECO/WKP 19, OECD.

Ahuja, M. K. and Carley, K. M. (1998), 'Network structure in virtual organizations', *Journal of Computer-Mediated Communication*, vol. 3, no. 4, June, available online at http://www.ascusc.org/jcmc/vol3/ issue4/ ahuja.html.

Álvarez de Toledo, P., Rojo, J., Toribio, A. and Usabiaga, C. (2000), 'Convergencia: un análisis conjunto de los sectores. Aplicación al caso de las regiones españolas', *Documento de Trabajo* 2000–06, FEDEA.

Amin, A. (1999), 'An institutional perspective on regional economic development', *International Journal of Urban and Regional Research*, vol. 23, no. 2, June, pp. 365–78.

Aramburu, N. and Iturrioz, C. (1998), 'Ibermática. Liderazgo del cambio en un entorno competitivo emergente', País Vasco: Cluster del Conocimiento.

Aramburu Irízar, J. J. and Escalada Garcés, J. M. (1999), 'La incidencia de la demanda pública en el valor añadido y en el empleo (1990–1995)', available online at http://www.eustat.es/spanish/estad/, EUSTAT, País Vasco.

Araujo, A. and Matey, J. (1998), 'Bultzaki. Creatividad de los recursos humanos: clave para la adaptación a las exigencias de los clientes', País Vasco: Cluster del Conocimiento.

Aroche-Reyes, F. (2001), 'The question of identifying industrial complexes revisited: a qualitative perspective', in M. L. Lahr and E. Dietzenbacher (eds), *Input–Output Analysis: Frontiers and Extensions*, New York: Palgrave, pp. 280–96.

Arrighetti, A., Seravalli, G. and Wolleb, G. (2001), 'Social capital, institutions and collective action between firms', EURESCO Conference on Social Capital, September, Exeter.

Arrow, K. (1962), 'The economic implications of learning by doing', *Review of Economic Studies*, vol. 29, no. 2, pp. 155–73.

Arrow, K. (1974), 'Limited knowledge and economic analysis', *American Economic Review*, vol. 64, no. 1, pp. 1–10.

Asheim, B. and Dunford, M. (1997), 'Regional futures', *Regional Studies*, vol. 31, no. 5, pp. 445–55.

Aunger, R. (1995), 'On ethnography: storytelling or science?', *Current Anthropology*, vol. 36, no. 1, special issue: Ethnographic authority and cultural explanation, February, pp. 97–130.

Azpilikueta, S., Igarza, R. and Ulazia, J. M. (1998), 'Gasnalsa. Liderazgo ejemplarizante: la satisfacción del cliente a través de la satisfacción del personal', País Vasco: Cluster del Conocimiento.

Baker, W. E. (1992), 'The network organization in theory and practice', in N. Nohria and R. G. Eccles (eds), *Networks and Organizations. Structure, Form and Action*, Boston, Massachusetts: Harvard Business School Press, ch. 15.

Baker, W. E. and Faulkner, R. R. (1993), 'The social organization of conspiracy: illegal networks in the heavy electrical equipment industry', *American Sociological Review*, vol. 58, no. 6, December, pp. 837–60.

Barro, R. (1991), 'Economic growth in a cross-section of countries', *Quarterly Journal of Economics*, vol. 106, no. 2, pp. 407–33.

Barro, R. and Sala i Martín, X. (1999), *Economic Growth*, Cambridge: MIT Press.

Barsky, N. P. (1999), 'A core/periphery structure in a corporate budgeting process', *Connections,* vol. 22, no. 2, pp. 1–29.

Bærenholdt, J. O. and Aarsæther, N. (2000) 'Coping strategies and regional policies: the intersection of social capital and space', MOST CCPP Workshop, November, Joensuu, Finland.

Batagelj, V. and Mrvar, A. (2003), *Pajek, Programme for Large Network Analysis*, available online at http://vlado.fmf.uni–lj.si/pub/networks/pajek/.

Becattini, G. (1989), 'Sectors and/or districts: some remarks on the conceptual foundations of industrial economics', in E. Goodam, J. Bamford and P. Saynor (eds), *Small Firms and Industrial Districts in Italy*, London: Routledge.

Bell, D. (1973), *The Coming of Post–Industrial Society: A Venture in Social Forecasting*, New York: Basic Books.

Benson, J. K. (1975), 'The interorganizational network as a political economy', *Administrative Science Quarterly*, 20, pp. 229–49.

Berkowitz, S. D. (1988), 'Markets and market–areas: some preliminary formulations', in B. Wellman and S. D. Berkowitz (eds), *Social Structures: A Network Approach*, Cambridge: Cambridge University Press.

Bernal, A. M. and Parejo, A. (2001), 'La economía andaluza: atraso y frágil vertebración', in L. Germán, E. Llopis, J. Maluquer de Motes and S. Zapata (eds), *Historia Económica Regional de España Siglos XIX y XX*, Barcelona: Crítica.

Beugelsdijk, S. and van Schaik, T. (2001), 'Social capital and regional economic growth', *CentER Discussion Paper* no. 2001–102, Tilburg University, The Netherlands.

Beugelsdijk, S., de Groot, H. L. F. and van Schaik, A. B. T. M. (2002), 'Trust and economic growth', *Tinbergen Institute Discussion Paper TI* 2002–049/3.

Beugelsdijk, S., de Groot, H. L. F. and van Schaik, A. B. T. M. (2004), 'Trust and economic growth: a robustness analysis', *Oxford Economic Papers*, vol. 56, no. 1, pp. 118–34.

Bharadwaj, K. R. (1966), 'A note on structural interdependence and the concept of "key" sectors', *Kyklos*, vol. 19, pp. 315–9.

Bian, Y. (2002), 'Social capital of the firm and its impact on performance: a social network analysis', in A. S. Tsui and C. Lan (eds), *The Management of Enterprises in the People's Republic of China*, Norwell, Massachusetts: Kluwer, ch. 12.

Bjørnskov, C. and Svendsen, G. T. (2003), 'Why does the Northern light shine so brightly?', *Aarhus School of Business Department of Economic Working Paper* no. 02–15.

Bolton, M. K., Malmrose, R. and Ouchi, W. G. (1994), 'The organization of innovation in the United States and Japan: neoclassical and relational contracting', *Journal of Management Studies*, vol. 31, no. 5, September, pp. 653–79.

Bonacich, P. (1987), 'Power and centrality: a family of measures', *American Journal of Sociology*, vol. 92, pp. 1170–82.

Borgatti, S. P. (1994), 'A quorum of graph theoretic concepts', *Connections*, vol. 17, no. 1, pp. 47–9.

Borgatti, S. P. and Feld, S. L. (1994), 'How to test the strength of weak ties theory', *Connections*, vol. 17, no. 1, pp. 45–6.

Borgatti, S. P. (1997), 'Structural holes: unpacking Burt's redundancy measures', *Connections,* vol. 20, no. 1, pp. 35–8.

Borgatti, S. P. (ed.) (1998), 'A socnet discussion on the origins of the term social capital', *Connections,* vol. 21, no. 2, pp. 37–46.

Borgatti, S. P., Jones, C. and Everett, M. G. (1998), 'Network measures of social capital', *Connections,* vol. 21, no. 2, pp. 27–36.

Borgatti, S. P. and Everett, M. G. (1999), 'Models of core/periphery structures', *Social Networks*, vol. 21, pp. 375–95.

Borgatti, S. P., Everett, M. G. and Freeman, L. C. (2002), *Ucinet for Windows: Software for Social Network Analysis*, Harvard: Analytic Technologies.

Boucher, M. (1976), 'Some further results on the linkage hypothesis', *Quarterly Journal of Economics*, vol. 90, no. 2, May, pp. 313–8.

Bouty, I. (2000), 'Interpersonal and interaction influences on informal resources exchanges between R&D researchers across organizational boundaries', *Academy of Management Journal,* vol. 43, no. 1, pp. 50–65.

Brass, D. J. and Burkhardt, M. E. (1992), 'Centrality and power in organizations', in N. Nohria and R. G. Eccles (eds), *Networks and Organizations. Structure, Form and Action*, Boston, Massachusetts: Harvard Business School Press, ch. 7.

Bradach, J. L. and Eccles, R. G. (1989), 'Markets versus hierarchies: from ideal types to plural forms', in W. R. Scott (ed.), *Annual Review of Sociology*, vol. 15. Palo Alto, CA: Annual Reviews Inc, pp. 97–118.

Brandenburger, A. M. and Nalebuff, B. J. (1997), *Co-opetition*, New York: Currency Doubleday.

Breiger, R., Boorman, S. and Arabie, P. (1975), 'An algorithm for clustering relational data, with applications to social network analysis and comparison with multi-dimensional scaling', *Journal of Mathematical Psychology*, vol. 12, pp. 328–83.

Breiger, R. L. (1981), 'Structures of economic interdependence among nations', in P. M. Blau and R. K. Merton (eds), *Continuities in Structural Inquiry*, Newbury Park, CA: Sage, pp. 353–80.

Breschi, S. (2000), 'The geography of innovation: a cross-sector analysis', *Regional Studies*, vol. 34, no. 3, pp. 213–29.

Buchan, N. R., Croson, R. T. A. and Dawes, R. M. (2002), 'Swift neighbors and persistent strangers: a cross-cultural investigation of trust and reciprocity in social exchange', *American Journal of Sociology*, vol. 108, no. 1, July, pp. 168–206.

Bunge, M. (1985), *Economía y Filosofía*, 2nd ed, Madrid: Tecnos.

Burkhardt, M. E. (1994), 'Social interaction effects following a technological change: a longitudinal investigation', *Academy of Management Journal*, vol. 37, no. 4, pp. 869–98.

Burt, R. S. (1976), 'Positions in networks', *Social Forces*, vol. 55, pp. 93–122.

Burt, R. S. (1980), 'Models of network structure', *Annual Review of Sociology*, vol. 6, pp. 79–141.

Burt, R. S. (1982), *Towards a Structural Theory of Action: Network Models of Social Structure, Perception and Action*, New York: Academic Press.

Burt, R. S. (1987), 'Social contagion and innovation: cohesion versus structural equivalence', *American Journal of Sociology*, vol. 92, no. 6, May, pp. 1287–335.

Burt, R. S. (1992), *Structural Holes: The Social Structure of Competition*, Cambridge: Harvard University Press.

Burt, R. S. (2000), 'The network structure of social capital'. University of Chicago and Institut Européen D'administration D'affaires (INSEAD); pre-print for a chapter in *Research in Organizational Behavior*, vol. 22, edited by Robert I. Sutton and Barry M. Staw, Greenwich, CT: Jai Press; available online at http://gsbwww.uchicago.edu/fac/ronald.burt/research/.

Burt, R. S., Hogarth, R. M. and Michaud, C. (2000), 'The social capital of French and American managers', *Organizational Science*, vol. 11, no. 2, March–April, pp. 123–47.

Burt, R. S. (2001), 'The social capital of structural holes' in M. F. Guillén, R. Collins, P. England and M. Meyer (eds), *New Directions in Economic Sociology*, New York: Russell and Sage Foundation, ch. 7.

*Cámaras de Comercio* (2003), 'La sociedad de la información en España y en las comunidades autónomas', available online at http://www.camaras.org.

Campbell, J. (1970), 'The relevance of input–output analysis and digraph concepts to growth pole theory', PhD dissertation, University of Washington, Washington State.

Cappellin, R. and Batey, P. W. J. (eds) (1993), *Regional Networks, Border Regions and European Integration*, London: Pion Limited.

Carter, M. R. and Castillo, M. (2002), 'The economic impacts of altruism, trust and reciprocity: an experimental approach to social capital', *Wisconsin-Madison Agricultural and Applied Economic Staff Papers*, no. 48.

Casadesus-Masanell, R. and Khanna, T. (2003), 'Globalization and trust: theory and evidence form cooperatives', Conference on Trust, Institutions and Globalization, 14–16 March, Aspen, Colorado, The William Davidson Institute and The Aspen Institute Initiative for Social Innovation through Business.

Casson, M. (1997*), Information and Organization. A New Perspective on the Theory of the Firm*, Oxford: Oxford University Press.

Casson, M. and Della Giusta, M. (2004), 'The costly business of trust', *Development Policy Review*, vol. 22, no. 3, pp. 321–42.

Castilla, E. J., Hwang, H., Granovetter, E. and Granovetter, M. (2000), 'Social networks in Silicon Valley', in Ch.-M. Lee, W. F. Miller, M. G. Hancock and H. S. Rowen (eds) *The Silicon Valley Edge: A Habitat for Innovation and Entrepreneurship*, Stanford: Stanford University Press, ch. 11.

Chase, I. (1992) 'Dynamics of hierarchy formation: the sequential development of dominance relationships', *Behavior*, vol. 80, pp. 218–40.

Chenery, H. B. and Watanabe, T. (1958), 'International comparisons of the structure of production', *Econometrica*, vol. 26, no. 4, October, pp. 487–521.

Cilleruelo, E. and Zubillaga, J. (1998), 'Gamesa. Un proyecto empresarial innovador', País Vasco: Cluster del Conocimiento.

Cohen, S. and Zysman, J. (1987), *Manufacturing Matters: The Myth of Post-Industrial Economy*, New York: Basic Books.

Cohen, S. S. and Fields, G. (1999), 'Social capital and capital gains in Silicon Valley', *California Management Review*, vol. 41, no. 2, pp. 108–30.

Coleman, J., Katz, E. and Menzel, H. (1957), 'The diffusion of an innovation among physicians', *Sociometry*, vol. 20, no. 4, December, pp. 253–70.

Coleman, J. S. (1973), *The Mathematics of Collective Action*, Chicago IL: Aldine.

Coleman, J. S. (1988), 'Social capital in the creation of human capital', *American Journal of Sociology*, vol. 94, supplement: Organizations and institutions: sociological and economic approaches to the analysis of social structure, S95–S120.

Contractor, N., Whitbred, R., Fonti, F., Hyatt, A., O'Keefe, B. and Jones, P. (1997), 'Self–organizing communication networks in organizations: validation of a computational model using exogenous and endogenous theoretical mechanisms', manuscript submitted to special issue on 'Applications of complexity theory to organization science'. Available online at http://www.tec.spcomm.uiuc.edu/nosh/comp/comp.htm.

Contractor, N., Whitbred, R., Fonti, F., Hyatt, A., O'Keefe, B. and Jones, P. (2000), 'Structuration theory and the evolution of networks', 2000 Winter Organizational Science Conference.

Cook, K. S., Emerson, R. M., Gillmore, M. R. and Yamagishi, T. (1983), 'The distribution of power in exchange networks: theory and experimental results', *American Journal of Sociology*, vol. 89, pp. 275–305.

Cooke, P. and Morgan, K. (1993), 'The network paradigm: new departures in corporate and regional development', *Environment and Planning D: Society and Space*, vol. 11, pp. 543–64.

Cooke, P. and Wills, D. (1999), 'Small firms, social capital and the enhancement of business performance through innovation programmes', *Small Business Economics*, vol. 13, no. 3, pp. 219–34.

Cooke, P. and Morgan, K. (2000), *The Associational Economy. Firms, Regions and Innovation*, Oxford: Oxford University Press.

Cuadrado Roura, J. R., Mancha Navarro, T. and Garrido Yserte, R. (1998), *Convergencia Regional en España*, Madrid: Fundación Argentaria-VISOR.

Cuello, A. F. and Mansouri, F. (1992), 'The identification of structure at the sectoral level: a reformulation of the Hirschman–Rasmussen key sector indices', *Economic Systems Research*, vol. 4, no. 4, pp. 285–96.

Czamanski, S. (1971), 'Some empirical evidence of the strengths of linkages between groups of related industries in urban–regional complexes', *Papers, Regional Science Association*, vol. 27, pp. 137–50.

Dasgupta, P. and Serageldin, I. (eds) (1999), *Social Capital: A Multifaced Perspective*, Washington: World Bank.

Dasgupta, P. and Serageldin, I. (eds) (2005), *Social Capital: A Multifaceted Approach*, Oxford: Oxford University Press.

Dasgupta, P. (2003), 'Social capital and economic performance: analytics', in E. Ostrom and T. K. Ahn (eds), *Foundations of Social Capital*, Cheltenham, UK and Northampton, MA, USA: Edward Elgar.

De Clercq (2003), 'Human capital, social capital and innovation: a multi-country study', *Vlerick Leuven Gent Working Paper Series*, 2003/18.

De la Fuente, A. (1996), 'Economía regional desde una perspectiva neoclásica. De convergencia y otras historias', *Revista de Economía Aplicada*, vol. IV, no. 10, pp. 5–63.

De la Fuente, A. and Freire Serén, M. J. (2000), 'Estructura sectorial y convergencia regional', *Documentos de Economía*, vol. 2, Fundación Caixa Galicia.

De Mesnard, L. (2001), 'On boolean topological methods of structural analysis', in M. L. Lahr and E. Dietzenbacher (eds), *Input–Output Analysis: Frontiers and Extensions*, New York: Palgrave, ch. 3.

DeBresson, C., Sirilli, G., Hu, X. and Luk, F. K. (1994), 'Structure and location of innovative activity in the Italian economy, 1981–85', *Economic Systems Research*, vol. 6, pp. 135–58.

Degenne, A. and Forsé, M. (1999), *Introducing Social Networks*, London: Sage.

Delgado Cabeza, M. (1993), 'Las tres últimas décadas de la economía andaluza', in M. Martínez Rodríguez (ed), *Estructura Económica de Andalucía*, Madrid: Espasa Calpe, pp. 73–111.

Desrochers, P. (2001), 'Geographical proximity and the transmission of tacit knowledge', *The Review of Austrian Economics*, vol. 14, no. 1, pp. 25–46.

DiMaggio, P. J. and Powell, W. W. (1983), 'The iron cage revisited: institutional isomorphism and collective rationality in organizational fields', *American Sociological Review*, vol. 48, no. 2, April, pp. 147–60.

DiMaggio, P. J. and W. W. Powell (1991), 'The iron cage revisited: institutional isomorphism and collective rationality in organizational fields', in W. W. Powell and P. J. DiMaggio (eds), *The New Institutionalism in Organizational Analysis*, Chicago: University of Chicago Press, pp. 63–107.

DiMaggio, P. (1992), 'Nadel's paradox revisited: rational and cultural aspects of organizational structure', in N. Nohria and R. G. Eccles (eds), *Networks and Organizations. Structure, Form and Action*, Boston, Massachusetts: Harvard Business School Press, pp. 118–42.

Dogan, M. (2001), 'Trust–mistrust in European democracies', *Sociologie Românească*, vol. 1, no. 4, pp. 1–19.

Dolado, J. J., González Páramo, J. M. and Roldán, J. M. (1993), 'Convergencia económica entre las provincias españolas: evidencia empírica (1955–1989)', VI Simposio de Moneda y Crédito, November, Madrid.

Domínguez Hidalgo, J. M. (1999), 'Articulación interna de la economía vasca en el periodo 1990–95', available online at http://www.eustat.es/spanish/estad/, EUSTAT, País Vasco.

Dominguez Martín, R. (2002), *La Riqueza de las Regiones. Las Desigualdades Económicas Regionales en España, 1700–2000*, Madrid: Alianza Editorial.

Doreian, P. (1974), 'On the connectivity of social networks', *Journal of Mathematical Sociology*, vol. 3, pp. 245–58.

Doreian, P. (2001), 'Causality in social network analysis', *Social Methods and Research*, vol. 30, no. 1, August, pp. 81–114.

Doreian, P. (2002) 'Event sequences as generators of social network evolution', *Social Networks*, vol. 24, pp. 93–119.

Dorfman, R., Samuelson, P. A. and Solow, R. M. (1958), 'The statistical Leontief system', in R. Dorfman, P. A. Samuelson and R. M. Solow (eds), *Linear Programming and Economic Analysis*, New York: McGraw-Hill, ch. 9.

Dorfman, R., Samuelson, P. A. and Solow, R. M. (1958), 'The statistical Leontief system (continued)', in R. Dorfman, P. A. Samuelson and R. M. Solow (eds), *Linear Programming and Economic Analysis*, New York: McGraw-Hill, ch. 10.

Drejer, I. (1999), 'Comparing patterns of industrial interdependence in national systems of innovation. A study of Germany, Great Britain, Japan and the United States', Druid Summer Conference on National Innovation Systems, Industrial Dynamics and Innovation Policy, June, Rebild, Denmark.

Echebarría Miguel, C. and Larrañaga Sarriegui, M. (1999), 'Análisis y evolución de la estructura productiva y comercial de la industria manufacturera de la CAPV en base a las tablas Input–Output', available online at http://www.eustat.es/spanish/estad/, EUSTAT, País Vasco.

The Economist Intelligence Unit (2000), 'A country of many faces', *The Economist, A Survey of Spain*, 25 November–1 December.

Edquist, C. (ed.) (1997), *Systems of Innovation, Technologies, Institutions and Organisations*, London: Pinter.

Elzo, J., Orizo, F. A., Barreda, M. A., Garmendia, F., Blasco, P. G. and Santacoloma, J. F. (1992), *Euskalerria ante la encuesta europea de valores. ¿Son los vascos diferentes?*, Bilbao: Universidad de Deusto, Deiker.

Emirbayer, M. and Goodwin, J. (1994), 'Network analysis, culture, and the problem of agency', *American Journal of Sociology*, vol. 99, no. 6, May, pp. 1411–54.

Enders, W. and Sandler T. (1996), 'Terrorism and foreign direct investment in Spain and Greece', *Kyklos*, vol. 49, no. 3, pp. 331–52.

EUROSTAT (1988), *Sistema Europeo de Cuentas Económicas Integradas SEC*, Brussels: CECA–CEE–CEEA.

EUSTAT (1998), *Tablas input–output de la comunidad de Euskadi*, EUSTAT, País Vasco.

Evans, P. (1997a), 'Government action, social capital and development: reviewing the evidence on synergy', in P. Evans (ed), *State–Society Synergy: Government and Social Capital in Development*, University of California Press/University of California International and Area Studies Digital Collection, edited volume, 94, pp. 178–209.

Evans, P. (ed.) (1997b), *State–Society Synergy: Government and Social Capital in Development*, University of California Press/University of California International and Area Studies Digital Collection, edited volume, 94.

Everett, M. G. and Borgatti, S. P. (1999), 'Peripheries of cohesive groups', *Social Networks*, vol. 21, pp. 397–407.

Everett, M. and Borgatti, S. P. (1999), 'The centrality of groups and classes', *Journal of Mathematical Sociology*, vol. 23, no. 3, pp. 181–201.

Fararo, T. J. (1989), *The Meaning of General Theoretical Sociology: Tradition and Formalization*, New York: University of Cambridge Press.

Fararo, T. J., Skvoretz, J. and Kosaka, K. (1994), 'Advances in E–state structuralism: further studies in dominance structure formation', *Social Networks*, vol. 16, pp. 233–65.

Feldman, T. R. and Assaf, S. (1999), 'Social capital: conceptual frameworks and empirical evidence. An annotated bibliography', *Social Capital Initiative Working Paper*, no. 5, The World Bank.

Fernández de Pinedo, E. and Fernández, E. (2001), 'De la primera industrialización a la reconversión industrial: la economía vasca entre 1841 y 1990', in L. Germán, E. Llopis, J. Maluquer de Motes and S. Zapata (ed.), *Historia Económica Regional de España Siglos XIX y XX*, Barcelona: Crítica.

Feser, E. J. and Bergman, E. M. (2000), 'National industry cluster templates: a framework for applied regional cluster analysis', *Regional Studies*, vol. 34, no. 1, pp. 1–19.

Flegg, A. T. and Webber, C. D. (2000), 'Regional size, regional specialization and the FLQ formula', *Regional Studies*, vol. 34, no. 6, pp. 563–9.

Florax, R. J. G. M., de Groot, H. L. F. and Heijungs, R. (2002), 'The empirical economic growth literature: robustness, significance and size', *Tinbergen Institute Discussion Paper*, no. TI 2002–040/3.

Flury, B. (1988), *Common Principal Components and Related Multivariate Models*, New York: John Wiley & Son.

Fontela, E., López, A. and Pulido, A. (2000), 'Structural comparison of input–output tables', 13th International Conference on input–output techniques, August, Macerata, Italy.

Francois, P. and Zabojnik, J. (2002), 'Trust as social capital and the process of economic development', available online at http://www.econlubc.ca/asiwan/542hmpg.htm.

Freeman, L. C., Fararo, T. J., Bloomberg Jr., W. and Sunshine, M. H. (1963), 'Locating leaders in local communities: a comparison of some alternative approaches', *American Sociological Review*, October, vol. 28, no. 5, pp. 791–8.

Freeman, L. C. (1992), 'The sociological concept of "group": an empirical test of two models', *American Journal of Sociology*, vol. 98, no. 1, July, pp. 152–66.

Freeman, L. C. (1996), 'Some antecedents of social network analysis', *Connections*, vol. 19, pp. 39–42.

Freeman, L. C. (1997), 'Uncovering organizational hierarchies', *Computational and Organizational Theory*, vol. 3, no. 1, pp. 5–18.

Freije, I. and Aláez, M. A. (1998), 'Goizper. La visión estratégica o de largo plazo: la carrera de fondo', País Vasco: Cluster del Conocimiento.

Friedman, M. (1953), *Essays in Positive Economics*, Chicago: University of Chicago Press.

Fukuyama, F. (2000), 'Social capital and civil society', *IMF Working Paper*, 00/74.

Fukuyama, F. (2001), 'Culture and economic development: cultural concerns', International Encyclopedia of the Social Behavioral Sciences, Amsterdam: Elsevier.

Fundación BBV (1999), *Renta Nacional de España y su Distribución Provincial. Serie Homogénea Años 1955 a 1993 y avances 1994 a 1998*, Bilbao: Síntesis.

Fundación Vasca para la Calidad (2001), *Irizar-European Quality Prize EFQM 2000*, País Vasco: Fundación Vasca para la Calidad.

Fundación Vasca para la Calidad (2002), *Avanzando hacia la excelencia: 12 ejemplos prácticos del País Vasco*, País Vasco: Fundación Vasca para la Calidad.

García Delgado, J. L. (ed.) (1999), *Estructura Económica de Madrid*, Madrid: Civitas.

García Delgado, J. L. and Carrera Troyano, M. (2001), 'Madrid, capital económica', in L. Germán, E. Llopis, J. Maluquer de Motes and S. Zapata (eds), *Historia Económica Regional de España Siglos XIX y XX*, Barcelona: Crítica.

García Greciano, B. and Raymond, J. L. (1999), 'Las disparidades regionales y la hipótesis de convergencia: una revisión', *Papeles de Economía Española*, vol. 80, pp. 2–18.

García Milá, T. and Marimon, R. (1999), 'Crecimiento de las regiones españolas: estructura sectorial, dinámica regional y distribución de rentas', *Economic Working Paper*, no. 228, Universitat Pompeu Fabra.

García Milá, T. and McGuire T. (1996), 'Do interregional transfers improve the economic performance of poor regions? The case of Spain', *Economic Working Paper*, no. 207, Universitat Pompeu Fabra.

García Montoya, M. A., Zárraga Castro, A. and Castro Iñigo, B. (1999), 'Relaciones intersectoriales en la C. A. de Euskadi en base a las tablas Input–Output 1995: Análisis factorial y comparación con los resultados de 1990', available online at http://www.eustat.es/spanish/estad/, EUSTAT, País Vasco.

Garofoli, G. (ed.) (1992), *Endogenous Development and Southern Europe*, Aldershot: Avebury.

Garrido Espinosa, P. and Garcia Olea, M. V. (1999), 'La dependencia exterior vasca en el periodo 1990–1995', available online at http://www.eustat.es/spanish/estad/, EUSTAT, País Vasco.

Gibson, J. L. (2001), 'Social networks, civil society, and prospects for consolidating Russia's democratic transition', *American Journal of Political Science*, vol. 45, no. 1, pp. 51–68.

Glaeser, E. L., Laibson, D. I., Scheinkman, J. A. and Soutter, C. L. (2000), 'Measuring trust', *Quarterly Journal of Economics*, vol. 115, no. 3, pp. 811–46.

Gnanadesikan, R. (1977), *Methods for Statistical Data Analysis of Multivariate Observations*, New York: John Wiley & Son.

Goerlich, F. J. and Mas, M. (1999), 'Medición de la desigualdad: contribución a una base de datos regional', *IVIE Documento de Trabajo*, Instituto Valenciano de Investigaciones Económicas.

Gould, R. V. (1987), 'Measures of betweenness in non-symmetric networks', *Social Networks*, vol. 9, pp. 277–82.

Granovetter, M. (1973), 'The strength of weak ties', *American Journal of Sociology*, vol. 81, pp. 1287– 303.

Granovetter, M. (1985), 'Economic action and social structure: the problem of embeddedness', *American Journal of Sociology*, vol. 91, no. 3, November, pp. 481–510.

Granovetter, M. (2005), 'The impact of social structure on economic outcomes', *Journal of Economic Perspectives*, vol. 19, no. 1, pp. 33–50.

Grootaert, C. (1998), 'Social capital: the missing link?', *Social Capital Initiative Working Paper*, no. 3, World Bank, p. 15.

Grootaert, C. (1999), 'Social capital, household welfare and poverty in Indonesia', *Policy Research Working Paper*, no. 2148, World Bank Social Development Department.

Guang-Zhen, S. and Yew-Kwang, N. (2000), 'The measurement of structural differences between economies: an axiomatic characterization', *Economic Theory*, vol. 16, pp. 313–21.

Gulati, R. (1995), 'Does familiarity breed trust? The implications of repeated ties for contractual choice in alliances', Special research forum: Intra and inter organizational cooperation, *Academy of Management Journal*, vol. 38.

Harrigan, F., McGilvray, J. and McNicoll, I. (1980), 'A comparison of regional and national technical structures', *Economic Journal*, vol. 90, no. 360, December, pp. 795–810.

Harris, R. I. D. and Liu, A. (1998), 'Input–output modelling of the urban and regional economy: the importance of external trade', *Regional Studies*, vol. 32, no. 9, pp. 851–62.

Harrison, B. (1992), 'Industrial districts: old wine in new bottles?', *Regional Studies*, vol. 26, no. 5, pp. 469–83.

Hazari, B. R. (1970), 'Empirical identification of key sectors in the Indian economy', *The Review of Economics and Statistics*, vol. 52, no. 3, August, pp. 301–5.

Healy, T. (2001), 'Networks and social norms can be good for business: the role of social capital in organisations', EURESCO Conference on Social Capital, University of Exeter, September.

Hedström, P. and Swedberg, R. (1998), 'Social mechanisms: an introductory essay', in P. Hedström and R. Swedberg (eds), *Social Mechanisms: An Analytic Approach to Social Theory*, Cambridge: Cambridge University Press, pp. 1–31.

Helliwell, J. F. (1996), 'Economic growth and social capital in Asia', *NBER Working Papers*, no. 5470, National Buerau of Economic Research, Inc.

Helliwell, J. F. and Putnam, R. D. (1995), 'Social capital and economic growth in Italy', *Eastern Economic Journal*, vol. 21, no. 3, pp. 295–307.

Helliwell, J. F. (ed) (2001), *The Contribution of Human and Social Capital to Sustained Economic Growth and Well-being*, Ottawa, Canada: HRDC and OECD.

Henderson, D. (1995), *Innovation and Technology Support Infrastructure in Wales*, Centre for Advanced Studies in the Social Sciences, Cardiff: University of Wales.

Hewings, G. J. D. (1982), 'The empirical identification of key sectors in an economy: a regional perspective', *The Developing Economies*, vol. XX, no. 2, June, pp. 173–95.

Hirschman, A. (1958), 'Interregional and international transmission of economic growth', in A. Hirschman (ed), *The Strategy of Economic Development*, New York: W. W. Norton, ch. 6.

Hirschman, A. O. (1959), 'Interdependence and industrialization', in A. O. Hirschman (ed.), *The Strategy of Economic Development*, New Haven: Yale University Press, ch. 6.

Hjøllund, L. and Svendsen, G. T. (2000), 'Social capital: a standard method of measurement', *Working Paper*, 00–9, Aarhus School of Business, Department of Economics.

Hubbell, C. H. (1965), 'An input–output approach to clique identification', *Sociometry*, vol. 28, pp. 377–99.

Hudson, R. (1997), 'Regional futures: industrial restructuring, new high volume production concepts and spatial development strategies in the new Europe', *Regional Studies*, vol. 31, no. 5, pp. 467–78.

Hummon, N. P. and Fararo, T. J. (1995), 'Assessing hierarchy and balance in dynamic networks', *Journal of Mathematical Sociology*, vol. 21, pp. 145–59.

Iacobucci, D. (1994), 'Graphs and matrices', in S. Wasserman and K. Faust (eds), *Social Network Analysis. Methods and Applications*, Cambridge: Cambridge University Press, ch. 4.

Idígoras, I. and Mitxeo, J. (1998), 'Batz, S. Coop. El reto de la tecnología y la calidad en una empresa internacional', País Vasco: Cluster del Conocimiento.

INE (1984), *Clasificación Nacional de Actividades Económicas Año 1974*, Madrid: INE.

INE (1993), *Clasificación Nacional de Actividades Económicas 1993 (CNAE–93)*, Madrid: INE.

INE (1994), *Estadística sobre las actividades en investigación científica y desarrollo tecnológico (I+D) 1991*, Madrid: INE.

INE (2002), *Anuario estadístico de España 2001*, Madrid: INE.

INE (2003), *Estadística sobre las actividades en investigación científica y desarrollo tecnológico (I+D) 2001*, Madrid: INE.

Inglehart, R. and Baker, W. E. (2000), 'Modernization, cultural change and the persistence of traditional values', *American Sociological Review*, vol. 65, February, pp. 19–51.

Instituto de Estadística de Andalucía (1998), *Sistema de Cuentas de Andalucía. Marco Input–Output*, Andalucía: Instituto de Estadística.

Isaksen, A. (1996), 'Regional clusters and competitiveness: the Norwegian case', no. 199616, *STEP Report*, Oslo.

Isaksen, A. (1998), 'Regionalisation and regional clusters as development strategies in a global economy', no. 199801, *STEP Report*, Oslo.

Israd, W. and Smolensky, E. (1963), 'Application of input–output techniques to regional science', in T. Barna (ed), *Structural Interdependence and Economic Development*, London: Macmillan.

Johannisson, B. (2002), 'Entrepreneurship in Scandinavia. Bridging individualism and collectivism', *Enrepreneurship/SIREC (Scandinavian Institute for Research in Entrepreneurship)*, Vaxjo University, available online at www.ehv.vxn. se/forskn/entreprofil/ entrepreneurship%20in% scandinavia. pdf.

Johnson, J. C., Boster, J. S. and Palinkas L. (2003), 'Social roles and the evolution of networks in isolated and extreme environments', *Journal of Mathematical Sociology*, vol. 27, nos. 2–3, pp. 89–122.

Jones, C., Hesterly, W. S. and Borgatti, S. P. (1997), 'A general theory of network governance: exchange conditions and social mechanisms', available online at http://www.analytictech.com/borgatti/oppamr6z.htm.

Jones, L. P. (1976), 'The measurement of Hirschmanian linkages', *Quarterly Journal of Economics*, vol. 90, no. 2, May, pp. 323–33.

Judd, C. M., Smith, E. R. And Kidder, L. H. (2001), *Research Methods in Social Relations*, 7th edn, London: Wadsworth Publishing.

Kasmir, S. (1996), *The Myth of Mondragon. Cooperatives, Politics and Working-Class Life in a Basque Town*, Albany, NY: State University of New York Press.

Kilduff, M. and Krackhardt, D. (1994), 'Bringing the individual back in: a structural analysis of the internal market for reputation in organizations', *Academy of Management Journal*, vol. 37, no. 1, pp. 87–108.

Knack, S. and Keefer, P. (1997), 'Does social capital have an economic payoff? A cross-country investigation', *Quarterly Journal of Economics*, November, pp. 1251–88.

Knack, S. (2001), 'Trust, associational life and economic performance in the OECD', in OECD (ed.), *The Contribution of Human and Social Capital to Sustained Economic Growth and Well-being*, Ottawa, Canada: HRDC and OECD, ch. 9.

Krackhardt, D. (1992), 'The strength of strong ties: the importance of philos in organizations', in N. Nohria and R. G. Eccles (eds), *Networks in Organizations. Structure, Form and Actions*, Boston: Harvard Business School Press.

Krackhardt, D. and Hanson, J. R. (1993), 'Informal networks: the company', *Harvard Business Review*, vol. 71, no. 4, July–August, pp. 104–11.

Kraut, R. E., Rice, R. E., Cool, C. and Fish, R. S. (1998), 'Varieties of social influence: the role of utility and norms in the success of a new communication medium', *Organizations Science*, vol. 9, no. 4, July–August, pp. 437–53.

Kremen Bolton, M., Malmrose, R. and Ouchi, W. G. (1994), 'The organization of innovation in the United States and Japan: neoclassical and relational contracting', *Journal of Management Studies*, vol. 31, no. 5, September, pp. 653–79.

Krishna, A. and Uphoff, N. (1999), 'Mapping and measuring social capital: a conceptual and empirical study of collective action for conserving and developing watersheds in Rajasthan, India', *Social Capital Initiative Working Paper*, no. 13, The World Bank, Washington.

Krugman, P. (1995), *Development, Geography and Economic Theory*, Cambridge: MIT.

Kvale, S. (1996), *Interviews: An Introduction to Qualitative Research Interviewing*, London: Sage.

La Porta, R., López de Silanes, F., Shleifer, A. and Vishny, R. (1997), 'Trust in large organizations', *American Economic Review Papers and Proceedings*, vol. 87, no. 2, pp. 333–8.

La Porta, R., López de Silanes, F., Shleifer, A. and Vishny, R. (2000), 'Trust in large organizations', in P. Dasgupta and I. Serageldin (eds*)*, *Social Capital. A Multifaceted Perspective*, Washington: The World Bank, pp. 310–9.

Lacomba, J. A. (1993), 'Desde los inicios de la industrialización al plan de estabilización de 1959', in M. Martínez Rodríguez (ed.), *Estructura Económica de Andalucía*, Madrid: Espasa Calpe, pp. 21–72.

Lahr, M. L. and E. Dietzenbacher (2001), *Input–Output Analysis: Frontiers and Extensions*, New York: Palgrave.

Landry, R., Amara, N. and Lamari, M. (2001), 'Social capital, innovation and public policy', *Isuma*, vol. 2, no. 1, Spring.

Lantner, R. (2001), 'Influence graph theory applied to structural analysis', in M. L. Lahr and E. Dietzenbacher (eds), *Input–Output Analysis: Frontiers and Extensions*, New York: Palgrave, ch. 15.

Larrea Aranguren, M. (1999), 'Evolución de las economías de localización de los sistemas productivos locales de la CAPV', available online at http://www.eustat.es/spanish/estad/, EUSTAT, País Vasco.

Laumas, P. S. (1976), 'The weighting problem in testing the linkage hypothesis', *Quarterly Journal of Economics*, vol. 90, no. 2, May, pp. 308–12.

Lawson, C. (1999), 'Towards a competence theory of the region', *Cambridge Journal of Economics*, vol. 23, no. 2, March, pp. 151–66.

Lenski, G. and Nolan, P. D. (1984), 'Trajectories of development: a test of ecological–evolutionary theory', *Social Forces*, vol. 63, pp. 1–23.

Leoncini, R. and Montresor, S. (2000), 'Network analysis of eight technological systems', *International Review of Applied Economics*, vol. 14, no. 2, pp. 213–34.

Leontief, W. (1951), 'Input–output economics', in W. Leontief (1986), *Input–Output Economics*, 2nd ed., Oxford: Oxford University Press, reprinted, ch. 1.

Leontief, W. (1967), 'An alternative to aggregation in input–output analysis and national accounts', *Review of Economics and Statistics*, vol. 49, no. 3, August, pp. 412–9.

Leontief, W. (ed.) (1977), *Structure, System and Economic policy*, Cambridge: Cambridge University Press.

Leontief, W. (1985), 'Input–output analysis', in W. Leontief (1986), *Input–Output Economics*, 2nd edn, Oxford: Oxford University Press, reprinted, ch. 2.

Leontief, W. (1986), *Input–Output Economics*, 2nd edn, Oxford: Oxford University Press.

Levine, J. (1972), 'The sphere of influence', *American Sociological Review*, vol. 37, pp. 14–27.

Levine, J. (1985), *Atlas of Corporate Interlocks*, Hanover, NH: Worldnet.

Levine, J. (1987), 'The methodology of the atlas of corporate interlocks', *Bulletin de Méthodologie Sociologique*, vol. 17, pp. 20–58.

Leydesdorff, L. (1991), 'The static and dynamic analysis of network data using information theory', *Social Networks*, vol. 13, pp. 301–45.

Lin, N., Ensel, W. M. and Vaughn, J. C. (1981), 'Social resources and strength of ties: structural factors in occupational status attainment', *American Sociological Review*, vol. 46, no. 4, August, pp. 393–405.

Lin, N. (1999), 'Building a network theory of social capital', *Connections*, vol. 22, no. 1, pp. 28–51.

Lipshitz, G. and Ravem, A. (1998), 'Socio-economic differences among localities: a new method of multivariate analysis', *Regional Studies*, vol. 32, no. 8, pp. 747–57.

López Martínez, M. (1995), *Análisis de la industria agroalimentaria 1978–1989*, Madrid: Serie Estudios, Ministerio de Agricultura, Pesca y Alimentación, Secretaría General Técnica.

Lundvall, B.-A. (1992*), National Systems of Innovation: Toward a Theory of Innovation and Interactive Learning*, London: Pinter.

Lutz, M. A. (1997), 'The Mondragon co-operative complex: an application of Kantian ethics to social economics', *International Journal of Social Economics*, vol. 24, no. 2, pp. 1404–21.

Maddigan, R. J. (1981), 'The measurement of vertical integration', *Review of Economics and Statistics*, vol. 63, no. 3, August, pp. 328–35.

Maillat, D. and Grosjean, N. (1999), 'Globalisation and territorial production systems', *Working Papers, Université de Neuchatel*, December, no. 9906b.

Maravall, F. and Pérez Prim, J. M. (1975), 'Cambio estructural y crecimiento económico: un análisis del caso español (1962–1970)', *Fundación del Instituto Nacional de Industria, Programa de Investigaciones Económicas, Serie E*, no. 4, Madrid.

Markovsky, B., Patton, T. and Willer, D. (1988), 'Power relations in exchange networks', *American Sociological Review*, vol. 53, April, pp. 220–36.

Martín, C., Romero, L. R. and Segura, J. (1981), 'Cambios en la estructura interindustrial española (1962–1975)', *Fundación del Instituto Nacional de Industria, Programa de Investigaciones Económicas, Serie E*, no. 16, Madrid.

Martínez Rodríguez, M. (ed.) (1993), *Estructura Económica de Andalucía*, Madrid: Espasa Calpe.

Mas, M., Maudos, J., Pérez, F. and Uriel, E. (1994), 'Disparidades regionales y convergencia en las comunidades autónomas', *Revista de Economía Aplicada*, vol. II, no. 4, pp. 129–48.

McCann, P. and Dewhurst, J. H. L. (1998), 'Regional size, industrial location and input–output expenditure coefficients', *Regional Studies*, vol. 32, no. 5, pp. 435–44.

McEvoy, B. and L. C. Freeman (1987), *UCINET: A Microcomputer Package for Network Analysis*, Irvine, CA: University of California.

McGilvray, J. W. (1977), 'Linkages, key sectors and development strategy', in W. Leontief (ed.), *Structure, System and Economic Policy*, Cambridge University Press, pp. 49–56.

Ministerio de Educación (2002), *Estadística de las Enseñanzas no Universitarias*, Madrid: Ministerio de Educación.

Mintz, B. and Schwartz, M. (1981a), 'The structure of intercorporate unity in American business', *Social Problems*, vol. 29, pp. 87–103.

Mintz, B. and Schwartz, M. (1981b), 'Interlocking directorates and interest group formation', *American Sociological Review*, vol. 46, pp. 851–69.

Moesen, W., Van Puyenbroeck, T. and Cherchye, L. (2000), 'Trust as societal capital: economic growth in European regions', *Centre for Economic Studies Working Paper, February 2000*, Belgium: Catholic University of Louvain.

Monge, P. R. and Contractor, N. S. (2004), 'Emergence of communication networks', in F. M. Jablin and L. Putnam (eds), *The New Handbook of Organizational Communication: Advances in Theory, Research and Methods*, London: Sage Publications, ch. 12.

Morgan, K. (1997), 'The learning region: institutions, innovation and regional renewal', *Regional Studies*, vol. 31, no. 5, pp. 491–503.

Morgan, K. (1997), 'The regional animateur: taking stock of the Welsh development agency', *Regional and Federal Studies*, vol. 7, no. 2, pp. 70–94.

Morgan, M. S. (1997), 'Searching for causal relations in economic statistics: reflections from history', in V. R. Mackin and S. Turner (eds), *Causality in Crisis: Statistical Methods and the Search for Causal Knowledge in Social Sciences*, Notre Dame, IN: University of Notre Dame Press, pp. 47–80.

Mullins, N. C., Hargens, L. L., Hecht, P. K. and Kick, E. L. (1977), 'The group structure of citation clusters: a comparative study', *American Sociological Review*, vol. 42, August, pp. 552–62.

Muñoz Cidad, C. (1992), *Estructura Económica Internacional. Introducción al Crecimiento Económico Moderno*, Madrid: Civitas.

Narayan, D. and Pritchett, L. (1997), 'Cents and sociability: household income and social capital in rural Tanzania', *Policy Research Working Paper* 1796, July, World Bank.

Nelson, R. (1995), 'The agenda of growth theory: a different point of view', in J. de la Mothe and G. Paquet (eds), *Technology, Trade and the New Economy*, Programme of Research in International Management and Economy, University of Ottowa, ch. 1.

Nemeth, R. J. and Smith, D. A. (1985), 'International trade and world–system structure, a multiple network analysis', *Review: A Journal of the Fernand Braudel Center*, vol. 8, pp. 517–60.

Newcomb, T. M. (1961), *The Acquaintance Process*, New York: Holt, Rinehart and Winston.

Newton, K. and Norris, P. (2000), 'Confidence in public institutions: faith, culture or performance?', in S. J. Pharr and R. D. Putnam (eds), *Disaffected Democracies: What's Troubling the Trilateral Countries?*, Princeton: Princeton University Press, ch. 3.

Nielsen, K. (2000), 'Social capital and systemic competitiveness', *Research Paper Network Institutional Theory*, no. 2/00, Roskilde University.

Nielsen, K. (2003), 'Social capital and innovation policy', *Research Paper Network Institutional Theory*, no. 10/03, Roskilde University.

Nohria, N. (1992), 'Is a network perspective a useful way of studying organizations?', in N. Nohria and R. Eccles (eds), *Networks and Organizations. Structure, Form and Action*, Boston, Massachusetts: Harvard Business School Press, pp. 1–22.

Nolan, P. D. (1983), 'Status in the world economy and national structure and development', *International Journal of Comparative Sociology*, vol. 24, pp. 109–20.

Nolan, P. D. (1987), 'World system status, income inequality, and economic growth: a criticism of recent criticism', *International Journal of Comparative Sociology*, vol. 28, pp. 69–76.

Nolan, P. D. (1988), 'World system status, techno-economic heritage, and fertility', *Sociological Focus*, vol. 21, pp. 9–33.

Norris, P. (2003), 'Social capital and ICTs: widening or reinforcing social networks', International Forum on Social Capital for Economic Revival, March, Tokyo.

OECD (2001a), *The Well-being of Nations. The Role of Human and Social Capital*, Paris: OECD.

OECD (2001b), *Classification des Secteurs et des Produits de Haute Technologie*, Paris: OECD.

Oh, H., Chung, M-H. and Labianca, G. (2004), 'Group social capital and group effectiveness: the role of informal socializing ties', *Academy of Management Journal*, vol. 47, pp. 860–75.

Osberg, L. and Sharpe, A. (2000), 'Comparison of trends in GDP and economic well-being. The impact of social capital', Symposium on the Contribution of Human and Social Capital to Sustained Economic Growth and Well-Being, March, Quebec.

Osberg, L. (ed), (2003). *The Economic Implications of Social Cohesion*, Toronto: University of Toronto Press.

Ouchi, W. G. (1980), 'Markets, bureaucracies and clans', *Administrative Science Quarterly*, vol. 25, no. 1, March, pp. 129–41.

Padulo, L. and Arbib, M. (1974), System Theory: *A Unified State–Space Approach to Continuous and Discrete Systems*, Philadelphia: W. B. Saunders.

Palazuelos, E. (2000), *Contenido y Método de la Economía Mundial*, Madrid: Akal.

Palmer, D., Friedland, R. and Singh, J. V. (1986), 'The ties that bind: organizational and class bases of stability in a corporate interlock network', *American Sociological Review*, vol. 51, pp. 781–96.

Parejo Barranco, A. (1997), *La Producción Industrial de Andalucía (1830–1935)*, Seville: Instituto de Desarrollo Regional.

Peeters, L., Tiri, M. and Berwert, A. (2001), 'Identification of techno-economic clusters using input–output data: application to Flanders and Switzerland', *CEST* 2001/9, July, Centre for Science and Technology Studies, Switzerland.

Pérez, P. (2000), 'Dinámica de las regiones en España (1955–1995)', *Revista de Economía Aplicada*, vol. VIII, no. 22, pp. 155–73.

Pérez García, F. (ed.) (2005), *La Medición del Capital Social. Una Aproximación Económica*, Madrid: Fundación BBVA.

Perroux, F. (1972), I*ndependencia de la Economía Nacional e Interdependencia de las Naciones*, Madrid: ICE.

Perroux, F. (1984), *El Desarrollo y la Nueva Concepción de la Dinámica Económica*, Barcelona: Serbal.

Perrow, C. (1992), 'Small-firm networks', in N. Nohria and R. G. Eccles (eds), *Networks and Organizations. Structure, Form and Action*. Boston, Massachusetts: Harvard Business School Press, ch. 17.

Pfeffer, J. and Salancik, G. (1978), *The External Control of Organizations*, New York: Harper and Row.

Porter, M. (1996), 'Competitive advantage, agglomeration economies and regional policy', *International Regional Science Review*, vol. 19, nos. 1–2.

Porter, M. E. (2003), 'The economic performance of regions', *Regional Studies*, vol. 37, no. 67, pp. 549–78.

Prado Valle, C. (1999), 'Cambios de las relaciones de la industria y los servicios en la economía vasca durante el periodo 1985–1995: Terciarización de la economía e integración de los servicios', available online at http://www.eustat.es/spanish/estad/, EUSTAT, País Vasco.

Prado Valle, C. and González Gómez, N. (2001), 'Análisis de la dimensión económica de la nueva economía en la CAPV', *Ekonomi Gerizan*, no. 9.

Pryor, F. L. (1996), *Economic Evolution and Structure: The Impact of Complexity on the U.S. Economic System*, Cambridge: Cambridge University Press.

Pulido, A. (ed.) (2000), *Informe Sobre la Evolución del Empleo en España Ante las Nuevas Tecnologías*, Madrid: Instituto Kelin, UAM Centro de Predicción Económica (CEPREDE).

Putnam, R. (1993), 'The prosperous community', *The American Prospect Online*, vol. 4, no. 13, 21 March, available online at http://www.prospect.org/print/V4/13/putnam–r.html.

Putnam, R. D. (1995), 'Bowling alone: America's declining social capital', *Journal of Democracy*, vol. 6, pp. 65–78.

Putnam, R. D. (2000), *Bowling Alone: The Collapse and Revival of American Community*, New York: Simon and Schuster.

Putnam, R. D. (2001), 'Social capital measurement and consequences', *Isuma*, vol. 2, no. 1, Spring.

Putnam, R. D. (ed.) (2002), *Democracies in Flux: The Evolution of Social Capital in Contemporary Society*, Oxford: Oxford University Press.

Putnam, R. D. and Goss, K. A. (2002), 'Introduction', in R. D. Putnam (ed.), *Democracies in Flux: The Evolution of Social Capital in Contemporary Society*, Oxford: Oxford University Press.

Ramaswamy, S., Kelly, T. and Isham, J. (eds) (2002), *Social Capital, Economic Development and the Environment*, Cheltenham, UK and Northampton, MA, USA: Edward Elgar Publishing.

Rasmussen P. N. (1956), 'Structural analysis: theory', *Studies in Inter-Sectoral Relations*, Kbenhavn: Einar Harcks Forlag, ch. 8.

Rasmussen P. N. (1956), 'Structural analysis: empirical findings', *Studies in inter–sectoral relations*, Kbenhavn: Einar Harcks Forlag, ch. 9.

Raymond, J. L. and García, B. (1994), 'Las disparidades en el PIB per capita entre comunidades autónomas y la hipótesis de convergencia', *Papeles de Economía Española*, no. 59, pp. 37–58.

Redman, J. M. (1994), *Understanding State Economies Through Industry Studies*, Washington: Council of Governors' Policy Advisors.

Riedel, J. (1976), 'A balanced-growth version of the linkage hypothesis: a comment', *Quarterly Journal of Economics*, vol. 90, no. 2, May, pp. 319–22.

Rodero Cosano, J., Martínez López, D. and Pérez Sánchez, R. (2003), 'Convergencia entre Andalucía y España: una aproximación a sus causas (1965–1995). ¿Afecta la inversión pública al crecimiento?', *Documento de Trabajo*, E2003/05, Fundación Centro de Estudios Andaluces.

Roepke, H., Adams, D. and Wiseman, R. (1974), 'A new approach to the identification of industrial complexes using input–output data', *Journal of Regional Science*, vol. 14, no. 1, pp. 15–29.

Romer, P. (1994), 'The origins of endogenous growth', *Journal of Economic Perspectives*, vol. 8, no. 1, pp. 3–22.

Rosenfeld, S. (1995), *Industrial Strength Strategies: Regional Business Clusters and Public Policy*, Washington: Aspen Institute.

Routledge, B. R. and von Ambsberg, J. (2003), 'Social capital and growth', *Journal of Monetary Economics*, vol. 50, no. 1, pp. 167–93.

Sáez, F. (1993), 'Cambio técnico, procesos productivos y factor trabajo. Un análisis económico del caso español', *Economía Industrial*, no. 289, January – February.

Sampedro, J. L. and Martinez Cortiña, R. (1973), *Estructura Económica. Teoría Básica y Estructura Mundial*, 3rd edn, Madrid: Ariel.

Sampson, S. F. (1968), 'A novitiate in a period of change: an experimental and case study of social relationships', PhD thesis, Cornell University, Ithaca, NY.

Santamaría Martínez, M. P., Redondo Mediavilla, M. J. and Caminero Martín, E. (1999), 'Análisis del sistema agroalimentario vasco. Una aproximación a través de las tablas input–output 85–90–95'; available online at http://www.eustat.es/spanish/estad/, EUSTAT, País Vasco.

Saxenian, A. (1994), *Regional Advantage: Culture and Competition in Silicon Valley and Route 128*, Cambridge, MA: Harvard University Press.

Schnabl, H. (2001), 'Structural development of Germany, Japan and the USA, 1980–90: a qualitative analysis using Minimal Flow Analysis (MFA)', in M. L. Lahr and E. Dietzenbacher (eds), *Input–Output Analysis: Frontiers and Extensions*, New York: Palgrave, pp. 245–67.

Schultz, S. (1977), 'Approaches to identifying key sectors empirically by means of input–output analysis', *Journal of Development Studies*, vol. 14, no. 1, October, pp. 77–96.

Scott, J. (1987), 'Intercorporate structure in Western Europe', in M. S. Mizruchi and M. Schwartz (ed.), *Intercorporate Relations: The Structural Analysis of Business*, Cambridge: Cambridge University Press, pp. 208–32.

Scott, J. (1991), *Social Network Analysis. A Handbook*, London: Sage.

Scott, M. (1984), 'The history of the theory of the firm from Marshall to Robinson and Chamberlin: the source of positivism in Economics', *Economica*, new series, vol. 51, no. 203, pp. 307–18.

Segura, J. and Restoy, F. (1986), *Una explotación de las tablas input–output de la economía española para 1975 y 1980*, Madrid: Fundación Empresa Pública, Programa de Investigaciones Económicas, Documento de trabajo 8608.

Skidmore, D. (2000), 'Civil society, social capital and economic development', *Columbia International Affairs Online, CIAO*, Date 9/00.

Smith, D. and White, D. (1992), 'Structure and dynamics of the global economy: network analysis of international trade 1965–1980', *Social Forces*, vol. 70, p. 857–93.

Snyder, D. and Kick, E. (1979), 'Structural position in the world system and economic growth 1955–70: a multiple network analysis of transnational interactions', *American Journal of Sociology*, vol. 84, pp. 1096–1126.

Stephenson, K. and Zelen, M. (1989), 'Rethinking centrality: methods and applications', *Social Networks*, vol. 11, pp. 1–37.

Stinchcombe, A. L. (1998), 'Monopolistic competition as a mechanism: corporations, universities and nation-states in competitive fields', in P. Hedström and R. Swedberg (eds), *Social Mechanisms: An Analytic Approach to Social Theory*, Cambridge: Cambridge University Press, pp. 267–305.

Stokman, F. N. and Wasseur, F. W. (1985), 'National networks in 1976: a structural comparison', in F. N. Stokman, R. Ziegler and J. Scott (eds), *Networks of Corporate Power: A Comparative Analysis of Ten Countries*, Cambridge: Polity.

Storper, M. and Harrison, B. (1991), 'Flexibility, hierarchy and regional development: the changing structure of industrial production systems and their forms of governance in the 1990s', *Research Policy*, vol. 20, pp. 407–22.

Storper, M. (1995), 'Regional technology coalitions. An essential dimension of national technology policy', *Research Policy*, vol. 24, pp. 895–911.

Storper, M. and Scott, A. J. (1995), 'The wealth of regions. Market forces and policy imperatives in local and global context', *Futures*, vol. 27, no. 5, pp. 505–26.

Storper, M. (1997), *The Regional World: Territorial Development in a Global Economy*, New York: Guilford Press.

Storper, M., Chen, Y. and De Paolis, F. (2000), 'The effects of globalization on location of industries in the OECD and European Union', *DRUID Working Paper*, no. 00–7, February.

Strassert, G. G. (2001), 'Interindustry linkages: the flow network of a physical input–output table (PIOT): theory and application for Germany', in M. L. Lahr and E. Dietzenbacher (eds), *Input–Output Analysis: Frontiers and Extensions*, New York: Palgrave, ch. 2.

Streit, M. E. (1969), 'Spatial associations and economic linkages between industries', *Journal of Regional Science*, vol. 9, no. 2, pp. 177–88.

Tassey, G. (1991), 'The functions of technology infrastructure in a competitive economy', *Research Policy*, vol. 20, pp. 345–61.

Teece, D. (1981), 'The market for know-how and the efficient international transfer of technology', *Annals, American Academy of Political and Social Sciences*, vol. 458, pp. 81–96.

Thorelli, H. B. (1986), 'Networks: between markets and hierarchies', *Strategic Management Journal*, vol. 7, pp. 37–52.

Tichy, N. M., Tushman, M. L. and Fombrun, C. (1979), 'Social network analysis for organizations', *Academy of Management Review*, vol. 4, pp. 507–19.

Tomlinson, M. (1997), 'The contribution of services to manufacturing industry: beyond deindustrialised debate', *CRIC Discussion Paper*, no. 5.

Travers, J. and Milgram S. (1969), 'An experimental study of the small world problem', *Sociometry*, vol. 32, no. 4, December, pp. 425–43.

Trigilia, C. (2001), 'Social capital and local development', *European Journal of Social Theory*, vol. 4, no. 4, pp. 427–42.

Trincado, I. and Etxabe, A. M. (1998), *Orkli. El compromiso de un colectivo con su proyecto socio-empresarial*, País Vasco: Cluster del Conocimiento.

Tsai, W. (2000), 'Social capital, strategic relatedness and the formation of intraorganizational linkages', *Strategic Management Journal*, vol. 21, pp. 925–39.

Uslaner, E. M. (2003), 'Trust in the knowledge society', International Forum on Social Capital for Economic Revival, March, Tokyo.

Uzzi, B. (1996), 'The sources and consequences of embeddedness for the economic performance of organizations: the network effect', *American Sociological Review*, vol. 61, August, pp. 674–98.

Van Schaik, T. (2002), 'Social capital in the European values study surveys', International Conference on Social Capital Measurement, September, London.

Vivarelli, M. (1997), *The Economics of Technology and Employment: Theory and Empirical Evidence*, Cheltenham, UK and Lyme, USA: Edward Elgar.

Wasserman, S. and Pattison, P. (1996), 'Logit models and logistic regressions for social networks: an introduction to Markov graphs and $p$', *Psychometrika*, vol. 61, pp. 401–25.

Wasserman, S. and Faust, K. (1994), *Social Network Analysis, Methods and Applications*, Cambridge: Cambridge University Press.

Watts, D. J. (1999), 'Networks, dynamics, and the small-world phenomenon', *American Journal of Sociology*, vol. 105, no. 2, September, pp. 493–527.

Whiteley, P. F. (2000), 'Economic growth and social capital', *Political Studies*, vol. 48, pp. 443–66.

Wilkinson, F. (1983), 'Productive systems', *Cambridge Journal of Economics*, vol. 7, nos. 3/4, September/December, pp. 413–29.

Williamson, O. E. (1983), *Markets and Hierarchies. Analysis and Antitrust Implications. A Study in the Economics of Internal Organization*, New York: The Free Press.

Wolfe, D. A. (2000), 'Social capital and cluster development in learning regions', *ISRN Working Paper*, 2000–8, University of Toronto.

Woolcock, M. (2001), 'The place of social capital in understanding social and economic outcomes', in J. Helliwell (ed.), *The Role of Human Capital and Social Capital in Economic Growth and Well–being*, Paris: OECD and HRDC, ch. 5.

World Bank Group (2003), 'Social capital and development', available online at http://www.iris.umd.edu/socat/concept/concept.htm.

Yli-Renko, H., Autio, E., Sapienza, H. J. and Hay, M. (1999), 'Social capital, relational learning and knowledge distinctiveness in technology-based new firms', Babson-Kauffman Entrepreneurship Research Conference, University of South Carolina.

Yotopoulos, P. A. and Nugent, J. B. (1973), 'A balanced-growth version of the linkage hypothesis: a test', *Quarterly Journal of Economics*, vol. 87, no. 2, May, pp. 157–71.

Yotopoulos, P. A. and Nugent, J. B. (1976), 'In defense of a test of the linkages hypothesis', *Quarterly Journal of Economics*, vol. 90, no. 20, May, pp. 334–43.

Zak, P. J. and Knack, S. (2001), 'Trust and growth', *Economic Journal*, vol. 111, April, pp. 295–321.

Zurbano Irizar, M. and Moreno Díaz, J. (1999), 'Cambio en la estructura productiva y desarrollo terciario, 1990–1995. Un análisis sobre la base de las tablas input–output de la Comunidad Autónoma de Euskadi', available online at http://www.eustat.es/spanish/estad/, EUSTAT, País Vasco.

# Index